THOEMMES PRESS
IDEALISM SERIES

T0345947

THOEMMES

ALSO AVAILABLE

Perspectives on the Logic and Metaphysics of F. H. Bradley

Edited and Introduced by W. J. Mander

ISBN 1 85506 432 4 : 306pp : Pb : £14.95
ISBN 1 85506 433 2 : 306pp : Hb : £45.00

Philosophy after F. H. Bradley

Edited with a Preface by James Bradley

ISBN 1 85506 485 5 : 390pp : Pb : £16.95
ISBN 1 85506 484 7 : 390pp : Hb : £48.00
October 1996

The Politics of Conscience: T. H. Green and his Age

Melvin Richter

ISBN 1 85506 487 1 : 415pp : 1964 edition : Pb : £14.95
ISBN 1 85506 486 3 : 415pp : 1964 edition : Hb : £45.00
October 1996

Printed in England by Antony Rowe Ltd

Current Issues in
IDEALISM

Edited and Introduced by
Paul Coates
and
Daniel D. Hutto

THOEMMES PRESS

© Thoemmes Press, 1996
except the essay
Subjective, Intersubjective, Objective
© Donald Davidson, 1991

Published by
Thoemmes Press
11 Great George Street
Bristol BS1 5RR
England

Current Issues in Idealism

ISBN 1 85506 434 0 – Paperback
ISBN 1 85506 435 9 – Hardback

British Library Cataloguing-in-Publication Data
A CIP record of this book is available from the British Library

CONTENTS

INTRODUCTION

At the start of this century the refutation of idealism was announced by G. E. Moore. Despite this, idealist views have remained influential, and as the century draws to a close the idealism/realism debate is still very much with us.

Idealism stands opposed to the form of realism which claims, at one extreme, that there can exist independent physical objects whose exact nature would forever lie beyond the power of the human mind to ascertain. A simple, though contentious, argument for such a realist view might run as follows. Our pre-theoretical view of the world – what might be claimed to be the natural view – involves our conceiving ourselves as inhabiting a world of discrete, though causally related objects. Our existence and our mental life are contingent features of that world, which largely consists of material things. But if that is so, then it makes perfect sense to envisage a variant of that same physical world which lacks the presence of minds (for an elaboration of this position see Nagel, 1986). On this account, the natural conception we have of ourselves, which is implicitly contained and reflected in what we ordinarily say and do, is a conception that allows for our own absence from the world; the world would be the same world, even if there were no human knowers contained within it; it just happens that we are a part of the causally connected set of things that make up the world.

Moreover, it is equally a contingent matter that we are able to form a conception of the character of at least part of that world, and we should not expect that conception, or any possible extension of our present conception, to be complete. As Nagel also argued, such a realist position countenances radical sceptical possibilities.

In his paper, Sorell defends aspects of the Nagelian realist position and offers us reasons to think that philosophy requires the notions of transcendence and objectivity. In doing so, he focuses his critique on Rorty's new style of philosophy, his 'pragmatism without method', and argues that it is incapable of taking us happily 'beyond realism and idealism'.

Nevertheless, this line of argument is open to challenge on a number of fronts, and each move away from the extreme realist position is considered by some as a move towards idealism. Two parallel methods whereby the realist view can be attacked focus on the very fact that the realist's conception of the world is of a world that he is able both to perceive and think about.

One important line of attack, which derives from reflections on the nature of perceptual experience, can trace its ancestry back to Berkeley even though it has not been without notable exponents in the present century (for example, it forms an important consideration in the overall arguments of two leading contemporary idealist philosophers, Sprigge and Foster). The essential thought behind such idealism is as follows: merely to perceive an object is for that object to exist as an entity in one's mind. Hence, such Berkeleyan idealism can sponsor an ontological thesis which insists that the only constituents of reality are minds, human or divine, and their contents. An analysis of perception can, in this way, provide one path towards idealism.

It is partly such a conception of perceptual experience that Moore reacted against, by insisting on the distinction between the act of perception and its object. However, as Wilson emphasizes in his contribution to this volume, Moore's paper contained a further strand of argument: he recognized that the idealist analysis of experience rested on a more fundamental thesis involving the ideality of relations, a thesis which Wilson claims Moore was right to reject.

Most philosophers today would accept as a common-place Moore's claim that perception involves some sort of distinction between the act of perception and its object. Nevertheless, it is arguable that some recent writers have attempted to defend the idea that perceptual experience provides us with a unique form of direct access to the physical objects which is over and above whatever relation we have to the world by virtue of the thoughts we entertain when we perceive objects. Coates, in his essay, suggests that such a move returns us to a form of idealism that has aspects in common with Berkeley's.

But Berkeley's form of idealism is not the only one. Another, influential, form of idealism has its roots in Kantian philosophy. Supporters of this alternative version of idealism argue that notwithstanding any distinctions which may legitimately be drawn between mental and physical existents, the sum total of what exists is limited to what can be grasped by human thought. There cannot, on this version, be any aspect of the world which is forever beyond human conceivability. Reality is necessarily graspable, and perhaps always in principle knowable. This second strand of idealism has been the focus of a great deal of attention in the twentieth century and has provided an undercurrent to much debate in the philosophy of language, as well as in metaphysics and epistemology.

Kantian idealists claim that the very categories of generality and existence are constrained by human concept-forming mechanisms, so that in the end the only coherent conceptions available to us are of a world which is bounded by human conceivability. Such a position is equally well supported if we replace the reference to 'concept-forming mechanisms' with an appeal to 'linguistic practices' which are responsible for the formation and development of our conceptual categories. Thus, given analytical philosophy's linguistic turn, it is often thought that a Kantian style version of transcendental idealism has been replaced by a linguistic version endorsed by analytic philosophy. This fact is nicely chronicled by Rorty who writes:

> Philosophers in the English-speaking world seem fated to end the century discussing the same topic – realism – which they were discussing in 1900. In that year, the opposite of realism was still idealism. But by now language had replaced mind as that which, supposedly, stands over and against 'reality'.... (Rorty, 1991, p. 2)

In his paper, Marsonet suggests the idealist strain in analytical philosophy is 'a 'natural continuation' of the Kantian viewpoint'. Surprisingly, he maintains that idealist overtones are present even in the work of that long-time supporter of scientific ontology, Quine. And this is interesting because Marsonet's main critique of what he calls linguistic idealism revolves around the fact that it overlooks that language has origins in the natural world which need explaining by science.

The accusation that Quine is a closet idealist has echoes of Williams' accusation that the later Wittgenstein was a transcendental idealist. If true, such a classification of Wittgenstein has widespread implications for those who, in one fashion or another, have followed in his footsteps. Against this, Hutto claims that if we understand Wittgenstein's philosophy sympathetically, we find ourselves unable to make sense of *any* form of metaphysical idealism or realism. He uses the work of Wittgenstein in his early and later periods and the work of Davidson to make this point. For Davidson too has strived for a long time to sail between the Scylla and Charybdis of metaphysical idealism and realism – but more often than not he is accused of sponsoring some form of idealism. This is apparent from the work of Nagel (1986), Papineau (1987) and McDowell (1994).

In his important contribution to this volume Davidson himself makes it clear that the conditions that underpin an understanding of both the objective and subjective must be intersubjective. On this view, which is driven by his complex theory of interpretation, minds cannot be 'independent' of reality because, in an important sense, the objects of the world help to fix the content of minds. Such a position would rule out the extreme forms of both realism and idealism.

In a different type of bid to stave off the kind of conceptual relativism that allegedly attaches itself to many pluralist attempts to accommodate the ontologies of our various forms of discourse, Stock attempts to define a privileged place for what he calls 'the world of human history'. Following in Bradley's footsteps he carefully draws the distinction between the real world and the metaphysician's ultimate reality, and claims that the former must be assigned a special status if we are to speak of a plurality of worlds at all. In doing so his position also appears to fall somewhere between realism and idealism.

But not everyone is content to 'resolve' the tension between realism and idealism by locating a safe haven between two extremes. Two contributors argue for idealism in more indirect ways, by appealing to the fact that certain problems only allow of a solution if we adopt an idealist point of view. For example, Armour argues that we need to adopt an idealist conception of a person in order to provide a satisfactory answer to problems in the sphere of ethics. Without such a return to idealism Armour claims we are unable to reconcile our notions of happiness and duty into a workable moral philosophy.

Ferreira puts forward a similar claim with respect to the nature of necessity. On his view, the idealist account of inference, which takes into account the context of a thought, avoids the pitfalls of alternative accounts, and is in particular to be preferred to a formalist approach.

A final paper explores the applications of idealism to matters of contemporary debate. Sprigge discusses ethical views relating to the environment and shows how an idealist ethic provides a natural support for some of our deeper intuitions about environmental issues.

Taken together, the collection reveals the lively nature, and philosophic importance, of the current debate between realism and idealism. It is hoped that the exploration of the themes which crop up over and again in a number of the papers will provide a stimulus to further debate on this topic.

The editors would like to record their gratitude to Stuart Brown whose contribution to the organization of the British Society for the History of Philosophy's conference on Idealism in the Twentieth Century, held at the University of Hertfordshire in 1994, provided the impetus for this volume. Many of the papers that appear here originate from that conference. We would also especially like to thank Margaret Mitchell-Jubb for her indispensable and capable administrative support, and Jenefer Coates for her invaluable editorial assistance.

Paul Coates and Daniel D. Hutto, 1996

REFERENCES

John McDowell, *Mind and World* (Cambridge, Mass: Harvard University Press, 1994).

George E. Moore, 'The Refutation of Idealism', *Mind*, vol. 12 ns (1903), reprinted in his *Philosophical Studies* (London: Routledge and Kegan Paul, 1922).

Thomas Nagel, *The View From Nowhere* (Oxford: Oxford University Press, 1986).

David Papineau, *Reality and Representation* (Oxford: Basil Blackwell, 1987).

Richard Rorty, *Objectivity, Relativism, and Truth*, Philosophical Papers, vol. 1 (Cambridge: Cambridge University Press, 1991).

Bernard Williams, 'Wittgenstein and Idealism', reprinted in his *Moral Luck* (Cambridge: Cambridge University Press, 1981).

IDEALISM, REALISM AND RORTY'S PRAGMATISM WITHOUT METHOD

Tom Sorell

In this paper I focus on some recent opposition to idealism – Thomas Nagel's – and Richard Rorty's opposition to that opposition (cf. Nagel, 1986, chap. 6; Rorty, 1991, Introduction and part 1). Rorty maintains that idealism and realism are dead ends and that somewhere beyond them is a better philosophy – a special kind of pragmatism – without the pretensions or illusions of what it supersedes. The preferred philosophy offers to conjure out of the idea of a certain kind of democratic community something as good as Nagel extracts from the ideas of objectivity and transcendence. Given the inconclusiveness of realist arguments against idealism and idealist arguments against realism, the strategy of adjudicating disputes with idealism by reference to wider views of philosophy seems a promising one. Unfortunately, the view of philosophy that Rorty himself puts forward is neither independently attractive nor easy to understand as a wholesome middle way between idealism and realism. In some ways it is hard to recognize it as a view of *philosophy* at all. I argue for something closer to Nagel's view of philosophy, and Nagel's realism

I

Nagel attacks an argument for a modern form of idealism. It is a sort of linguistic idealism, rather than the kind that throws doubt on a reality independent of mind. It holds that what is real or true is determined by what is humanly thinkable or sayable, so that there couldn't be truths that were totally inconceivable or unthinkable or inexpressible in language. The idea that there *are* such truths or objects overtaxes any applicable concept of truth, or of reality, according to the idealist, for an applicable concept of truth is one that we succeed now in applying or that we could succeed in applying, and what is in question is whether there are truths in the range of the concept of truth that we could *never* recognize as truths. Either the supposedly inconceivable truths lie in the range of application of our concept of truth, say at some point far in the future, in which case they are not totally inconceivable, or else they do lie outside that range, in which case we are unable to understand or express the possibility of their lying outside that range.

One way of countering this argument is to challenge its general assumption about the applicability of concepts – to the effect that conditions under which concepts recognizably *do* apply determine whether and how far concepts *can* apply. Nagel does challenge this assumption (Nagel, 1986, pp. 97–8, p. 105). But he goes further to show that the inconceivability he believes in, and that the idealist denies, is just a straightforward analogue of a kind of inconceivability *everyone* believes in, and that the idealist *cannot* deny. This is the inconceivability one encounters when truths within the grasp of intellectually very able human beings are out of the reach of the very young, or out of the reach of the mature but less intelligent. Nagel constructs the fiction of a community of congenital nine-year-olds. Many actual adults can understand things that actual nine-year-olds cannot yet understand; so many actual adults can understand things that congenital nine-year-olds could never understand. To see how truths could be permanently beyond human beings, then, one has only to imagine beings who stand to humans as human adults stand to the congenital nine-year-olds. Nagel anticipates the objection that the analogy does not hold, on the ground that the nine-year-olds could not themselves have a concept of truths beyond their grasp, whereas we are supposed to. But he makes a persuasive case for the proposition that the nine-year-olds could have a version of this concept, and, anyway, that idealists would be committed to crediting them with one (Nagel, 1986, pp. 96 ff.).

He admits that his general argument is essentially negative (Nagel, 1986, p. 95). Instead of leading directly to the conclusion that realism is correct, it works by showing that we have to give up many deeply held pre philosophical views to accept idealism, while realism is consistent with, and probably presupposed by, much that we thought all along. Behind the argumentative strategy there appears to be a certain understanding of philosophy and philosophical method which Nagel has articulated in a number of places. Philosophy derives its problems from, and its solutions have to do justice to, pre-philosophical beliefs and tensions between these beliefs. These beliefs go deeper than culture or language.[1] They have their source, if I

---

[1] 'Philosophy is not like a particular language. Its sources are preverbal and often precultural, and one of its most difficult tasks is to express unformed but intuitively felt problems in language without losing them' (Nagel, 1986, p. 11).

understand Nagel, in something like human nature. Not all of our pre-philosophical beliefs are beyond criticism or correction by philosophy; but philosophical arguments have to produce conviction (Nagel, 1979, p. xi). If a philosophical argument leaves us with a nagging sense of artificiality, or the strong suspicion that it leaves something important out of account, then one needs a new argument, not fresh intuitions.

How does this theory of philosophy bear on the issue between realism and idealism? According to Nagel, there is a 'natural picture' of the relation of human beings to reality according to which we are much smaller than it is, and only partially adapted to understanding it. On the other hand:

> [t]he idea that the contents of the universe are limited by our capacity for thought is easily recognised as a philosophical view, which at first sight seems crazily self-important given what small and contingent pieces of the universe we are. It is a view no one would hold except for philosophical reasons that seem to rule out the natural picture. (Nagel, 1986, p. 92)

Realism is consistent with the 'natural picture'; idealism is not, even after reflection; nor does idealism give us compelling reasons for dropping the 'natural picture'. So if the choice is between realism and idealism, realism is philosophically preferable.

Although I am sympathetic to Nagel's conception of good philosophical practice, I do not think the associated view of philosophy is entirely trouble-free, and his apparent application of it in his controversy with the idealists raises a number of questions.[2] To

---

[2]   In stressing the authority of intuitions, Nagel's views have something in common with those of a host of otherwise disagreeing philosophers, including Kripke, Strawson, Malcolm and Wittgenstein.

begin with, is his 'natural picture' supposed to be one of those manifestations of intuitions that run as deep in us as our humanity? Or is it a by-product of what most educated people grasp of evolutionary theory? Or does the 'natural picture' have elements contributed by primordial thought *and* by science and perhaps other things as well? The more eclectic and the more removed from the pre-philosophical it is, the less its 'naturalness' can count in its favour and the 'philosophical' character of its rival count against it. I think it can be shown that the 'natural picture' is indeed eclectic, but that it has authority despite that. To account for its authority Nagel's vision of philosophy needs to be adjusted so that the test of convincingness of a solution or theory is its convincingness in the light of everything we defensibly believe, without the pre-philosophical being accorded a special added authority. This means thinking twice before invoking naturalness.

To apply these considerations let us return to the 'natural picture' that predisposes us, if Nagel is right, to resist the idealist and side with the realist:

> The picture is that the universe and most of what goes on it are completely independent of our thoughts, but that since our ancestors appeared on Earth we have gradually developed the capacity to think about, know about, and represent more aspects of reality. There are some things that we cannot now conceive but may yet come to understand; and there are probably still others that we lack the capacity to conceive not merely because we are at too early a stage of historical development, but because of the kind of beings we are. About some of what we cannot conceive we are able to speak vaguely – this may include the mental lives of alien creatures, or

what went on before the Big Bang – but about some of it we may be unable to say anything at all, except that there might be such things. The only sense in which we can conceive of them is under that description – that is, as things of which we can form no conception – or under the all-encompassing thought 'Everything', or the Parmenidean thought 'What is'. (Nagel, 1986, p. 92)

If the 'natural picture' is supposed to be a pre-philosophical and a pre-scientific one, then this description seems to bring in too many post-philosophical and post-scientific elements. The description starts appropriately enough, for it does seem to be a natural thought that the universe and what goes on it is completely independent of our thoughts; but it is unclear that we bring to philosophy even rudimentary thoughts about how our capacities for thinking about the world have evolved, or any thoughts about how humanity interferes with some kinds of understanding. Again, from the fact that the universe is completely independent of our thoughts it does not follow that we can never understand all of it. And it may be difficult to find a pre-philosophical thought from which it does follow. Of course, the pre-philosophical thought about the independence of the universe leaves it open that we will never be able to understand everything; but then the idealism that Nagel objects to leaves it open that we will never reach the point in our historical development when we will understand everything. These need not strike pre-philosophical people as hugely distinct thoughts. So perhaps the pre-philosophical cannot be used to adjudicate between realism and idealism.

Further doubts about Nagel's hold on the pre-philosophical emerge when he ascribes a certain 'general concept of reality' to everyone who thinks that they are much smaller than the world is and only partially adapted to understanding it:

> Creatures who recognise their limited nature and their containment in the world must recognise both that reality must extend beyond our conceptual reach and that there may be concepts that we could not understand. This condition is met by a general concept of reality under which one's actual conception, as well as all possible extensions of that conception, falls as an instance. This concept seems to me to be adequately explained through the idea of a hierarchical set of conceptions, extending from those much more limited than one's own but contained in it to those much larger than one's own but containing it – of which some are reachable by discoveries one might make but others, larger still, are not. (The hierarchy could also include parallel conceptions, not intersecting our own but joined with it only in a larger one.) We could ascribe this concept to the philosophical nine-year-olds in our example, and I maintain it is the same as our general concept of what there is. It seems to me so clear that we have this concept that any theory of thought our reference which implies that we can't have it is for that reason deeply suspect. (Nagel, 1986, p. 98.)[3]

---

[3] Compare this passage with a couple of sentences in the Introduction to *A View from Nowhere*: 'We may think of reality as a set of concentric spheres, progressively revealed as we detach ourselves from the contingencies of the self. This will become clearer when we discuss the interpretation of objectivity in relation to specific areas of life and understanding' (Nagel, 1986, p. 5). This looks similar to the general concept that we all have (cf. Nagel, 1986, p. 98); yet it seems to be presented in the Introduction as a philosophical picture, which subsequent material will clarify. If it were pre-philosophical, it would presumably be clear from the start.

It seems to me doubtful that the general concept of reality, if it belongs to pre-philosophical thought at all, takes the form that Nagel indicates. I would have supposed it takes the form of a picture of a world outside my mind, affecting me to a far greater extent than I affect it, for the most part out of my control, unaffected by my mere wishes or desires, having to be investigated in order to be known, having to be acted upon if it is to satisfy my desires.

I infer that there is no easily identified 'natural picture' that supports realism and that has greater authority than the merely 'philosophical' picture one gets from idealism. That is, there is no easily identified 'natural picture' with which realism, and only realism, squares. This does not mean that Nagel has no argument for realism; only that he does not have an argument from naturalness. Whether the picture he describes is natural or not, whether the general concept of reality he describes is natively shared, the picture and the concept *are* needed. They are needed to describe certain kinds of intellectual advances, the kinds that Nagel labels 'objective advances', and they are needed to expose the presumption of thinking that all truths lie within the path of human objective advance. Objective advances are leaps in knowledge that result in an appearance/reality distinction being drawn, and that explain why what emerges as appearance was previously mistaken for what was real. Nagel gives as example of objective advances the primary/secondary quality distinction and Einstein's theory of special relativity (Nagel, 1986, pp. 74–7). Let us consider the former. Prior to the drawing of the primary/ secondary quality distinction, the explanation of why objects appeared to have colours was that they were intrinsically coloured. This naive conception clashed, however, with facts about the conditions under which objects appear to change and lose colour. It resolved this conflict to suppose that objects did not have intrinsically the colours they appeared to have, but only had shape, size, position, number and so on, which explained their appearing as coloured to creatures with senses like ours. The new hypothesis that objects have intrinsically only their primary qualities bears all the marks of an objective advance on the hypothesis that objects have colours intrinsically. The new hypothesis says that material objects objectively have shape, position, number and so on; that we are constituted to have experiences of colour when viewing material things in certain conditions; that visual experiences can be fully explained in terms of our interactions between our sense-organs and external things with primary qualities and that therefore the appearance of objects having colours intrinsically is pure appearance. In this way the more objective conception of material objects, like any other such conception, contributes to the explanation of '(1) what the world is like; (2) what we are like; (3) why the world appears to us in certain ways as it is and in certain ways as it isn't; (4) how beings like us can arrive at such a conception' (Nagel, 1986, p. 74).

It is as a device for explaining objective advances that Nagel's hierarchical set of conceptions comes into its own. It is needed to distinguish an objective advance from a simple accumulation of knowledge at a level prior to advance. As for his 'natural picture', it is needed to indicate the limits of objective advance. The natural picture is authoritative, because objective advances take place in the face of obstacles thrown up by the loosely connected evolutions of humans and the world: realism in Nagel's preferred sense falls into place as the thought that some conceptions can probably never be represented to ourselves as mere appearances, so that there are probably limits for us to objective advance, and perhaps different and more remote limits for other conceivers.

On my understanding of Nagel's 'natural picture' and his 'general concept of reality', then, neither need be regarded as pre-philosophical, or as deriving its authority from is naturalness. But without being natural or pre-philosophical, each can give support to realism.

II

The general concept of reality, with its hierarchy of conceptions, comes into more than Nagel's attack on idealism; it is the device by which he is able to unify a wide range of recognized philosophical problems as specimens of a general problem of the relation between the subjective and objective. If Nagel is right, many human conceptions of subject matters can give way to others which owe less and less to what humans are like, and which constitute objective advances on the native human conception of those subject matters. Some subject matters have already undergone successive objective advances; others only appear to admit of these advances because the method of understanding them is incorrectly modelled on the methods of physics. Thus, according to Nagel, there are demonstrable limits on our conception of mental life, with certain negative consequences for attempts to colonize the mind for physics or the brain sciences. On the other hand, certain subject matters promise more in the way of objective advance than they have so far delivered. Thus, according to Nagel, there are possibilities of far greater objective understanding in ethics, though the methods of achieving this understanding are as yet not very refined.

Here is where Rorty comes in. He thinks that Nagel's approach in philosophy gives too much importance to objectivity, and that it indulges rather than stifles the urge to do the impossible and climb outside of one's mind. Not only that, it fails to learn from the history of philosophy that these attempts at transcendence:

> have been fruitless and undesirable... [T]hese efforts generate the sort of pseudoproblems which Wittgenstein hoped to avoid by abandoning the picture which held him captive when he wrote the *Tractatus*. Wittgenstein was not insane when he wrote that book, but he was right when he later described himself as having been buzzing around in a fly-bottle... He was suggesting that questions which we should have to climb out of our own minds to answer should not be asked. He was suggesting that both realism and idealism share representationalist presuppositions which we would be better off dropping. (Rorty, 1991, p. 7)

There is a short and a long answer to Rorty. The short answer is that Nagel only indulges the transcendental urge within limits, and only *has* to indulge that urge within limits to confront the problem of idealism. The questions which he addresses are not ones we have to climb out of our minds to answer, but in answering them Nagel does make use of conceptions in which certain parochially human elements, those contributed by our sensory constitution, for example, have been eliminated. So there is at best a limited transcendental strategy, and the absurdity or extravagance which Rorty thinks Nagel cannot avoid does not arise in the first place.[4]

The longer answer depends on confronting an approach to philosophy which Rorty urges as the alternative to Nagel's, and which he outlines in essays such as 'Solidarity or Objectivity'. Rorty summarizes his position by saying that:

> whatever good the ideas of 'objectivity' and 'transcendence' have done for our culture can be attained equally well by the idea of a community which strives after both intersubjective agreement and novelty – a democratic, pluralist community of the sort of which Dewey dreamt. If one reinterprets objectivity as intersubjectivity, or as solidarity, ...then one will drop the question of how to get in touch with 'mind-independent and language-independent reality'. One will replace it with questions like 'What are the limits of our community? Are our encounters sufficiently free and open? Has what we gained in solidarity cost us our ability to listen to outsiders who are suffering? Do the outsiders have new ideas?' These are political questions rather than metaphysical or epistemological questions. Dewey seems to me to have given us the right lead when he viewed pragmatism not as grounding, but as clearing the ground for, democratic politics. (Rorty, 1991, p. 13)

A certain kind of pragmatism, not quite Dewey's, but in sympathy with Dewey's, is prescribed as the antidote to

---

[4]   On other occasions Rorty has claimed that representationalists need access to a non-existent point of view of the world or of God for their project to make sense. This claim, too, deserves short shrift. It does get short shrift in my 'The World From its own Point of View' (Sorell, 1990, pp. 11–21).

Nagel's representationalism. Rorty calls it 'pragmatism without method'.

This pragmatism has something in common with idealism, for with idealism it is sceptical of the idea that truth is correspondence. It holds that truth is made rather than discovered, and it is holistic about meaning (Rorty, 1991, p. 64). It also 'exalts spontaneity at the cost of receptivity', that is, considers human beings to be related to causal forces primarily as harnessers of them rather than as passive sensors of them (Rorty, 1991, p. 81). The debts of pragmatism without method to realism are less clear. There is an acknowledgement of the causal forces acting upon people, and, to that extent, a conception of a reality independent of the will; there is an acknowledgement of something impinging on human beings that needs to be 'coped' with. On the other hand, and now by contrast with a more mainstream pragmatism, there is no favouritism of science over religion or the arts, no insinuation of a distinction between methods of finding out and methods of being consoled about what we cope with (Rorty, 1991, p. 76). Rorty calls it 'pragmatism without method', because the pragmatist's allegiance to science, and the pragmatist's belief in method, are subtracted.

One could ask whether what remains after the subtraction deserves to be called 'pragmatism' at all, but I am more concerned with Rorty's claims for his approach than with its nomenclature. He writes as if the key to the pragmatist approach is its refusal to allow metaphysical and epistemological questions to be pursued independently of considerations of the preferred form of community. Thus he is drawn to the idea that truth is what emerges from communal enquiry in a democratic setting, and unmoved by the metaphysical realist's suggestion that truth, or at any rate some truths, might totally elude any of a community's, indeed any of a species', enquiries. His claim, already quoted, is that 'whatever good the ideas of "objectivity" and "transcendence" have done for our culture can be attained equally well by the idea of a community which strives after both intersubjective agreement and novelty – a democratic, pluralist community of the sort of which Dewey dreamt'. This does not mean that, armed with Deweyan materials, one can solve the problems which philosophers like Nagel invoke objectivity and transcendence to describe and solve; it is rather that, because these problems are insoluble or pseudoproblems, it does more good to pursue another agenda.

If correct, this line of thought probably proves more than that one *style* of philosophy ought to be abandoned in favour of another. It probably proves that philosophical activity of *all* kinds is better given up in favour of other cultural activity. In a sense this *is* what Rorty is driving at, for in his hands the difference between philosophy and a certain story-telling about culture that is perhaps more familiar from literary criticism, virtually disappears. In 'Texts and Lumps', an essay in which he argues that literary critics are on the wrong track when they invoke the authority of philosophy or philosophers to justify interpretations of texts or hypotheses about canon-formation, Rorty describes a sort of pragmatism that brings philosophy very close to a kind of textual criticism:

> [T]he pragmatist does not try to justify his metaphors [of linguistic behaviour as tool-using, of language as a way of grabbing hold of causal forces] by philo-

sophical argument – by claiming to have made some new discovery about the nature of the universe or of knowledge which shows that the nature of truth is quite different than had been thought. He abjures Aristotelian appeals to the nature of this and that. Instead, like Dewey, he tells stories about how the course of Western thought has been stultified by the metaphors he dislikes. His own technique in philosophy is that same Homeric, narrative style which he recommends to the literary critic. His recommendation to the critic is thus not grounded in a theory about literature or criticism, but in a narrative whose details he hopes the literary critic will help him fill in. The pragmatist philosopher has a story to tell about his favourite, and least favoured, books – the texts of, for example, Plato, Descartes, Hegel, Nietzsche, Dewey, and Russell. He would like other people to have stories to tell about other sequences of texts, other genres – stories which will fit together with his. His appeal is not to the latest philosophical theories about the nature of science or language, but to the existence of views on these matters which chime in with views other people (for example, contemporary critics looking for the big picture) hold about other matters. (Rorty, 1991, pp. 81–2)

The narrative technique does not appear to be suited to the solution of traditional philosophical problems, or, despite the 'pragmatist' label, to problem-solving of any kind. What makes it a *philosophical* technique? Is it the fact that it is a style for a narrative about views of knowledge or science, the staples of mainstream philosophy? Or is it the fact that it is a narrative mainly about the bad old philosophers and bad old philosophy, ie., *pre*-pragmatic philosophers or *pre*-pragmatic philosophy? I do not see that any other possibilities are implicit in Rorty's text. It does seem that the preferred pragmatic philosophy depends for its identity as philosophy on having the non-pragmatic philosophy to feed off. On this account, the non-pragmatic philosophers do turn out to have their uses after all – playing straight men to pragmatist deflators of philosophical pretensions and exposers of philosophical illusions. Certainly it is not an identifiable method of confronting the chosen texts, a method of analysis or argument, that turns pragmatist narrative into philosophy: that would be to take 'narrative' too narrowly. Narrative in Rorty's preferred sense is more closely tied to the invention and application of new metaphors, an activity it would take an argument to establish as philosophical.

If it *is* philosophy, Rorty's pragmatism without method has little in common with traditional philosophy, even traditional pragmatism. It purports to break also from a certain kind of non-traditional philosophy, namely the highly technical, highly profes-sionalized writing of late twentieth-century Anglo-American academic philosophical journals, and the esotericism of 'Continental' philosophy. Rorty advocates philosophy that is not separated from other cultural disciplines by the belief that it is the custodian of rarefied methods of clarification and argument, and that is not separated from the rest of society at a time and place by a preoccupation with 'deep' questions as against timely and pressing ones (Rorty, 1991, p. 77). What ties these two themes together is the liberal democratic strand in Rorty's pragmatism. Philosophy should speak to people, but not from a great height, and not from a great depth either. What is more, and here the democratic and the anti-metaphysical in Rorty meet, what philosophy should speak about is what it is possible for people to speak about, ie., not a set of problems whose investigation is obstructed by one's humanity, but a set of texts that are meant to provoke thought in people.

To what extent can one understand these aspirations to come down to earth as philosophical ambitions, and to what extent are they ways of wanting to stop doing philosophy and start doing something else? It focuses these questions to ask whether Rorty has an argument for dropping the older aspirations of philosophy – an argument other than that they lead to the interminable contest of idealism vs. realism. I do not detect anything beyond an argument from interminability, and there is an answer to such an argument. The interminability of a contest between say, realism and idealism, does not show there is nothing to fight over, and the possibility that the controversy may be endless should be no more repellent than the possibility of a conversation being extended indefinitely, which Rorty approves of. Rhetoric about fruitless activity in philosophy and about philosophical problems going stale does not seem to prove that one should abandon the old problems, unless it is also true that philosophers can no longer infect others with, or elicit from others, a *sense* of a problem where traditional philosophy or mainstream philosophy says there is one (Nagel, 1976).[5] Philosophers still *can* call up this sense of a problem. If they could not, there would be nothing for Rorty to diagnose as a pseudoproblem. And because there is still a communicable sense of what is a problem in

---

[5]   This rhetoric is as much at home in scientistic writing as in Rorty's (cf. Sorell, 1991, chap. 1, chap. 6).

philosophy, one need not be at a loss to say what would make philosophy fruitful. Fruitfulness would consist of solving the problems or of making the sense of the problem disappear.

Now there are philosophers who offer to solve the recognized problems of philosophy, and philosophers who offer to dissolve them. Rorty is neither a solver nor a dissolver. The focus of his writing since *Philosophy and the Mirror of Nature* has not been the mainstream philosophical problem, or the effect of such a problem for better or worse on the human intelligence. Instead, Rorty has been concerned with the broad sweep of intellectual history and the metaphors supposedly captivating the great canonical figures. I am not sure whether this genre will catch on in the English-speaking world, but if it did, that would hardly be a reason for dropping the philosophical problem as the main unit of philosophical exchange. It would not even be a reason for dropping the traditional philosophical problem as a unit of philosophical exchange.

To insist on the importance of the old problems in philosophy is not, as Rorty thinks, to display a kind of bad faith about what a philosophy for people can be about. So long as the problems can come to be appreciated by a line of thought that starts with what we all admit, the problems are surely rooted in, or in something close to, our humanity. This can be as true in cases where the problems look insoluble as where they do not. The insolubility of a problem does not show that it lacks human roots. And apparent insolubility is not a reason for human beings to refuse to engage with the problems. To try to solve these problems may be futile, but to persist in a futile under-taking, or in an undertaking that may be doomed because it exceeds our capacities, is not to lose faith with our humanity. Persistence with the problems has as much of a place in a philosophy for people as a sense of the deep problems has in the people themselves. Moreover, to persist in an undertaking that does not achieve its ultimate objective is not necessarily to persist in a fruitless undertaking. For example, many philosophical advances have been made in the long engagement with scepticism, even if no refutation of the sceptic is possible. And there has been progress with the question of why people should be moral, although no-one has discovered a knock-down argument against egoism.

These points ought to make one suspicious of a case for the abandonment of philosophical problems or philosophical efforts based on bald assertions of futility or failure. It ought to make one suspicious in particular of a case for the abandonment of realism and the belief in a limited transcendence of appearance that one finds in Nagel. Not even the tailoring of philosophical practice to a democratic politics puts realism or truth as correspondence in a bad light. On the contrary, famous conceptions of the open society, such as Popper's, are systematically tied to a realist conception of truth in and out of science. Openness to criticism may be desirable in social institutions, as in scientific theories, because it is easy to be wrong about what will benefit people and about the causes of natural phenomena, and because criticism roots out error. Liberal societies can be held to maximize the opportunity for criticism and so for protection from error; they need not only be held to maximize the scope for edification and creativity. Hence liberalism can be held to be a politics for realism *with* method just as much as for pragmatism without method. The same conclusion can be reached if one considers that a realist belief in a shared and vulnerable human nature is a more natural accompaniment to feelings of solidarity than the idea that truth is only a kind of intersubjective agreement.

Pragmatism without method does not seem to be a better match for a liberal democratic politics than some kinds of realism; and one does not have to be a pragmatist to believe it is good for philosophy to be accessible, to be in touch with other disciplines, and to engage with the cultural past. Indeed, all of these aspirations are represented in non-pragmatist Anglo-American philosophy as it is now being done, though admittedly not all of the time and not all at once. It may be true that what is most typical of Anglo-American philosophy is ahistorical, arcane and out of bounds to practitioners of other disciplines. Still, it seems in a way naive and in a way perverse to expect philosophy, even Rorty's reformed philosophy, to be otherwise. How can a subject that is in touch with the cultural past *not* be esoteric? How can stories about Plato, Descartes, Hegel, Nietszche, Dewey, and Russell fail to contain longueurs that are neither politically timely nor addressed to urgent questions? How can digressions on private languages, hylomorphisms, absolute conceptions, on Heidegger and Derrida not lose even Rorty some of his readers from other disciplines?

On the other hand, why should an approach to the subject which is in many ways antagonistic to Rorty's, which is unashamed about the professionalism of philosophy, and which self-consciously relegates its most accessible bits to a sector of itself called 'applied philosophy' – why should this have a smaller, less diverse, or less riveted audience than the products of 'pragmatism without method'? Why should not practitioners of this mainstream version of the subject make any fewer contacts with other disciplines or with the public via its accessible fringes than pragmatism makes from its supposedly accessible core? Why can't the right strategy in philosophy – even from a pragmatist point of view – be the development of all of those strands in the mainstream version of the subject that can enlarge the audience for philosophy? It would not be a matter of marshalling applied ethics only; it would be a matter of, for example, exploiting the possibilities philosophy offers with respect to the divide between the arts and sciences. As I have argued elsewhere, it is intelligible to assign philosophy the task of mediating between the arts and sciences, where mediation means something less exalted than sitting in judgement (Sorell, 1991, p. 112). Why shouldn't this be regarded as a better strategy than the cultivation of esoteric story-telling about esoteric texts?

If Rorty's case for pragmatism without method is compelling at all, that is not because there is no alternative. For all Rorty shows, Nagel's realism is an available option, even taken together with its commitment to the reality of the old problems in philosophy. Indeed, the attempt to adjudicate the dispute between idealism and realism by reference to a vision of philosophy that makes both sides in the dispute *passé*, seems not to work. Not even the strategy of giving democratic politics priority over metaphysics is proof against realism, for the importance of openness can be reinforced by a realist metaphysics.

REFERENCES

Thomas Nagel, *Mortal Questions* (Cambridge: Cambridge University Press, 1979).

————, *The View from Nowhere* (Oxford: Oxford University Press, 1986).

Richard Rorty, *Objectivity, Relativism, and Truth*, Philosophical Papers, vol. 1 (Cambridge: Cambridge University Press, 1991).

Tom Sorell, 'The World from its own Point of View' in Malachowski (ed.), *Reading Rorty* (Oxford: Blackwell, 1990).

————, *Scientism* (London: Routledge, 1991).

MOORE'S REFUTATION
OF IDEALISM

Fred Wilson

G. E. Moore's essay, 'The Refutation of Idealism' is apparently well known (Moore, 1922). Yet one can in fact find very few analyses of its argument. Even where these exist, they remain sketchy. Thus, the commentary by D. Lewis, admirable as it is, deals only with what Moore designates as the second part of his argument, bypassing the first as if it were unimportant (Lewis, 1966).[1] Yet, if it can simply be ignored, in the way in which Lewis ignores it, then why did Moore include it? Moore's argument is clearly important, if only symbolically: though others were making some of the same points as was Moore, it is Moore's essay that has come to mark the point at which idealism began its retreat

---

[1] More recently, David Crossley (Crossley, 1994), also ignores the first part of Moore's argument. John Skorupski, refers to Moore's 'The Refutation of Idealism', but mentions only the second part of Moore's argument, where he insists upon the act–object distinction as a way of refuting Berkeley (Skorupski, 1993, p. 152). This fits with Skorupski's reading of T. H. Green and the other idealists as beginning with a phenomenalism similar to that of Hume and Berkeley (Skorupski, 1993, p. 84), but in fact, as we shall see, the phenomenalism, or, what is the same, the idealism, is not a premise but a conclusion derived from the idealist account of relations. Skorupski does recognize the importance of the doctrine of relations (pp. 84ff), but does not probe it deeply enough to see how the idealism is implied by that account (see footnote 3). Since the idealism depends upon the doctrine of relations, and since the first part of Moore's argument in 'The Refutation of Idealism' is directed at that account of relations, we can see why Skorupski overlooked the signifi-

after its apparent triumph over empiricism in the final quarter of the nineteenth century. But if it is so important, then precisely what was that argument?

The general thrust of Moore's argument is of course to refute the principle that Berkeley was the first to defend, that *esse* is *percipi*, to use the Berkeleyan formula, which Moore in fact quotes, but which should more exactly be exp*ress*ed as the principle that *esse* must be *percipi*. Against this proposition Moore carefully distinguishes the intentional relation in which a mind stands to its object in perception from the relation of predication in which a mind stands to the properties that are predicated of it. What Moore points out is that there is nothing about the intentional relation, unlike the relation of predication, that can be taken to imply that the perceived object will cease to exist if it were unperceived.

> ...we recognise that this awareness is and must be in all cases of such a nature that its object, when we are aware of it, is precisely what it would be, if we were not aware.... (Moore, 1922, p. 29)

The argument is as clear in its simplicity as it is convincing. Who, in fact, would disagree? Certainly, if

cance of the first part of Moore's argument. More oddly, Alan White not only ignores the first part of Moore's argument but the second part also: Moore's essay on 'The Refutation of Idealism' is not even discussed (White, 1958). Unfortunately, Lewis's work (Lewis, 1966) appeared too late for White to be able to make use of its insights. Referring to it, White might have become able to see the significance of Moore's early arguments against the idealists, and their relevance for his (Moore's) defence of realism. White might also have benefited from Lewis's often very insightful account of Moore on perception. The notable exception to the rule that the first part of Moore's argument is ignored is Thomas Baldwin, who devotes a chapter to analysing Moore on idealism, both the arguments of 'The Refutation of Idealism' and also those elsewhere in Moore's work (Baldwin, 1990). We shall have something to say about Baldwin's discussion below.

one were to canvass philosophers today it is more than likely that many if not most would agree with Moore. To that extent Moore's argument has succeeded in persuading the twentieth century that idealism is wrong.[2]

But in fact, there were those who disagreed. Thus, Berkeley does, for one, as well as the idealists who form the immediate background to Moore's essay. But before turning to the latter, who were Moore's main target, we had best complete our task of unravelling the structure of Moore's essay.

Given the structure of Moore's essay, the second portion of the overall argument against idealism that we have just examined, the portion directed specifically at Berkeleyan idealism, is clearly intended to presuppose the first part. That is why Lewis is therefore wrong to ignore this first part of Moore's argument. For all that, it is not too hard to think why Lewis might have ignored this part. Here is how Moore summarized the case he is presenting in this portion of his argument:

'*Esse* is *percipi*', we have seen, asserts of two terms, as distinct from one another as 'green' and 'sweet' that

---

[2] Baldwin objects that Moore has not refuted phenomenalism (Baldwin, 1990). But that was not Moore's intention. Phenomenalism is not the same as idealism. The latter holds that there is an ontological dependence of sensations upon the mind; phenomenalism holds that sensations are causally dependent for their existence upon the state of our sense organs, and in this way causally dependent upon the perceiving of them. Hume was a phenomenalist but not an idealist; he is careful to argue that, although sensations depend for their existence upon our organs (Hume, 1740, [1978], bk. 1, pt. 3, sect. 2, pp. 210–11), it is logically or ontologically possible for them to exist apart from minds (Hume, 1740, [1978], bk. 1, pt. 3, sect. 2, p. 207). (On this point see, F. Wilson, 1989a, pp. 49–73 and 1989b, pp. 247–82). It is no doubt true that pains, if not sensations, exist depending upon the states of our bodily organs. Hume's point is that it is still logically and ontologically possible for these entities to exist apart from any perceiving mind.

whatever has the one has the other: it asserts that 'being' and 'being experienced' are necessarily connected: that whatever is is also experienced. And this, I admit, cannot be directly refuted. But I believe it to be false; and I have asserted that anybody who saw that '*esse*' and '*percipi*' were as distinct as 'green' and 'sweet' would be no more ready to believe that whatever is green is also sweet. (Moore, 1922, p. 16)

The conclusion of the first part of Moore's argument would thus seem to be the simple one that where things are distinct, they are distinct. It is a point that Moore's argument against Berkeley presupposes. For, after all, that argument depends upon his insisting that the relation of intentionality is distinct from the relation of predication. Moreover, the second part of the argument also presupposes that the sensation – what is perceived, the colour blue – is distinct from the perceiving of it – the act of awareness: the latter is a sensation of blue but is distinct from the blue. So the conclusion of the first part of Moore's argument is indeed necessary for the

---

Moore's is the same. What Moore establishes, in other words, is that even if pains are causally dependent upon the perceiving of them, nonetheless, to experience a pain is already to be outside the circle of ideas, that is, outside the circle of things that are predicated of the mind and in that sense are ontologically dependent upon the mind. This establishes that idealism is false, but not that phenomenalism is false. But Moore's point is to refute idealism, not phenomenalism. Douglas Lewis sees this quite clearly. Baldwin does not. So Baldwin ends up unfairly criticizing Moore's argument on the grounds that it fails to do what it did not set out to do! It should also be added that, while to get to the blue is to get one outside the circle of ideas, it does not necessarily get one to things in the sense of physical objects. This point has been made by others. Thus, Henry Baker proposed 'to use the word "object"...to denote what is actually experienced by the individual subject, and to use the word "thing" to denote the standardised object of ordinary speech' (Baker, 1912, p. 258). Douglas Lewis is also clearly aware of this distinction (Lewis, 1966). The point is, as Lewis emphasizes, that to refute idealism is not yet to secure realism.

second part, but at the same time it is a point about which it hardly seems worth arguing. It is that, in fact, which likely explains why Lewis did not think it worthwhile to examine this section in detail.

However, obvious as the point is, there were philosophers who were clearly prepared to deny it. Otherwise, why would Moore have included it? It is the philosophers who deny this who are his opponents. These opponents were the idealists. That *esse* must be *percipi* is defended by them in a variety of places. Moore refers to A. E. Taylor (cf. Taylor, 1902 and 1909). One also has John B. Watson (Watson, 1912), and W. M. Urban (Urban, 1909 and 1929), for example. Above all one has F. H. Bradley (Bradley, 1897). A succinct statement can be found in B. Bosanquet (Bosanquet, 1913). Reading these philosophers, it quickly becomes clear that the idealist argument is not simply Berkeley's, that it is a doctrine of relations that guarantees idealism: wherever there is a relation then there is consciousness, and that the unity achieved upon this account by relations implies inseparability of the relata, the parts of the unity. Bosanquet holds that the various parts of a sensation are related to one another by relations of similarity and dissimilarity; these relations create a unity; this relational unity cannot exist except through the activity of mind.

> How do the elements of the [sensation] hang together? What makes the blue reinforce or modify the blue? There is no push or pull between them. They work on each other through their identity and difference; or, to avoid disputes, here irrelevant, through their likeness and unlikeness. What sort of medium does such a unity involve? Surely, that of consciousness and no other. Blue, then, while it

retains the characters of blue, must have it in the life of the mind. (Bosanquet, 1913, p. 33)

Bosanquet emphasizes what Bradley, Taylor, Urban and Watson also emphasized, that relations not only imply consciousness but also the notion of a complete system. Moreover, the parts of this system cannot be as they are apart from the system: to be a sensation that is blue is for the sensation to be related to other entities, if only by relations of likeness and unlikeness, and to be related is to be inseparable from consciousness.

> ...no world can be synthetic in itself, that is, can possess universals as a part of its own nature, if its elements have not, pervading them, the living nexus and endeavour towards a whole which indicates participation in the nature of minds. I cannot understand any attempt to explain a universal which does not recognise that it absolutely consists in the effort of a content to complete itself as a system. (Bosanquet, 1913, p. 35)

What establishes idealism, on this view, is not the collapse of the act-object distinction, as in Berkeley. Rather, what establishes idealism is that there can be no structure apart from a structuring activity. 'There can be no concrete whole but a whole centring in mind, and no self-existent whole but a concrete whole' (Bosanquet, 1913, pp. 39–40). It is not so much that qualities, whether secondary or primary, are mind-dependent, as Berkeley would have it, that is, cannot exist save as predicated of a substantial mind. It is instead that they are parts of a unity that is achieved through the activity of consciousness: the idealist conclusion concerning all qualities:

...is drawn..., one might say, from their being mind-component; that is, possessing a logical character or implicity unity, which finds completion only in the focus of mind, which, in turn, it constitutes. (Bosanquet, 1913, p. 42)

The root of idealism:

...is not the failure to distinguish between an act and an object of mind. It is not any simple prejudice that mind can apprehend only what is part of itself. But it is the insight – an insight substantially just – that a universe severed from the life of mind can never fulfil the conditions of self-existence...to overlook the character of mind which bears on this point, when stating the simplest points of perception, is to be misled *ab initio*. Mind is always a world; its objects are always fragments. (Bosanquet, 1913, p. 38)[3]

As one explores the idealist account of relations, we find the following. This doctrine of relations must be such that where one has a relation predicated of two things, there is a third individual, the whole. The two relata are parts or aspects of this whole, and insofar as they are such parts or aspects they are not genuine individuals. The whole alone is a truly real individual. The whole itself not only has these aspects but is characterized as being a whole of a certain sort depending upon the way in which the parts are related. The original things are inseparable parts of the relational whole. Moreover, the whole is active: it causes its own differentiation into the parts according to the relational structure that characterizes it.

---

[3] Thus, phenomenalism, or idealism, is a consequence of the doctrine of relations, not a premise for the theory – contrary to what Skorupski suggests (Skorupski, 1993, p. 84). See footnote 1 above.

Unless the doctrine of relations had these features, the consequences held to follow from the fact of order by idealists such as Bosanquet, Taylor, Watson and Urban – and by Bradley, for it is above all his doctrine of relations that we are talking about – these consequences that the idealists draw simply would not follow from the fact that things do, really, stand in relations to one another.

Now, the classical empiricists – from Locke through Hume to the Mills – denied any ontological status to relations; they held what Russell later called a 'monadistic' account. The idealists are insisting against this view that order and relations must be given ontological status. Moore in fact agrees. That is why he can distinguish, for example, between the relation of predication and that of intentionality. But it is a non-idealistic view of relations. For, Moore insists upon the separability of the relata in the case of the intentional relation, something that the idealists deny. The question, then, for the idealists is this: Why does the fact of order imply that this view of relations is correct and that of Moore is wrong?

In fact, there is no argument. As Moore and Russell never refrained from pointing out, the doctrine of relations defended by the idealists was taken for granted. As Russell remarked in his review of Joachim's *The Nature of Truth*, 'The arguments in the pages we have been considering are...such as will only appear cogent to those who already admit the conclusions which the arguments are intended to prove' (Russell, 1906, p. 531; cf. Joachim, 1906). No arguments for the doctrine of relations were in fact offered – other than the arguments put forward by Watson, that this idealist account of relations, unlike the monadistic account found traditionally in empiricism, could account for order (Watson, 1912).

Moore, however, wants to do more than just show that the idealist doctrine of relations has nothing much in its favour. He wants to argue that the doctrine is false, to refute it. He proposes to show that idealism is false by showing the falsity of the central implication of the idealist account of relations, and, specifically, of the feature which implies that *esse* must be *percipi*, to wit, the doctrine that relata must always be inseparable. Now, while Moore proposes thus to argue against the idealist account of relations, it is also true that he, Moore, unlike the traditional empiricists, does not reject relations. Indeed, he accepts them, in contrast to the traditional empiricists. That, after all, is his point against Berkeley. What he does do is insist that things, properties, and relations are distinct, that, while they are related one to another, they are also separable. Moore urges, in other words, that by itself relatedness does not imply that distinct relata are logically inseparable.

The idealist, Moore suggests, holds that yellow and the sensation of yellow are indistinguishable. Hence, 'to assert that yellow is necessarily an object of experience is to assert that yellow is necessarily yellow – a purely identical proposition, and therefore proved by the law of contradiction alone' (Moore, 1922, p. 14). But unlike 'A is A', the proposition that yellow is a sensation is substantive, and worth defending. Hence, 'the proposition also implies that experience is, after all, something distinct from yellow – else there would be no reason for insisting that yellow is a sensation...' (Moore, 1922, p. 14). Thus, the very assertion of the idealist, that yellow is inseparable from the experiencing of it, is one that would not be made unless yellow and the experience of it were in fact distinct and therefore separable. The doctrine of relations proposed by the idealists maintains, since yellow and the experience are indeed related, they form a unified whole and therefore also maintains that yellow and the experience are inseparable and therefore not distinct. But to state the doctrine presupposes that yellow and the experience are distinct. The very attempt to state the doctrine of relations thus refutes that doctrine. The doctrine of relations thus does not so much establish that there is no distinction as obscure the fact that such a distinction exists.

> When, therefore, we are told that green and the sensation of green are certainly distinct but yet are not separable, or that it is an illegitimate abstraction to consider the one apart from the other, what these provisos are used to assert is, that though the two things are distinct yet you not only can but must treat them as if they were not. Many philosophers, therefore, when they admit a distinction, yet (following the lead of Hegel) boldly assert their right, in a slightly more obscure form of words, also to deny it. (Moore, 1922, p. 15)

Moore's argument is clear. It is in effect an appeal to the empiricist's Principle of Acquaintance (PA).[4] We do in fact know yellow; it is presented to us. We also know experience; this too is presented to us. These entities that are presented to us are presented as distinct. They are presented as self-complete, and to know the one does not require us to know the other. The entity

---

[4] For a discussion of this principle, see Wilson, 1970, 1983, 1969, and 1986.

yellow as we know it, as it is presented to us, is presented as an entity such that there is nothing about it that requires it to be connected inseparably with experience. To identify it as yellow does not require us to identify it as somehow connected to any other property, which would after all be required if it were, as the idealists assert, inseparably connected to some other entity, eg., experience.

This argument from acquaintance, that we are not presented with necessary connections, and we can therefore, by PA, not admit them into our ontology, can be found in earlier philosophers. It can be found, for example, in Locke (Locke, 1894, bk. 4, chap. 3, sect. 28).

It is this Lockean argument that Moore re-introduced into philosophy. In fact he had already made much the same point in his earlier essay (Moore, 1899). Moore makes the point that the idealist account – Bradley's account – of relations requires us to ascend to the Absolute before we can make any true judgement at all.[5] For Bradley, a sign is an entity with meaning; it could be linguistic or it could be mental (Bradley, 1922, pp. 3ff). But, contrary to the classical empiricists, the meaning is not an image: the details of images are irrelevant to the meaning they have for us. So far, Moore agrees with Bradley: meaning is not an image. Now, for Bradley, a sign, like any entity, has, in his terminology, a content: its content is the totality of its properties – 'the complex of qualities and relations that it contains' (Bradley, 1922, p. 3). A sign's meaning cannot be its total content, since several signs can have the same meaning. Its meaning is but a part of the content of the

---

[5] Moore does not add the further point that Russell makes, that even then we cannot make a true judgement.

sign, a part that is 'cut off, fixed by the mind, and considered apart from the existence of the sign' (Bradley, p. 4). Blue is, of course, the meaning of the awareness of blue. This implies that blue is only part of the content of the sign, the awareness. Insofar as this blue is isolated and abstracted from the totality of the relational complex, it is not grasped as it really is. In order to identify truly, or, more truly, precisely what it is that is presented to us, we must locate it relative to the other things to which it is related. Any two ideas, or, more generally, any two signs, will have different contents, if only because they will stand in different relations to different things. This implies that, if two ideas, perhaps both mine, or perhaps mine and thine, have the same meaning, then they have but part of their content in common. More accurately, each will have a part, and these parts will be the same. However, to say this is to place those parts in the context of certain relations of similarity and dissimilarity.[6] In order, therefore, to know that these contents are the same, we must become aware of the whole, the relational complex, by virtue of which they are the same. This is what is required by Bradley's idealist account of relations. In fact, in order to know precisely what the meaning of an idea is we must place it in its total context. Since everything, meanings included, is in the end related to everything else one way or another, it follows that with respect to any meaning, we cannot know precisely what it is, we cannot identify it as it is in itself, unless we proceed through all those relations to a grasp of the infinite whole. Thus, Moore correctly infers, we can know what really is the meaning of one of our ideas only if we have passed through an infinite

---

[6]   See the remarks of Bosanquet, discussed above.

regress of judgements: as Moore puts it, the task of knowing precisely what we mean requires 'the completion of an infinite number of psychological judgements before any judgement can be made at all' (Moore, 1899, p. 178). Again, the idealist account of relations

> ...presupposes that I may have two ideas, that have a part of their content in common; but...at the same time compel[s] us to describe this common part of content as part of the content of some third idea. (Moore, 1899, p. 178)

That is, Bradley's idealist account of relations requires the introduction of a third particular, the Whole, over and above the two particulars that stand in relation to each other. This relational whole is such that the one quality cannot be identified independently of its necessary connections to other qualities.[7] But, Moore indicates, in fact qualities can be identified as themselves without reference to the relations in which they stand to other qualities and other things. Moore makes the point with specific reference to the relation between qualities and the mind that knows them, in a way therefore that touches specifically on the concern of 'The Refutation of Idealism':

> It is indifferent to their nature whether anybody thinks them or not. They are incapable of change; and the relation into which they enter with the

---

[7] Thomas Baldwin takes Bradley's 'content' and 'part of the content' to be simply a collection of qualities, but has not explored the idealist account of relations sufficiently to note that when one speaks in the context of that account of relations of a quality which is a 'common part' to two contents one cannot identify that quality independently of its necessary connections to other qualities (Baldwin, 1990, p. 14). He thus fails, as he himself suggests, to understand the significance of Moore's argument.

knowing subject implies no action or reaction. (Moore, 1899, p. 179)[8]

Moore makes the point about qualities being identifiable apart from the relations in which they stand with specific reference to the cognitive relation, but he implies the point in full generality, and Russell was later to cite Moore's specific statement but only to assert it himself in that full generality (Russell, 1937, p. 449).

Moore and Russell, we see, appealed systematically to the empiricist's Principle of Acquaintance to make their case against the idealists. It was this appeal that Moore re-introduced into philosophy. Philosophers seem in fact to have found it fairly convincing. After all, the idealist doctrine of relations which denied that there are any real distinctions is no longer with us. Moore's argument is that a relational whole 'does contain analytically that which is said to be its part', contrary to the claim of the idealists that to analyse is to falsify (Moore, 1903, p. 34). Hence the origin of the designation 'analytical philosophy', which has come to characterize at least English-speaking philosophy ever since. That is how persuasive Moore's argument was, how persuasive his appeal to the empiricist's Principle of Acquaintance.

In fact, if we turn to more recent philosophers who have found various aspects of Bradley's philosophy attractive, at least so far as it emphasized things neglected by various other of their contemporaries, they have stated those points in a way that is compatible

---

[8] Thomas Baldwin misses this part of Moore's argument (Baldwin, 1990, pp. 13–15). Again, the failure to provide a detailed account of the idealist theory of relations leads Baldwin to fail to recognize the thrust of Moore's argument and how devastating Moore's appeal to our ordinary experience of qualities is to that account of relations, and therefore to the idealism which rests upon that account.

with Moore's appeal to the empiricist's PA. While these philosophers are inclined to emphasize, as did the idealists, the relational structure of the world, they do so in a way that allows that there are in fact real distinctions among things, properties and relations. But in allowing the latter they allow that there are aspects to the world – eg., mind and what the mind knows – which are not logically, or ontologically, inseparable.

Thus, to take one, though an important, example, consider some of the views of T. L. S. Sprigge (Sprigge, 1993). What Sprigge wants to do is to rehabilitate some of the idealist notions, particularly some of those concerning relations. One example is his attempt to render plausible the holistic principle of the idealists that 'to be related requires belonging together in a more genuine whole' (Sprigge, 1993, p. 267). He asks us to consider the streets of a town.

> ... one could say that the streets, understood as the full social realities which they are, belong together in the life of the town, region, or country, and that at some level one of these is going to be more of a genuine individual than the individual streets. It will be more of a genuine individual in that it makes more sense to try to understand it in its own terms. To try to understand one individual street, in the sense of explaining, or even giving much of a description of, what is going on there, while confining oneself simply to what lies within its bounds, would be hopeless; it requires rather a study of the town as a whole, or perhaps of the region or country to which it belongs. Thus if you take the street as a 'concrete' reality, as the whole of one distinguishable part of the universe, then it seems reasonable to say that its relations to other things are always a matter of how it unites with

them to constitute something larger which is more of a genuine individual than they are. (Sprigge, 1993, p. 267)

Now, if the empiricist knows what he or she is about, it is unlikely that they will disagree with this. What Sprigge is insisting is that in order to explain a social phenomenon, it is necessary to introduce social relations as relevant variables. Just as, in order to understand the motions of the planets, it was necessary for Newton to consider the distances of the bodies of the system relative to each other as among the relevant variables.[9] There have been those who neglected the role of social relations. This can be seen in those who demand individualistic explanations. It can be seen in those who insist that the atomistic economic man is the paradigm case for social explanations. It can be seen in some philosophies of the social sciences, John Stuart Mill's to give one notable example.[10] But that said, it is also true that there is nothing in empiricism that requires one to ignore either relations or social relations: the existence of the former generically and the latter specifically is quite compatible with accepting the injunction to do philosophy within the constraints established by PA. In any case, upon Sprigge's usage it is clear that a 'genuine individual' is one that is causally complete, one where the individuals within it exemplify jointly a complete set of relevant variables, and where no individual outside the system is (terribly) relevant.[11] Such a system is the ideal of scientific explanation – it is the sort of explanation achieved by Newton with regard

[9] Cf. Brodbeck, 1968 and also Addis, 1975.

[10] Cf. Wilson, forthcoming (b).

[11] Cf. G. Bergmann's notion of 'process knowledge'; see Bergmann, 1957; see also Wilson, 1985.

to the solar system. In contrast to the way in which a system that is complete and closed stands alone causally, completely determined within itself, individuals within such a system do not in terms of their causal relations stand alone. The point is that Sprigge is here not only correct but states a position that is quite compatible with an empiricism defined by the PA to which Moore appealed (Moore, 1922).

The point about causal relations was in fact emphasized by the idealists against those who had neglected it. The radical individualism that ignores social relations has returned in spite of the idealists. One can find it, for example, in Popperian 'methodological individualism'. It is good that Sprigge should recall to us the idealist insight that this is a view that simply will not do. The point is, however, that when Sprigge does so recall us he takes for granted Moore's critique of idealism, and recalls us in a way that turns out to be fully compatible with empiricism's PA to which Moore appealed.

This is also evident in another point made by Sprigge in defence of the idealists. Sprigge points out that 'the qualities which things exhibit when seen in isolation are incompatible with the qualities they present as elements in larger totalities' (Sprigge, 1993, p. 416). This is something with which no one who disagrees with the idealists need disagree. If we have a physical object moving in isolation, then it will have one velocity. If it moves into a certain relation with another object, then it will, by virtue of the interaction, move in a different way. In other words, it will have a property when it is related to another object that it would not have if it were not so related. Similar processes occur in perception. An object in isolation will present one colour to the observer, but if it is presented standing in certain relations to other individuals of a somewhat different colour, both those individuals will present a different colour to the observer. Again, put a straight stick in water and it appears bent, presents to one that geometrical shape where it presented before a different geometrical shape. Once one takes into account the causal relevance of relations none of this is problematic. In contrast, for the traditional empiricists it was indeed problematic, since their monadistic account of relations made it difficult for them to allow that relational as opposed to non-relational properties were causally relevant. The idealists made a sound point against this traditional empiricist position. But once relations are admitted, as Moore and Russell admit them, there is no reason why this point should not be granted. To grant it requires only that relations be admitted, not that the idealist account of relations be accepted. Sprigge in effect recognizes this when, having drawn attention to these cases, he does not proceed from them to the further conclusion, implied by the idealist account of relations, that the properties of the entities, either when they are related or when they are not, are so inseparably united that they are in the end not distinct. This implication, clearly suggested by, for example, Bosanquet's discussion above, is simply not accepted by Sprigge. To that extent, then, while he accepts insights defended by the idealists against the monadistic account of relations of the earlier empiricists, he rejects what Moore set out firmly to reject, the implication of the idealist account of relations that entities that are related lose their distinctness in an inseparable union. Sprigge, in other words, on this point accepts the conclusion justified by Moore's appeal to PA.

Sprigge's conformity to Moore's PA is still more clear in another appeal which he makes in defence of the idealists.

Russell argued against the idealists that their account of relations – what Russell called the monistic account of relations – could not in the end deal satisfactorily with a number of issues (Russell, 1937, pp. 448–9).[12] Bradley's was, of course, the best articulated of the idealist accounts of relations (Bradley, 1897 and 1935). As did the other idealists, Bradley insisted, against the traditional monadistic account of relations the empiricists had adopted, that there are relations which are genuine in the sense that their relata are not independent, or, equivalently, in the sense that the being of one relatum is not separable from the being of the other relatum.[13]

> If it [a relation] is to be real, it must be so at the expense of the terms, or, at least, must be something which appears in them or to which they belong. A relation between A and B implies really a substantial foundation within them. This foundation, if we say that A is like to B, is the identity X which holds these differences together. And so with space and time – everywhere there must be a whole embracing what is related, or there would be no differences and no relation. It seems as if a reality poss*ess*ed differences A and B, incompatible with one another and also with itself. And so in order, without contradiction, to retain its various properties, this whole consents to wear the form of relations between them. (Bradley, 1897, p. 18)

[12] Cf. also Wilson, forthcoming (a).

[13] Cf. Wilson, forthcoming (c).

But like the other idealists, Bradley insisted that where there is a relational fact there is an individual constituted by the two related individuals forming a whole which is a further individual. 'Nothing in the end is real but the individual...' is the way Bradley puts it, and therefore infers that the whole must itself be an individual (Bradley, 1935, p. 663). Bradley thus applies the dictum in particular to relations: 'A relation, to be experienced and to be actual, must be more than a mere abstraction. It must be an individual or particular fact, and, if less than this, it cannot be taken as itself' (Bradley, 1935, pp. 635–6).

Bradley concludes against the monadistic account that 'there must be a whole embracing what is related', and imposes the condition that the parts be inseparable in this whole. Thus, 'Your individual term is an abstraction always. It implies what we may call a selection from the concrete fact of the whole and entire experience' (Bradley, 1935, p. 646). This relational whole must furthermore be itself a substantial particular. From these two conditions Bradley infers his own account of the nature of this whole: the relata A and B are different things within a whole (A, B), which itself is an individual and which has those two terms as aspects. This whole then 'consents to wear the form of a relation'; thus, if A and B stand in the relation R, then the correct representation of this fact consists in attributing a property corresponding to R, say r, to (A, B). Thus, according to Bradley's account, the correct way to represent the fact reported by

(1)   a is R to b

is given by

(2)   (a, b) is r

or,

(3) r(a, b)

The whole (a, b) is itself a particular thing, of which the two terms a and b are but aspects, and where the arrangement r characterizes the whole. But this whole consists of the relata as parts. Thus, the relation holds of the relata, not separately as in the monadistic account, but jointly: 'where the whole, relaxing its unity, takes the form of an arrangement, there is co-existence with concord' (Bradley, 1897, p. 19).

Russell criticized this account on the ground, among others, that it did not account for the fact of order (Russell, 1937, p. 221). If we consider the example of a cup upon a saucer, the two particulars stand in a certain relation, namely that of being on top of. This relation orders the objects in the fact in a certain way: the relation goes from the cup to the saucer. But the two particulars are to be treated symmetrically, upon Bradley's analysis, relative to each other, relative to the whole of which they are both parts, and relative to the relational form exemplified by the whole: at no point are we able to distinguish, upon this account, whether it is the saucer that is upon the cup or the cup that is upon the saucer.

Sprigge has attempted to defend Bradley on this point. In fact, as it turns out, while his defence succeeds in making a valid phenomenological point, it fails to touch the substance of Russell's ontological critique of Bradley in particular and the idealist's monistic account of relations in general. More importantly, as we shall see, Sprigge's defence turns out to be compatible with Moore's critique of idealism.

Sprigge tells us that:

> The monist must interpret the proposition 'This cup is above the saucer' as a characterisation of a certain total situation comprising the cup and the saucer. Now certainly if he took it as the predication of a mere aboveness of that situation, then indeed he could not distinguish its significance from that of 'That saucer is above that cup'. It is evident, however, that he would take it as the application to a sensibly presented totality of the predication being (the totality) of a cup on top of a saucer, which is a quite different gestalt quality from that of being (the totality) of a saucer on top of a cup. (Sprigge, 1993, p. 407)

Sprigge argues that the judgement that the cup is on the saucer, understood as attributing a gestalt quality of the whole is not the same as a conjunctive judgement to the effect that 'This is a cup & that is a saucer & this is on top of that' (Sprigge, 1993, pp. 407–8). This is undoubtedly a correct phenomenological point. He also makes the point that in making the judgement our judgement is to the effect that 'This totality is a cup on a saucer', rather than a judgement in which we attend to two separate particulars (Sprigge, 1993, pp. 409–10). That is, the gestalt quality is predicated of a single subject; it is treated as a monadic predicate and not a dyadic predicate with two subjects. This, too, is a valid phenomenological point.

Now, it is clear that Sprigge does have a point, that if Russell insists that the predication of a gestalt quality is simply a conjunction of three predications, two non-relational and one relational, then Bradley does better justice to the phenomenology of judgement. But it is clear from the overall thrust of idealism that it is doing more when it asserts its theory of relations than simply insisting that there are circumstances in which we predicate gestalt qualities of totalities. The idealist theory involves much more than this; otherwise (what Sprigge does not note) the account of relations by itself would not imply idealism, the inseparability of any set of related things both from themselves and from mind. Still, it might nonetheless be true (as Sprigge does suggest) that predications of gestalt qualities enable one to capture, contrary to what Russell argues, the notion of order. This might not be the whole of the idealist account of relations, but it will be part of it.

Still, even if, as I think we must, we grant the correctness of Sprigge's phenomenological points about judgements involving gestalt qualities, it does not follow that Sprigge has shown that the idealist account of relations can capture, as Russell rightly insists it must, the relevant relational order. There is, to be sure, a problem that Sprigge creates for Russell, namely that of providing a way of formulating a text that at once expr*esse*s the content of the gestalt judgements to which Sprigge directs our attention, and does so in a phenomenologically correct way. But it does not follow that the notion of a gestalt quality captures the feature of order in a way that makes it possible for Bradley to avoid Russell's criticism.

In fact, what I want to suggest is that we can provide for Russell a phenomenologically adequate account of judgements which predicate gestalt qualities of totalities. It turns out, however, that these predications presuppose order rather than account for it. They therefore cannot provide a basis for defending Bradley's idealistic account of relations in which the relata always occur symmetrically relative to each other.

Now, to speak of a 'gestalt' quality is to speak of a

structure that is predicated of a whole. There certainly are such qualities. Think of four objects so arranged that the relations they are in determine that they form a square. This property, that of being a square, is one that is exemplified by the four objects jointly, by that totality, in other words, and not by any of the four individual objects that, related as they are, form that totality. Sprigge is quite correct when he points out that these gestalt qualities are often presented to us in experience. But do they provide any sort of defence of the idealist account of relations?

The question must become: What would Russell be able to say about such qualities?

In thinking about relations we must distinguish

(4)   < a, b >

from

(5)   < b, a >

as two different 'ordered pairs'. These ordered pairs are taken to satisfy such axioms as

(6)   < a, b > = < b, a > ↔ a = b

The usual axioms for ordered pairs establish that such pairs satisfy the same formal axioms as pairs ordered by relations. Sets of ordered pairs are what Russell called relations in extension. As for relations in extension, Russell introduces these into *Principia Mathematica* in section *21 (Russell, 1927, vol. 1, p. 200). He defines a predicate

(7)   xy[R(x, y)](u, v)

This is a predicate expression in just the sense in which 'R(u, v)' is a predicate expression. (7) is so defined that it holds of u and v if and only if

(8)   R(u, v)

(7) is a class of ordered pairs; it can be proved that the members of (7) satisfy the axioms that must be satisfied by ordered pairs. Specifically, (7) is the class of pairs ordered by the relation R; it is, in other words, the relation R considered in extension. The order in the pairs is that which is established by the relation R. Thus, the concept (7) does not introduce the notion of order but rather presupposes it.

Russell does not make use of the notion of *an* ordered pair, but his apparatus enables one to introduce such a notion. An ordered pair is a set, a totality; it is a set which has but two members, where these members are taken in a certain order. Recognizing this, we see that the ordered pair

(4)   < a, b >

can be defined as

(9)   xy[x = a & y = b](u, v)

(9) will hold of u and v just in case that we have

(10)   u = a & v = b

It is thus analytically true that (9) holds of the pair (a) and (b) and analytically false that it holds of any other pair. In particular, it is analytically false that (9) holds of the pair (b) and (a). Here again, (9) does not introduce order but rather presupposes it. The order which it presupposes is represented by the typographical order of the conjuncts in (9), or, what amounts to the same, in (10). If it is Bertrand who has selected the arrangement (10), then the order among the individuals (a) and (b) that is represented by the typographical order is given by the relational fact:

(11) (a) and (b) stand in the relation of prior to posterior in Bertrand's selection

(11) is of course an objective relational fact, though it is, to be sure, a fact that exists by virtue of an arbitrary choice made by Bertrand. In this sense, the arrangement is indeed arbitrary, but it is still an arrangement, a relational fact about the individuals (a) and (b). It is the relation (11) that orders the pair consisting of (a) and (b), and it is this order that is represented by the typographical order in (9). Here, as in the case of (7), we see that the defined predicate (9) does not introduce the notion of order but rather presupposes it.

The notation for an ordered pair allows us to refer to the pair of entities that are ordered or structured by some relation or other, but without making specific reference to the relation that does the ordering. The terms referring to ordered pairs can function grammatically as subject terms of sentences that are used to make statements about the structured wholes to which the term refers. Russell in this provides a notation for referring to the structured wholes to which Sprigge directs our attention. We can similarly introduce by contextual definition one-pace or monadic predicate terms that can be predicated of ordered pairs. Thus, we can introduce

(12) $R (< x, y >) = Df\ R(x, y)$

'R' is a one-place predicate that takes as its subject terms the special terms that refer to ordered pairs. Thus, to say that an ordered pair is R is to make a non-relational predication of a structured whole understood in context to be a single unified totality. Similarly, we can define

(13)   (F–R–G) (< x, y >) = Df Fx & R(x, y) & Gx

which again constitutes a one-place, or non-relational, predicate applying to ordered pairs understood in context to be single unified totalities.

Now, with regard to Sprigge's cup and saucer, what he is saying is that we often make judgements about such situations that cannot reasonably be expressed as merely conjunctive. Rather, they are judgements best seen as predicating a non-relational gestalt predicate of a single complex taken as a unitary whole. Neither Russell nor the empiricist need disagree with Sprigge that there is a phenomenological difference here in the two sorts of judgement that must be captured. What we have just seen is that Russell provides us with the resources for expressing this sort of difference on the side of the judgement. If a and b are Sprigge's cup and saucer, then what he is saying is that the judgement that is expressed by

(14)   (F–R–G) (< a, b >)

is different from the judgement that is expressed by

(15)   Fa & R (< a, b >) & Gb

or by

(16)   Fa & R (a, b) & Gb

The point that Sprigge is making concerns the text that is most appropriate for expressing a judgement. He insists, quite correctly, that certain judgements about wholes or totalities must be expressed by sentences making non-relational, non-conjunctive predications of wholes (Sprigge, 1993, pp. 407–408).

The issue is whether this supports the idealist account of relations or is, rather, compatible with the account of relations given by Russell. It is of course true that the phenomenological point about relations that Sprigge makes comes down on the side of Bradley against the monadistic account of relations that the early empiricists had taken over from the tradition. But it comes down equally in favour of any account that asserts, against the monadistic view, that relations must be given genuine ontological status. It thus tells equally in favour of Russell. It tells against Russell only if one insists upon accepting as a principle the thesis that different judgements expr*esse*d by sentences of different forms must be understood as being about different complexes. In the case of relations, the idealist account of relations forces us to accept something like this principle. But that presupposes that one has antecedently accepted that account for relations, where the issue that is now before us is whether we have any reason to accept that account of relations. The argument has to be from the principle to the account and not conversely. And unfortunately, perhaps, Sprigge gives us no reason to accept that principle. His example therefore provides no basis for rejecting Russell's view of relations and accepting that of the idealists.

Further, Sprigge, unlike the idealists, does not insist that the structured wholes are individuals over and above the related individuals, nor insist with the idealists that the related individuals somehow lose their individuality in the super-individual that constitutes their relatedness. The gestalt qualities and structured wholes or totalities to which Sprigge directs our attention thus presuppose a structure or ordering, and therefore presuppose the relation R that Russell insists is basic. Sprigge is thus allowing that (14) and (16) express different judgements but are nonetheless both about the same objective state of affairs. He is thus accepting that the various forms of judgement that we use to describe the cup being on the saucer all pre-suppose the ordering of the cup and saucer induced by the relation that holds between them. In short, Sprigge is in effect agreeing with Russell that the issue of order cannot be avoided.

Moreover, Sprigge does not suggest that the cup becomes inseparable from the saucer once the relation between them is recognized. The whole consisting of the cup and saucer, the former on top of the latter, is itself distinguishable from other wholes, and, moreover, the cup is distinguishable from the saucer. But this is to say that things are after all not inseparable. That is, he recognizes that one can consistently affirm both that

(17) Fa

and

(18) ~ R(a, b)

or that one could consistently affirm that the cup (a) is on the saucer (b) while denying that the saucer is on the table (c), even when it is in fact upon the table. In allowing that the parts that are related to each other are thus distinguishable from each other, and therefore separable, he is denying that his account of relations implies such inseparability. What this means is that Sprigge has accepted Moore's basic claim against the idealists and against their account of relations, that when things are related they become inseparable parts of a single whole.

Sprigge makes a good number of valuable, and valid points, in his defence of Bradley. He shows that Bradley is not simply the silly metaphysician that Ayer, for example, took him to be.[14] Indeed, he indicates his acceptance of several idealist theses, becoming thereby a major exponent in the late twentieth century of the idealist positions developed some hundred years earlier. But at the same time, as we now see, he also takes for granted the fundamental criticism, based in the empiricist's PA, that Moore offered of the idealist account of relations (Moore, 1922).

Now, the argument that Moore and others offer against Berkeleyan idealism has not universally been accepted. There are, for example, those who hold what has been called an 'adverbial' account of perception.[15] The philosophers who accept this adverbial account of perception have rejected the conclusion of the second half of Moore's argument. But these philosophers have also accepted, as we saw Sprigge accept, the conclusion of the first half of Moore's argument that things and their qualities are distinct from other things, they are what they are independently of other things and entities, including those entities to which they are related. In this case, it is the quality of, say, experiencing bluely that is distinct from and independent of other qualities. To this extent, contemporary philosophers have largely accepted the conclusion of the first half of Moore's argument in refutation of idealism.

[14] Cf. Wilson, forthcoming (a).

[15] Such a position was developed by C. J. Ducasse and has more recently been defended by R. Chisholm. The relevance of this example was pointed out to me by Paul Coates.

We started by wondering why it was that the first half of Moore's argument tended to be overlooked by those discussing Moore's paper (Moore, 1922). What I am now suggesting is that Moore's argument has become so thoroughly accepted by the philosophical community that we have tended to forget that once upon a time that argument really was needed. We have forgotten that there were those who denied Moore's conclusion, and therefore have forgotten not only that the argument was needed but therefore also exactly what its force is. It has become a puzzle. When idealism is now to be defended this is to be done, as it is by Sprigge and by the defenders of the adverbial account of perception, by means that are compatible with Moore's point, and, it would seem, with PA. That shows how much Moore's paper marks a real turn away from the idealism of Bradley in the twentieth century: whatever idealism we now have it is not that idealism, nor can it be based on the theory of relations that we find in Bradley and the other idealists against whom Moore was arguing. *Esse* may well be *percipi*, but that is hardly plausible unless one can somehow establish that it must be that way. Moore's point – or, what is the same, Locke's point – was that an appeal to PA argues against the inseparability of such connections, and against the idealist theory of relations that entailed such inseparability. This point and this principle seems by now to have securely precluded any possibility that we can conceive that Berkeley's principle that *esse* is *percipi* can be made plausible by an account of relations that, on the one hand, makes relational states dependent upon consciousness, and, on the other hand, concludes that related entities become so inseparable as to be indistinguishable.

REFERENCES

L. Addis, *The Logic of Society* (Minneapolis: University of Minnesota Press, 1975).

Henry Baker, 'Can There Be Anything Obscure or Implicit in a Mental State?', *Proceedings of the Aristotelian Society*, vol. 13 ns (1912), pp. 257–81.

Thomas Baldwin, *G. E. Moore* (London: Routledge, 1990).

Gustav Bergmann, *Philosophy of Science* (Oxford: Oxford University Press, 1957).

Francis H. Bradley, *The Principles of Logic*, 2nd edn (London: Oxford University Press, 1922).

————, 'Relations', in his *Collected Essays*, vol. 2, pp. 628–76 (London: Oxford University Press, 1935).

Bernard Bosanquet, *The Distinction between Mind and Its Objects* (Manchester: Manchester University Press, 1913).

May Brodbeck, 'Methodological Individualisms', in May Brodbeck (ed.), *Readings in the Philosophy of the Social Sciences* (New York: Macmillan, 1968), pp. 280–303.

David Crossley, 'Moore's *Refutation of Idealism*: The Debate about Sensations', *Idealistic Studies*, vol. 24 (1994), pp. 1–20.

David Hume, *A Treatise of Human Nature*, eds. L. A. Selby-Bigge and P. H. Nidditch, 2nd edn (Oxford: Oxford University Press, 1978).

Harold H. Joachim, *The Nature of Truth* (Oxford: Oxford University Press, 1906).

Douglas Lewis, 'Moore's Realism', in L. Addis and D. Lewis, *Moore and Ryle: Two Ontologists* (The Hague: Nijhoff, 1966), chap. 1.

John Locke, *Essay concerning Human Understanding*, 4th edn, ed. A. C. Fraser (Oxford: Oxford University Press, 1894; reprinted New York: Dover, 1959).

George E. Moore, 'The Nature of Judgement', *Mind*, vol. 8 ns (1899), pp. 176–93.

————— , 'The Refutation of Idealism', in his *Philosophical Studies*, pp. 1–30 (London: Routledge and Kegan Paul, 1922).

Bertrand Russell, *Principles of Mathematics*, 2nd edn (London: Allen and Unwin, 1937; 1st edn 1903).

————— , Review of Joachim's *The Nature of Truth*, *Mind*, vol. 15 ns (1906), pp. 528–33.

Bertrand Russell and Alfred N. Whitehead, *Principia Mathematica*, 2nd edn (Cambridge: Cambridge University Press, 1927).

John Skorupski, *English-Language Philosophy 1750–1945* (Oxford: Oxford University Press, 1993).

Timothy L. S. Sprigge, *James and Bradley: American Truth and British Idealism* (LaSalle, Illinois: Open Court, 1993).

Alfred E. Taylor, 'Mind and Nature', *Ethics* (formerly *The International Journal of Ethics*), vol. 13 (1902), pp. 55–86.

——— , *The Elements of Metaphysics*, 2nd edn (London: Methuen, 1909; 1st edn 1903).

W. M. Urban, *Valuation: Its Nature and Laws* (London: Swan Sonneschein, 1909).

——— , *The Intelligible World: Metaphysics and Value* (London: George Allen and Unwin, 1929).

John B. Watson, *The Interpretation of Religious Experience, Part Second, Constructive* (Glasgow: James Maclehose and Sons, 1912).

Alan White, *G. E. Moore* (Oxford: Blackwell, 1958).

Fred Wilson, 'The Role of a Principle of Acquaintance in Ontology', *The Modern Schoolman*, vol. 47 (1969), pp. 37–56.

——— , 'Acquaintance, Ontology and Knowledge', *The New Scholasticism,* vol. 54 (1970), pp. 1–48.

—————— , 'Effability, Ontology and Method', *Philosophy Research Archives,* vol. 9 (1983), pp. 419–70.

—————— , *Explanation, Causation and Deduction* (Dordrecht, Netherlands: Reidel, 1985).

—————— , 'The Lockean Revolution in the Theory of Science', in S. Tweyman and G. Moyal (eds.), *Early Modern Philosophy: Epistemology, Metaphysics and Politics* (New York: Caravan Press, 1986), pp. 65–97.

—————— , 'Was Hume a Sceptic with regard to the Senses?', *The Journal for the History of Philosophy,* vol. 27 (1989a), pp. 49–73.

—————— , 'Was Hume a Subjectivist?', *Philosophy Research Archives,* vol. 14 (1989b), pp. 247–82.

—————— , 'Bradley's Impact on Empiricism', in James Bradley (ed.), *Philosophy after F. H. Bradley,* forthcoming (Bristol: Thoemmes Press, 1996).

—————— , 'John Stuart Mill on Psychology and the Moral Sciences', in J. M. Skorupski (ed.), *Cambridge Companion to John Stuart Mill,* forthcoming (a).

—————— , 'Relations from Burgersdijck to Bradley', in a collection of essays on the ontology and epistemology of relations edited by K. Barber, forthcoming (b).

IDEALISM AND THEORIES OF PERCEPTION

Paul Coates

A large part of the development of epistemology in this century has involved attempts to defend some form of direct realism against alternative theories of perception such as, on the one hand, phenomenalism, and, on the other, various versions of the causal theory of perception.

In this paper I argue that direct realism is an unstable position. Attempts to clarify and defend it in a form that is clearly distinguishable from the causal theory of perception are doomed to failure. The only coherent options, I shall argue, are some form of causal theory, or some form of idealism. I shall focus upon recent attempts to defend direct realism, and suggest that they display some of the central characteristics of idealism.

Before examining the main argument I need to explain some matters of terminology, in order to locate the key issues more precisely. In particular, the notions of perceptual experience and direct realism require clarification, since they are used in a confusing variety of ways in the literature.

I

When a subject perceives an object, he has, in some

sense, a perceptual experience. When a subject hallucinates he has an experience which, from a subjective point of view at least, is qualitatively similar to the kind of experience he has when genuinely perceiving something. This paper's main focus will be the ontological question of how perceptual experiences are related to the physical objects we perceive, and this will involve a discussion of the intimately related question of whether perceptual and hallucinatory experiences involve some common sensory element, such as a sense datum or sense impression. But before approaching this central ontological issue, there is a second question to be addressed concerning the character of the content of perceptual and hallucinatory experiences. For this purpose the two kinds of experience may be considered together and I shall henceforth use the term 'experience' to cover both veridical and hallucinatory cases where the ontological status of the experience is not in question.

In common with a number of recent writers on the subject, I distinguish between the intentional or propositional content of the experience, and its non-conceptual or phenomenal aspect. Clearly, in some way experiences involve intentional states; they represent the world as being some way. This representational aspect of experience I shall describe by speaking of the perceptual thought involved. But there is a second, non-representational aspect to experience which distinguishes it from pure thought. Earlier this century C. I. Lewis defended a distinction between what he termed 'the sensuously given', and the conceptual element in experience; a view which has something in common with this tradition has more recently been defended by Peacocke, who, at least in his earlier writings on this topic, distinguished between the sensational and the representational properties of experience (cf. Peacocke, 1983, chap. 1). However, to make a contrast by invoking the idea of sensational properties might seem to beg the question against the form of direct realism I shall be concerned with. The distinction I have in mind is the more general one between the intentional or conceptual component of the perceptual experience, and the phenomenal aspect of consciousness, or sensory awareness, that many writers claim is appropriately described by a non-epistemic use of terms such as 'appears' and 'seems' and 'looks' (cf. Chisholm, 1957, chap. 4, Lowe, 1992, p. 86). Such a distinction is independent of the controversy between the direct realist and the causal theorist.

Thus, to illustrate, suppose I am perceiving a tree situated in front of me; the intentional content of my experience would be described, if I am a normal adult subject, as: 'That object which is in front of me is a tree', or by some such similar expression in propositional form. But there could be a parallel case where I occupy the same location on a dark night, and think about the tree which I know to be there and entertain a thought with similar intentional content. Admittedly, there is some difference in the demonstrative character of the two thoughts, in so far as in the second situation my thought does not occur in the context where, as Evans expresses the point, there is a *continuing* informational link between subject and object, between myself and the tree (cf. Evans, 1982, p. 146).[1] This point can be conceded, so long as it is also recognized

---

[1] Considerations concerning various types of blindsight cases would, I believe, reinforce the claim made here that there are differences to be accounted for over and above any differences in the continuing informational link.

that there is a further difference between the two cases: what is also part of my experience in the perceptual case, and is lacking in the parallel case, is any sensory awareness, such that there is an appearance (in the non-epistemic sense) of a tree to me. I shall therefore distinguish the representational aspect of the subject's perceptual thought from his sensory awareness (or what I shall call, simply, his awareness). What is essential to sensory experience is that it involves the subject's phenomenal consciousness – it involves the subjective awareness of what it is like for the subject to have that kind of experience.[2]

Distinguishing the two aspects of perceptual experiences does not yet commit us to any claim about the ontological status of what sensory awareness involves, and this brings me to the main issue with which this paper is involved: according to one traditional account of perception, what a subject is aware of in perceptual experience is always an entity which is distinct from the physical objects in his surroundings; thus according to one version of this traditional type of account, the subject is aware of a sense datum which is caused by some physical object in his environment.[3] The direct

[2]   Some writers argue that what I have here termed the sensory awareness aspect of experience is also representational, though it involves a different kind of representational state from belief or pure thought (eg., Tye, 1992). In virtue of what I have just claimed, I am committed to rejecting this type of account of experience. But then so also is the direct realist, as I shall suggest. Hence in making the assumption that the sensory aspect of perceptual experience is distinct from the representational content I am not thereby begging any questions that support the case I put forward against the direct realist's position.

[3]   See for example Frank Jackson's excellent defence of the sense data view. Although I do not accept Jackson's claim that sense data are located in physical space, in most other respects I am in agreement with his claims (cf. Jackson, 1977, p. 103). I have defended the existence of sense data elsewhere (cf. Coates, 1976).

realist opposes this view. The label 'direct realism' has been appropriated to cover a number of slightly different views (see for example Armstrong's application of this term to a version of the causal theory).[4] However, the version I shall be concerned with, and which I believe captures what is central to the opposing tradition, is a version in which it is claimed that the subject is aware, in the sensory sense distinguished above, of the physical objects themselves, and not of any intermediary entity or 'perceptual deputy'.

A clear statement of this position is provided in Dretske (1969). Dretske argues that there is a non-conceptual aspect to perceptual experience, and treats this as an irreducible relation which holds directly between the perceiver and the physical object he perceives. He denies that this aspect of perception can be analysed further in terms of the causation of items like sense data. In a standard case of perception, as when we see a coffee pot in normal circumstances, 'it is the coffee pot itself which looks some way to us'.[5]

Dretske's position may be viewed as a precursor to the position more recently advanced by Paul Snowdon (1981) and John McDowell (1982, 1986 and 1994a), which has been called 'the disjunctive view'. The essential feature of this view can be brought out by reference to its treatment of hallucinatory experiences. On the traditional causal account sketched above, which the disjunctive view opposes, the subject is aware of the same ontological type of item, such as a sense datum, whether he is hallucinating, or perceiving an object veridically. The difference between the two lies

---

[4] Though as Armstong subsequently acknowleged, his use of the term was potentially misleading (cf. Armstrong, 1968, p. 227).

[5] Compare this with Dretske's account (Dretske, 1969, p. 71).

in the causal ancestry of the sense datum that the subject is aware of. Whereas, roughly speaking, in the case of veridical perception the sense datum is caused in the appropriate way by a physical object outside of the subject's awareness, in most cases of hallucination there is no such appropriately placed object in the subject's environment (leaving aside problem cases involving deviant causal chains). For the causal theorist there is in all cases one general type of state of affairs whose obtaining makes 'looks' ascriptions true (compare Snowdon, 1981, p. 186).

The disjunctive theorist, in contrast, argues that we must distinguish between two kinds of entity that a subject can be aware of; in hallucination the subject is aware of a *mere* appearance, or mind dependent entity. But in ordinary perception the subject is aware of a physical object (or possibly some *fact* directly involving the physical object itself). In McDowell's words, '...appearances are no longer conceived of as in general intervening between the experiencing subject and the world' (McDowell, 1988, p. 211); and elsewhere McDowell speaks of 'the object itself [being] presented to one's awareness' (McDowell, 1994a, p. 192).

It is this key idea, that ordinary perception provides the subject with some form of direct sensory access to the physical world, some form of direct encounter with the environment of the perceiver, over and above any relation arising from our perceptual thoughts, that I want to focus on. But before I do so, it will help to have before us a slightly fuller characterization of the alternative causal picture of perception, and I wish in particular to emphasize two points in connection with this alternative view.

First, nothing I have said so far commits me to any

claim about incorrigibility. It is not a necessary feature of the causal view that the subject has incorrigible knowledge about the way things appear to him. A second important point relates to the role of the subject's perceptual thought, that is, to the representative aspect of his experience. Causal theorists have been guilty in the past of postulating phenomenologically implausible claims about rapid processes of inference on the part of the subject, from thoughts about the sensory awareness of mind-dependent items, to judgements about the physical objects that lie beyond immediate awareness. This version of the causal theory, which may be called 'representative realism', is rejected in this paper.

A rather more plausible account of the perceptual thought was put forward at the beginning of this century by the unjustly neglected group of Critical Realists, amongst whose members were George Santayana, Arthur Lovejoy and Roy Wood Sellars. According to the critical realist view, in perceiving an object in normal circumstances we are directly caused to have a thought about that object. The sensory appearance is not the object of the intentional aspect of perceptual experience. It is not normally the focus of our attention. Our perceptual thoughts relate directly to the objects in our physical environment. In modern terminology, although the perception of objects is mediated by sensory awareness, it is judgementally or cognitively direct.[6] This squares with the fact that most of the time the perceiver is concerned with objective features of the physical things he perceives, and not with how they appear to him. In seeing an object, I

[6] A modern version of this view is argued by John Mackie (cf. Mackie, 1976, chap. 2 passim).

represent it as being of a certain objective size and distance away from me, and I do not normally form concepts about the appearance it presents to me (in looking out of a window I am not usually aware that I see the window frame as double).

II

With these preliminary points of clarification completed, I now want to consider how the phenomena of hallucination bear upon the disagreement between the critical realist and the disjunctive theorist. I shall try to show that the direct realist view is ultimately unstable, and that attempts to uphold it collapse into idealism.

It is necessary to distinguish between two quite different kinds of argument in which possibilities about hallucination are brought to bear upon the proper analysis of perception. On what may be termed 'the sceptical version' of the argument, the chief concern is with the justification we have for making the ordinary types of perceptual claims that we do. Thus Ayer attempts to undermine the direct realist view by describing a situation in which he has an experience of a cigarette case (cf. Ayer, 1956, chap. 3, sect. iii). He then raises the familiar sceptical doubts as to whether he is in fact perceiving any physical object at all, and concludes from this that he is not directly aware of the cigarette case; this leads on to the general claim that we are only ever aware of sense data. The trouble with this approach, it is now recognized, is that the attempt to cast sceptical doubt on *all* experiences is highly questionable, and hence any general conclusions based upon the sceptical possibilities in a single example are unfounded.

But there is a second way in which the phenomena of hallucination can be marshalled to attack the disjunctive view which does not rely on any kind of sceptical consideration. I call this version of the argument 'the Modal Argument'.[7]

Imagine a normal situation where a subject faces an object such as a tree. It is stipulated not just that he thinks he sees a tree, but that he actually does see it. It follows that in some sense which requires explication, he has an experience of a tree, involving the sensory awareness of, let us say, something green. The subject's experience is a genuine perceptual experience. The modal argument revolves around a certain counterfactual claim:

(A)   It is possible that the experience the subject is having in seeing the tree might have arisen in some other way, as in a hallucination, even though there were no tree present.

The subject might, for example, have followed H. H. Price's advice and tried out the effect of taking mind-altering drugs. But if it is a genuine counterfactual possibility that the experience might have been caused by some means which did not involve the tree that in the actual circumstances was perceived, then it follows that the tree which the subject perceives and the experience he has in seeing it are distinct entities. The experience could have occurred even if the tree was not in existence. The argument does not deny that in the actual example initially envisaged there is a *contingent* connection between the subject's experience and the

[7]   This version of the argument was originally prompted by many helpful discussions with J. J. Valberg, who considers a related argument in his recent monograph (Valberg, 1992, cf. also Coates, 1976).

tree in an ordinary case of veridical perception; it is simply claimed that the counterfactual possibility shows that there is no *necessary* connection between them.

I shall shortly consider a reply to this line of reasoning; but if the argument works, then it follows that even in ordinary perception we are never directly aware of the physical object (in the sensory sense outlined earlier) because what we are aware of in a sensory way depends solely upon the character of the perceptual experience we have, and the conclusion of the modal argument is that the perceptual experience is logically distinct from what is perceived. We cannot therefore be directly aware in a sensory manner of the objects we perceive. We do, however, have concepts which relate directly to the perceived object, as the critical realist allows, and in this sense perception is direct and immediate. But that object is external to the experience the perceiver has. Perceptual experiences, so far as their sensory aspect is concerned, are as much states of the subject's mind as experiences of pains and other bodily sensations.

For the remainder of this paper I wish to consider an important line of objection to the modal argument that an upholder of the disjunctive theory might advance. I shall suggest that the price paid by the disjunctive theorist in trying to avoid the critical realist position is that his own view collapses into a form of idealism.

III

The modal argument turns on the acceptance of a certain counterfactual claim: the subject might have had the same experience that he had when seeing the tree, even if he had not seen the tree. The objection the direct realist makes in reply is that the modal argument wrongly interprets this claim: when we speak of same experience here, only qualitative sameness is involved. According to the direct realist, if a subject has a given experience in genuinely seeing an object, then that experience directly involves the object he sees, without there being any intermediary entity involved. So although it may be true that he could be in a state that from a subjective standpoint would be qualitatively indistinguishable even if he were hallucinating, this by itself does not show that hallucination and ordinary perception involve the same kind of entity.

This point is emphasized in recent papers by John McDowell and Paul Snowdon defending the disjunctive view. McDowell attacks what he labels the 'highest common factor' view, claiming that there is no single type of entity common to both perceptual and hallucinatory experiences. The sensory awareness in each type of case is subjectively similar, but the entity involved is different. In the case of the ordinary perception of a physical object, the very object itself is, in McDowell's words, 'directly presented to view'; 'appearances are no longer conceived as in general intervening between the experiencing subject and the world' (McDowell, 1988, pp. 212, 211); and also, 'it is the relevant tract of the environment that is present to consciousness' (McDowell, 1994a, p. 191).[8]

What this means is that in a case of genuine perception it is not possible for us logically to separate the perceiver's experience from the object he perceives, as the modal argument assumes; they are necessarily connected, in the sense that the experience could not

---

[8] I have not here tried to take into account McDowell's more recent book (McDowell, 1994b).

have occurred unless the perceived object also existed. At best, it may be allowed that when a perceiver has a given perceptual experience of a tree, there is from his point of view an *epistemic* possibility that no tree exists in front of him. But from this mere epistemic possibility no metaphysical consequences follow about the distinctness of this particular perceptual experience from the perceived object.[9]

What I shall now argue is that although it appears that the disjunctivist can thus put forward a *prima facie* reply to the modal argument, he faces a major problem in arriving at a satisfactory explication of his positive position. Difficulties arise when we try to give a clear account of the relation which the disjunctivist claims to hold between a perceiver's experience and the object perceived. It may seem plausible to speak of physical objects being directly present to the perceiver's experience, and so forth, but unless these somewhat metaphorical claims can be unpacked his thesis has a dubious status.

On the rival causal account of perception, to say that a subject has an experience of an object is to say that he has a certain kind of mental state caused by that object. There is no metaphysical problem in accounting for the connection between the subject's experience and the object he perceives, beyond that of accounting for the causal link between them. How does the disjunctivist elucidate the alternative claim that an object is so much a part of our experience that it is necessarily connected with it? The key issue is whether there is a coherent interpretation of the disjunctivist's claim. I shall argue that we cannot make sense of the combination of the

---

[9] Compare the important distinction made by Saul Kripke (Kripke, 1980, p. 103).

two central theses that the disjunctivist is committed to:

(1) *The Necessary Connection Thesis*: In a case of genuine perception, the perceiver's experience is necessarily connected with the object he perceives.

(2) *The Realism Thesis*: The physical objects we perceive are of an ontologically distinct kind from our mental states.

There is a further consideration, in that it can also be argued that there are no compelling positive grounds for preferring the disjunctive view to that of the highest common factor view favoured by the critical realist, but I shall not discuss this here except in so far as it is bound up with the above mentioned difficulty.[10]

IV

What reasons could there be for claiming that the experience is necessarily connected with the perceived object, in the sense that it could not exist unless the perceived object also existed?

One position in which this entailment follows straightforwardly is that of the subjective idealist: we can't make sense of the claim that a perceptual experience is (altogether) distinct from the object perceived, because those experiences go to form that object; objects are, roughly speaking, extended patterns of experiences, and hence are mental. A position of this sort could be appealed to by way of a reply to the modal argument. The crucial question, therefore, is whether we can make sense of the disjunctivist's commitment to a necessary connection between the

---

[10] I hope to be able to show in a further paper that there are no good phenomenological or similar reasons for preferring the disjunctivist view.

perceptual experience and object perceived, without his position collapsing into some form of idealism.[11]

One way in which the disjunctivist might attempt to explain his view is by drawing parallels with recent theories which construe thought and belief as object-involving, and this seems to be part of McDowell's motive for defending the disjunctive view. The argument would be that content of the perceptual experience gains its identity in part from the physical context in which the perceiver is located. Thus, suppose that on the basis of his perceptual experience, a subject has a perceptual thought about the object in front of him, which could be expressed by the demon-strative claim 'that is a tree'. On one line of thought, which I take to be in keeping with Putnam's views, the content of this perceptual thought is fixed in part by the object external to the mind; on McDowell's view, we should, rather, conceive of the mind as extending outside the subject's physical body and including the object which is the focus of the demonstrative thought involved. But irrespective of these differences, the same claim would be arrived at, that the perceptual thought involves the tree essentially.[12] The conclusion would then be that the perceptual experience could only be identified in terms of the thought about the object it is an experience of, and hence could not exist indepen-dently of that object (cf. McDowell, 1986, p. 153, no. 29).

---

[11] At least as far as we are concerned with the existence of the object whilst it is being perceived – I am not here concerned with the problem of the relation of the perceived to unperceived object, though I believe that this is a further difficulty for the disjunctivist.

[12] A useful discussion of the possible variants here is given by Timothy Sprigge (Sprigge, 1988).

However, this general attempt to elucidate the disjunctive view is too swift. For it does not capture the full immediacy which the direct realist has traditionally claimed to be a feature of perceptual consciousness, and which underlies the disjunctivist's claims about the presence of the perceived object in experience. The content of the perceptual experience which is appealed to in the above reply to the modal argument relates to its conceptual or propositional aspect, and not to its phenomenal character. But although the experience as a whole may be essentially connected with the perceived object, in virtue of the perceptual thought involved, the causal theorist may still argue that that object is external to and contingently connected with the subject's phenomenal consciousness in the sense which relates to his sensory awareness. The above reply does not distinguish between critical realism and the disjunctive theory. The direct realist needs to make a stronger claim. He has to say that over and above any object-involving thoughts that occur in perception, there is some further kind of direct contact with the perceived object which arises from the sensory awareness involved; what is present in the phenomenological sense is the very object itself, and not some sort of sense impression that is part of the subject's mind.

We might therefore envisage a supporting argument for such a claim on behalf of the disjunctivist to the effect that the sensory aspect of experience itself should be construed analogously to the propositional aspect, as also essentially object-involving. But we must distinguish different motives for putting forward this claim.

On the one hand it might perhaps be held that the perceiver's sensory experience is essentially identified by reference to physical causes. Yet although this anti-individualist claim may be argued with respect to the sensory awareness *types*[13] this does not in itself establish a necessary connection in the particular case between a token sensory awareness and the individual physical object perceived. The sensory aspect of a token experience may be picked out via a contingent identifying reference to the physical object that, as a matter of fact, it happens to be caused by, perhaps with some accompanying indication of its sensory-awareness-type; thus I might pick out a part of my sensory experience as the white left-hand image of a candle I am seeing double (cf. Kripke, 1980, p. 55). There is therefore no ground for saying that the perceived object is necessarily connected with what the subject is sensorily aware of.

On the other hand, the claim might be based, as Sprigge (1988) points out, on a more interesting thesis about a necessary connection between things perceived and the subject's consciousness, and it is this possibility that I now wish to explore. The idea is that we interpret the disjunctivist's claim as implying that, while being perceived, the perceived object is in some sense included in the subject's sensory experience as part of what he is phenomenally conscious of.

The difficulty now lies in how we should understand the notion of 'included in' here. Is this to be modelled on spatial inclusion? If we do understand the disjunctive claim in this way, the resulting thesis is that the object which is perceived is a part of the perceiver's experience. But this leads straightforwardly to the idealist conclusion. What is in the subject's experience in the sense of being in his consciousness is a part of the

---

[13] This is in effect the argument put forward by Tyler Burge (Burge, 1986, cf. also Davies, 1991).

subject's mind. Therefore the physical object perceived, to the extent that the subject has an experience of it, is a mental item.

To resist this simple argument the disjunctivist needs a conception of experience that can include non-mental items. What might encourage the illusion that such a conception is available is the ambiguity between the broad and narrow sense of the term 'experience'. There is certainly a broad and innocuous sense of the word which is used in such expressions as: 'We experienced a minor earthquake in Greece' or 'Seeing the production of Lear was an overwhelming experience'. However, such uses are perfectly compatible with the causal theories of perception, since they describe or imply the entire process of perception of physical objects, of which the subject's sensory awareness is but a part, whereas the present issue concerns the strict and narrow sense of the term which relates to this sensory awareness itself, to what is in the subject's consciousness. The broad conception of experience does not give the disjunctivist what he wants. Part of the trouble here is that in our unreflective transactions with the world we do not find the notion of perception puzzling enough. It may seem, before we reflect closely upon matters, that perception can be analysed in terms of facts about a subject's experiences and facts about the existence of an object appropriately placed in the subject's vicinity. Such an analysis is, for example, advocated by Alan White, when he writes:

… the existence of X and the fact that it looks to me as if there were an X or as if there were other than an X provide the necessary and sufficient conditions of my seeing an X. (White, 1956, p. 119)

Unfortunately they do no such thing; I may be hallucinating in the presence of an X. Even if we tack on
specific details of the physical conditions which prevail,
these will not guarantee that the object is in the subject's
experience. The causal theorist is content with this
conclusion, for his account accepts that experiences in
the narrow sense of mental occurrences are distinct
from the perceived objects. An object is present to a
subject's experience, in the broad sense of that term, if
it is the cause of his having a conscious experience,
understood in the narrow sense.[14]

There are, in sum, two conceptions of experience
available to the disjunctivist: in the narrow sense, being
in a subject's experience is equated with being in the
subject's mind, in the ordinary sense that pains and
other bodily sensations are in a person's mind. To say
that a perceived object is in this sense in a person's
experience is to capitulate to the main idealist thesis.
Alternatively, one can construe experiences in the broad
sense outlined above, but this then fails to provide the
disjunctivist with the intimate relation between mind
and object that he is after. For what the disjunctivist is
trying to capture is a special kind of relation between
consciousness and the objects we perceive, which
somehow unites mind and world in a non-causal way.
The idea is that conscious experience, understood in
the narrow sense, somehow reaches right up to the
physical object, and is thus directly connected with it,
while at the same time the object retains a separate
identity as something distinct from and outside the
mind. But an entity is either in our conscious
experience as a part of that experience, or it is outside

----

[14] I ignore here problems which arise from deviant causal chains; the
assumption is that the object causes the experience in the right way.

it; there is no third mode of existence. The dilemma for the disjunctivist is that if the object is in experience, then it must be a mental item, whereas if it is outside of experience, then it seems as if it must be logically distinct and only contingently related to it. If the latter case is correct, the modal argument succeeds.

I suspect that underlying the disjunctivist's claims that the physical objects we perceive are somehow directly accessible to subjective experience is a deeper confusion over the nature of properties and relations.[15] On the one hand, the experience is treated as a relation between the subject and the object perceived, so as to capture the fact that in perception two separate and different kinds of items are brought together and connected; but on the other hand the disjunctivist also thinks of the experience as equivalent to a part of the subject's conscious state of mind, and therefore, in some sense, as a complex property of the perceiver, with the result that the existence of the perceived object ends up in the mind. But this attempt to have things both ways leads to incoherence, as we have just seen: if the object is within the subject's experience, it must be a mental entity, and comparable to the subject's sensations and feelings and so on. It cannot consistently be claimed that the physical object, to the extent that it is directly experienced, is also distinct from the subject's mind. I conclude that the disjunctivist ought either to embrace the idealist conclusion that physical objects are mental, at least when they are being perceived, or to abandon his attempt to provide an alternative to a version of the causal theory of perception.

Nothing in what I have argued so far impugns the status of physical objects when they are not being

---

[15] Compare McDowell's account (McDowell, 1986, p. 150).

perceived. That would be the subject of further argument. But I suspect that if the main argument of this paper is correct, the disjunctivist cannot avoid the choice between idealism or some version of the causal theory. The reason is that he must provide some account of what it is that unifies our conception of physical objects, both through the phases when they are perceived and also during those when they are not. If the same type of entity is held to continue through both phases, then it looks very much as if he must move towards a thoroughgoing idealism. The alternative move is to accept the mental status of what is directly experienced, while insisting on the distinct physical character of the physical objects outside our experience. But that amounts to abandoning the disjunctive account and accepting the alternative causal theory as the only way of avoiding the idealist position.

REFERENCES

David Armstrong, *A Materialist Theory of Mind* (London: Routledge and Kegan Paul, 1968).

Alfred J. Ayer, *The Problem of Knowledge* (London: Macmillan, 1956).

Tyler Burge, 'Individualism and Psychology', *Philosophical Review*, vol. 95 (1986), pp. 3–45.

Roderick Chisholm, *Perceiving* (New York: Cornell University Press, 1957).

Paul Coates, 'Critical Realism and the Causal Theory of Perception' (Ph.D Thesis, University of London, 1976).

Martin Davies, 'Individualism and Perceptual Content', *Mind*, vol. 100 (1991), pp. 461–84.

Fred Dretske, *Seeing and Knowing* (London: Routledge, 1969).

Gareth Evans, *The Varieties of Reference* (Oxford: Oxford University Press, 1982).

Frank Jackson, *Perception* (Cambridge: Cambridge University Press, 1977).

Saul Kripke, *Naming and Necessity* (Oxford: Basil Blackwell, 1980).

Clarence I. Lewis, *Mind and the World Order* (New York: Charles Scribners & Sons, 1929).

E. J. Lowe, 'Experience and its Objects', in Tim Crane (ed.), *The Contents of Experience* (Cambridge: Cambridge University Press, 1992).

John McDowell, 'Criteria, Defeasibility and Knowledge', *Proceedings of the British Academy*, vol. 68 (1982), pp. 455–79; reprinted with revisions in Jonathan Dancy (ed.), *Perceptual Knowledge* (Oxford: Oxford University Press, 1988).

————— , 'Singular Thought and the Extent of Inner Space', in Philip Pettit and John McDowell (eds.), *Subject, Thought and Context* (Oxford: Clarendon Press, 1986).

————— , 'The Content of Perceptual Experience', *The Philosophical Quarterly*, vol. 44 (1994a), pp.190–205.

————— , *Mind and World* (Cambridge, Mass: Harvard University Press, 1994b).

John Mackie, *Problems from Locke* (Oxford: Clarendon Press, 1976).

Christopher Peacocke, *Sense and Content* (Oxford: Oxford University Press, 1983).

Paul Snowdon, 'Perception, Vision, and Causation', *Proceedings of the Aristotelian Society*, vol. 81 (1981), pp. 175–92.

Timothy Sprigge, 'Intrinsic Connectedness', *Proceedings of the Aristotelian Society*, vol. 88 (1988), pp. 129–45.

Michael Tye, 'Visual Qualia and Visual Content', in Tim Crane (ed.), *The Contents of Experience* (Cambridge: Cambridge University Press, 1992).

Jerry Valberg, *The Puzzle of Experience* (Oxford: Oxford University Press, 1992).

Alan White, 'The Causal Theory of Perception', *Supplementary Proceedings of the Aristotelian Society*, vol. 35 (1961), pp. 153–68.

LINGUISTIC IDEALISM IN ANALYTIC PHILOSOPHY OF THE TWENTIETH CENTURY

Michele Marsonet

I

Introduction

In the model of philosophical inquiry envisioned by the logical empiricists, analysis of scientific language becomes something similar to a metaphysical endeavour which is meant to establish the bounds of sense, and this stance may be easily traced back to Wittgenstein's *Tractatus Logico-Philosophicus*. On the other hand, the analytic tradition transferred this conception to the analysis of ordinary language, and this move, eventually, was able to restore the confidence of many philosophers in their own work. After all, they were doing something important and worthwhile, that is to say, something no one else was doing, since linguists are certainly concerned with language, but from quite a different point of view.

At this point we may well ask ourselves: *What* is wrong with this kind of approach, given the present crisis of the analytic tradition and the growing success of the so-called post-analytic thought? At first sight it looks perfectly legitimate and, moreover, it produced important results, as anybody can verify just reading the masterpieces of contemporary analytic philosophy. To answer the question: *What is wrong?*, we must first of all take into account language itself and check what it is meant to be within the analytic tradition. This will give our question a clear answer. We have to verify, furthermore, what kind of knowledge philosophy needs to be equipped with if it wants to preserve its autonomy. The logical positivists clearly claimed in their program that there is no synthetic a priori knowledge such as the one envisioned by Immanuel Kant. There is, however, an analytic and a priori knowledge which is supplied by mathematics and logic alone. Within this field, the techniques of contemporary formal logic are exalted because they allow us to build artificial languages which – at least theoretically – eliminate the ambiguities of everyday speech.

Richard Rorty claimed recently that the linguistic turn was an attempt to find a substitute for Kant's transcendental standpoint (Rorty, 1993, pp. 337–57). He is right in this respect, but I also think that it would be better to speak of a 'natural continuation' of the Kantian viewpoint. The question to be asked now is the following: what are the philosophers supposed to do if the vision of philosophical work endorsed by logical positivism is correct? It is clear, in fact, that we cannot invent an activity just to allow philosophers to have a job and survive: this is, after all, a matter of intellectual honesty. In other words, *if* logical positivists and the large majority of analytic thinkers are right, ie., *if* philosophy has been completely displaced by science so that it no longer is a kind of knowledge independent of the scientific one, *then* we are bound to conclude that there is no need for philosophy any more.

According to the neopositivists, the sole true knowledge is empirical and based on immediate observative data; furthermore, they reject the Kantian synthetic a priori, even though Kant's influence on their philosophical outlook is quite strong. Neopositivists attribute a pivotal role to formal logic because, in their opinion, it allows us to formalize, in a rigorous manner, the intuitive inferential processes of ordinary language. Logical positivism is currently less popular than it had been a few decades ago, although it still maintains a considerable influence (not only in Great Britain and North America, but in continental Europe as well). The so-called 'post-empiricist turn' questioned practically every single point of its general outlook on philosophy and the world (an outlook that is often defined as the *received view*, just to stress the fact that, despite its many shortcomings, it is the starting point of a trend of thought whose importance within contemporary philosophy cannot be denied). In my view, however, it is not correct to claim – as many contemporary authors do – that the neopositivists are *completely* wrong. This is clearly an overstatement, because the members of the Vienna Circle – along with their German and Polish allies of the Berlin Circle and of the Lvov-Warsaw School – can at least be credited with one great merit: they compelled philosophers to take science seriously in a period when it was largely believed that philosophy and science were totally independent fields of inquiry.

If we try to identify the position of logical positivism on the map of contemporary philosophy, we will soon find out that it can be characterized by a few basic and radical theses:

(A) first, neopositivism is not a philosophical system but, rather, a general *attitude* towards philosophy

which denies any validity to the way philosophical
work has been carried out in the past centuries;

(B) second, the logical positivists think that
philosophy is not a speculative discipline: it is, rather,
a logico-linguistic activity aimed at clarifying scientific
propositions;

(C) third, there are only analytic (a priori) and
synthetic (a posteriori) propositions. The first class is
formed by logical and mathematical sentences, and
the second by the sentences that can be found in the
empirical sciences (where physics has a predominant
role). As we said before, there is no Kantian
'synthetic a priori'.

It follows that the whole of human knowledge can be
reduced to the two classes of sentences just mentioned,
and this means that the only possible knowledge is
given by science. Metaphysics becomes thus
meaningless, because its sentences do not comply with
the rules set forth by logical analysis of language.
What, then, is the philosopher's job? The members of
the Vienna Circle answer that his task is to clarify the
concepts used within empirical and formal sciences,
while analytic philosophers stress instead the importance of ordinary language's analysis. But the outcome
is in both cases clear: philosophy *is* linguistic analysis.
It may be observed that neopositivism certainly has
some ancestors in the history of philosophy: the
sophists of ancient Greece like Protagoras, the
nominalists of the Middle Ages like Ockham, the
classical British empiricists (and especially Hume), the
positivists of the nineteenth century like Comte. Their
radicalism, however, is rather new. The logical
positivists want to rebuild philosophy *ab initio*, just
making *tabula rasa* of what has been said and done in

many centuries of philosophical speculation. And their attitude is based on two undeniable facts:

(a) the enormous results, both speculative (knowledge of empirical reality) and practical (technological applications) accomplished by modern science from Galileo on; and

(b) the spectacular achievements of formal logic which, starting from Frege and Russell, set forth the project of accomplishing the Leibnizian dream of the *calculemus*, ie., the complete formalization and mechanization of human reasoning.

II

The Metaphysical Tenets of Logical Positivism

Let us now display some metaphysical tenets which, although unconsciously endorsed by the neopositivists, are not usually taken seriously into account. If we examine the famous distinction between pseudo-problems (which are, more or less, all those problems addressed by traditional philosophy) and the true ones, it is easy to realize that, according to neopositivism, the difference between philosophy and science is the same difference holding between *language* on the one side, and the *world* described by language on the other. My thesis is that we can identify here a clear Kantian descent. Kant's work, while showing that metaphysics – conceived of in scientific terms – is impossible, linked science to the perceptual and conceptual characteristics of human experience. Acting that way, the philosopher of Königsberg hoped to avoid both the sceptical doubts put forward by David Hume and the metaphysical excesses often endorsed by the rationalists. It may be noted, however, that by limiting scientific discourse to a domain explicitly identified with *appearance*, Kant's writings prompted a growing interest in the *transcendent* domain which, if we take his words seriously, must exist somewhere beyond appearance itself.

The neopositivists, on the other hand, meant to solve this problem by rejecting the Kantian 'synthetic a priori', and by reducing all knowledge to (i) purely empirical and (ii) purely linguistic factors, with nothing else left behind. The founder of the Vienna Circle, Moritz Schlick, claimed that between philosophy and science there is no conflict, but just a differentiation of their respective fields of inquiry: philosophy looks for *meaning*, and science is interested in *truth*. It follows that philosophers must only concern themselves with clarifying the meaning of scientific sentences, thus reconstructing the language of science in a clear and rigorous manner. Scientists, in turn, use language in order to ascertain the truth (or falsity) of those sentences concerning the world, and build theories which must be empirically verifiable.

What happens, then, if physicists want to discover the meanings of the assertions that are made within their discipline? According to the neopositivist doctrine, if they do that, they become, *ipso facto*, philosophers. But on the other hand philosophers, in determining both the nature and the extension of meaningful discourse, set up the the boundaries of scientific inquiry, and this means, more or less, that philosophers themselves establish the *conceptual limits* of scientific inquiry. At this point nobody can deny that this is an extremely important job: the philosopher, in fact, becomes a kind of *super-scientist*. They *bestow meaning*, and any operative scientist is practically compelled to ask for their – the philosopher's – opinion.

Let us now ask ourselves: what does logico-linguistic analysis become *if* it is conceived of in these terms? The answer is that it becomes something which is enormously more important than the mere scrutiny of terms and sentences. It turns out to be a sort of *first philosophy*, ie., a super-discipline which is meant to establish the conditions that make all knowledge possible. If we, for some reason, do not want to call it 'metaphysics', a different name may still be found for it. But it is quite clear that the substance of the argumentation does not change. And, in fact, in Wittgenstein's *Tractatus* we find the following claims:

> Philosophy settles controversies about the limits of natural science. It must set limits to what can be thought; and, in doing so, to what cannot be thought. It must set limits to what cannot be thought by working outwards through what can be thought. It will signify what cannot be said, by presenting clearly what can be said. (Wittgenstein, 1961, propositions 4.113–4.115, p. 49)

If this is the situation, it becomes evidently misleading to speak of a 'long' Kantian descent. Kant's presence in the neopositivist theoretical building is, instead, well-perceivable, and any difference must be attributed, in the final analysis, to the changes occurring in the historical context. So we find a *first* analogy between the Kantian reaction to rationalism and the neopositivist and analytic reaction to idealism. We also find a *second* analogy between Kant's desire to save scientific knowledge from Hume's sceptical doubts and the analytic attempt to assure safe logical foundations to that same knowledge. Not only that. More generally, we may recall that for Kant the perception of reality is possible only if it is somehow *mediated* by conceptualization: our knowledge of the world always needs the application of categories, which in turn give shape to human experience. By adopting such an approach, it is no longer possible to speak of an *absolute* knowledge of reality, but only of a type of knowledge which is necessarily *relative* to our conceptual apparatus.

Exactly the same preoccupation is common to neopositivist and analytic philosophers, with only one important difference. For Kant the conceptual apparatus filtering experience is located in human intellect, while the analytic philosophers of our century locate it in *language*. In both cases we have preconditions of knowledge: categories for Kant and language for the analytic tradition. So we are entitled to claim that contemporary analytic philosophy replaces the Kantian question: *what are the conditions that make human knowledge possible?* with the following – and rather similar – query: *what are the conditions that make meaningful discourse possible?* Since the philosopher's task is just to answer this second question, the philosophical activity of bestowing meaning becomes – as Moritz Schlick used to claim – the beginning and the end of all knowledge. And it may even be noted that the problems foreseen by Kant about the possibility of mapping our conceptualizations onto reality-in-itself find a precise correspondence in the problems – underlined by neopositivist and analytic thinkers – concerning the possibility of mapping the characteristics of linguistic systems onto the reality they purport to name and describe.

But, at this point, the objections to the Kantian outlook are, *mutatis mutandis*, the same objections that can be addressed to linguistic philosophy. We can in fact claim that Kant, by positing limits to knowledge, assumed *de facto* the existence of something that lies beyond those limits. Similarly – as Wittgenstein, for instance, pointed out – to set up limits to meaningful discourse implies, *ipso facto*, assuming the existence of something that transcends those limits. We can thus conclude that, while according to Kant our knowledge of the world is relative to human conceptualization and categorization, for the analytic tradition this same knowledge, on a par with the meaningfulness of any discourse regarding the world, is relative to *language*. By choosing this path, conceptualization is transferred from human nature to language, and such a move is very important because it guarantees – theoretically, at least – the logical independence of the new linguistic philosophy not only from the old metaphysics, but also from natural science. This strategy favours, in particular, the detachment of philosophical inquiry from all kinds of psychological introspection, as Ludwig Wittgenstein underlines once again in his *Tractatus Logico-Philosophicus*:

> Psychology is no more closely related to philosophy than any other natural science... Does not my study of sign-language correspond to the study of thought-processes, which philosophers used to consider so essential to the philosophy of logic? Only in most cases they got entangled in inessential psychological investigations. (Wittgenstein, 1961, proposition 4.1121, p. 49)

The antimetaphysical stance of linguistic philosophy is thus based on the assumption that our knowledge of the world is always relative to language and to our conceptual schemes, and the 'Kantian flavour' of this position is neatly perceivable in a famous metaphor introduced by Otto Neurath, one of the founding fathers of the Vienna Circle. According to Neurath, in fact, we are all embarked since our birth on a sort of *conceptual ship*; if one wants to modify this ship, one cannot step ashore, but is rather compelled to rebuild it bit by bit in the open sea. This means that human beings cannot modify their conceptual schemes in order to make them more suitable to an – alleged – external reality, since this same reality (the world) turns out to be perceivable *only* through conceptual schemes. It is here that we find the roots of what I call *linguistic idealism*, a theme about which we shall have more to say later on. It is not possible, therefore, to justify language by appealing to what reality is; adopting such a strategy, we are likely to return immediately to some old brand of metaphysics which, as it was already pointed out, is for analytic philosophy a bunch of sentences devoid of meaning. And Neurath's metaphor is, as we shall see later, very important for under-standing the theses (or, at least, their early formulation) of a philosopher like Willard V. Quine, who says in this regard:

> It is meaningless, I suggest, to inquire into the absolute correctness of a conceptual scheme as a mirror of reality. Our standard for appraising basic changes of conceptual scheme must be, not a realistic standard of correspondence to reality, but a pragmatic standard (on this theme see Duhem). Concepts are language, and the purpose of concepts and of language is efficacy in communication and in prediction. Such is the ultimate duty of language, science, and philosophy, and it is in relation to that

duty that a conceptual scheme has finally to be appraised. (Quine, 1963, p. 79)

It is correct to claim, at this point, that the purported analytic elimination of metaphysics is more theoretical than real. The absoluteness of traditional metaphysical questions like: 'What is the structure of reality?', 'Of what does it really consist?', has a punctual correspondence in the absoluteness of such linguistic questions as: 'What is the structure of our language?', 'What entities can we talk about?'. The analytic tradition turned, in sum, the metaphysical absoluteness into a linguistic one, and this explains why Rudolf Carnap – just to take a famous example – meant to translate the traditional metaphysical and ontological assertions into sentences concerning the syntactic and semantic structure of language. And so, any sentence about *what there is* corresponds to a sentence about what *we say* there is. In Carnapian terms, the sentences of the metaphysical/ontological object-language must be translated into sentences belonging to the metalanguage of a philosophy conceived of as mere linguistic analysis (cf. Carnap, 1947).[1]

It is obvious, however, that this stance is nothing but the linguistic translation of metaphysical positions quite common in the history of Western philosophical thought. On the one hand, the possibility of pronouncing meaningful statements on an alleged extralinguistic reality is denied, but, on the other, we are supposed to pronounce definitive truths on the way in which we describe that same reality. According to this view, men would be unable to take directly into account

---

[1] This theme was also developed by Polish thinkers like Tadeusz Kotarbinski and Kazimierz Ajdukiewicz.

the categories of existence, but would at the same time be able to examine in absolute terms their linguistic representations of reality. It is not difficult to understand that by acting that way the analytic philosophers, far from 'eliminating' metaphysics, give rise to their own brand of metaphysics, with only one very important *caveat*: the world conceived of as reality, the Aristotelian being-*qua*-being, is replaced by Language (which must be written now with a capital L), thus going back to some form of rationalism. The alleged elimination of metaphysics through logical analysis of language is, therefore, a mere illusion, and it is much better to turn our attention, instead, to the symmetry existing between the analytic outlook and the positions endorsed by many traditional metaphysicians. No matter what the analytic thinkers claim, we have once again a distinction – in most cases *unconscious* – between science and metaphysics. As we observed previously, the analyst of language gives rise to a kind of first philosophy which is meant to bestow meaning on human knowledge conceived as a whole. And thus a growing gap appears between *practical-operative* scientific activity on the one hand, and linguistic analysis on the other. Abstract and purely speculative problems are privileged by many analytic philosophers, including traditional metaphysical and ontological problems which are now taken into account by using the tools of formal logic and the logical analysis of language. It is not at all surprising, thus, that the analytic thinkers have in most cases become the *linguistic counterparts* of those metaphysicians they originally meant to fight and destroy.

Within the analytic tradition, old distinctions are reproposed which have always been objects of inquiry in traditional metaphysics: for instance the distinction between platonists and nominalists. The clarification of the traditional philosophical problems obtained thanks to the linguistic turn, in other words, does not succeed in hiding the much more important fact that many old quarrels show up again within the analytic field. Let us only mention the dispute about the opportunity of using a nominalist or a platonist language in the philosophy of logic and mathematics. This is not a merely linguistic controversy but, rather, the re-proposal of problems thriving already in ancient and medieval philosophy. The step toward recognizing that metaphysics, after all, cannot be eliminated, is rather short.

Carnap's answer was that the analytic discussions about platonism and nominalism do not regard the problem of the existence of universals, but rather the choice of which language is more useful for dealing with themes related to the foundations of mathematics. It is evident, however, that this answer is far from being satisfactory. Platonists and nominalists fight each other not for linguistic reasons, but because they do not agree on what kinds of entities have to be admitted into *ontology*. The real nature of the dispute is ontological and metaphysical, and not linguistic. So the anti-metaphysical stance turns out to be more an 'ideological prejudice' (just to borrow a term belonging to political philosophy) than a thesis which can be reasonably argued for.

It may then be noted that the absolutism of the analytic conception of language, which is based on the thesis that our talk about the world is meaningful only in so far as it is referred to as some system of linguistic representation, practically assumes that language itself is *not* a part of the world. In other terms, we must ask a question that neopositivist and analytic philosophers tend – strangely – to ignore: *how* was language born and *where* does it come *from?* This is one of the reasons why Quine (or, at least, the Quine of the 1950s) rejects the analytic/ synthetic distinction insisting, instead, on language conceived of as a *tool* created by mankind for practical purposes (Quine, 1963, pp. 20–46). The early Quine, thus, overcomes the strictures of a purely analytic conception of language resorting to the pragmatist – and typically American – tradition represented by thinkers like Charles S. Peirce and John Dewey.

Let us conclude this section by noting that, despite what many authors nowadays keep saying, (i) metaphysics has not been eliminated, and (ii) logical analysis of language may instead be extremely useful for examining the traditional metaphysical problems in a more precise manner. This explains why, within the analytic school itself, a great deal of attention is currently paid to such old problems as the platonism/nominalism distinction, the status of modal propositions and the meaning of negative existential sentences (Quine, 1963, pp. 1–19).[2]

III

Quine and the Primacy of Language
If there is any analytically oriented philosopher who often writes about ontology, it is Quine. Throughout his writings, in fact, we constantly find the following question: 'What kinds of objects do exist?'. On the

---

[2]   A clear example of analytic metaphysics is given in the well-known book by Alvin Plantinga (Plantinga, 1974, cf. also Strawson, 1992).

other hand the so-called 'ontic decision', that is the decision concerning what objects should be admitted into ontology, is the cornerstone of his philosophical quest. A central position has been given to these problems in Quine's works since the late 1930s, and important formulations may be found in such writings as 'On What There Is', *Word and Object* and 'Ontological Relativity'. Given this fact, one would be inclined to think that in those works a precise and well-constructed ontology can be found. The real situation, however, does not meet these expectations.

Quine firmly believes that ontological problems can be addressed (and eventually solved) *only* by means of symbolic logic. But one has to be very careful in pronouncing such a statement. I do not mean to deny that formal logic is a very important tool when ontological questions are coped with, since this fact may be easily recognized by anyone trained in analytic philosophy. In Quine's view, however, the aforementioned statement is much stronger, since he claims sometimes that ontological problems *are*, at bottom, logical and linguistic matters: standard quantification theory, and in particular existentially quantified sentences, are in his opinion the ontological idiom *par excellence*. It follows that, should we not possess first order logic, we would not even be able to express ontological questions properly.

This is indeed a tough-minded position, and it takes us back to the relationship between *language* and the *world* which plays a crucial role in logical positivism and in the analytic tradition at large. Why does Quine assume such a stance? In order to answer this question, one must be audacious enough to challenge Frege's paradigm which identifies *existence* on the one side and *logical quantification* on the other, a challenge that very few authors today feel inclined to make.[3] In fact, Quine is one of the champions of this identification of existence with standard logical quantification, a very important move indeed, since it was – and still is – endorsed by the absolute majority of the authors belonging to the analytic tradition. So, if we want to answer the question posed above, I think that there are two possible replies, which are in turn interconnected:

(A) Only formal logic can adequately describe reality; and
(B) It is impossible to make a distinction between logic, language and reality.
But the real question at stake here is no doubt the following:
(C) Is there a world (reality) independent of the language we use for *talking about* reality?

Let us note that Quine underlines, here and there in his writings, that this – ie., (C) – is precisely the problem we have to solve in order to get a satisfactory comprehension of what ontology is and what it means to formulate ontological questions. And in fact, when posing existential problems in his works, Quine always adopts this formulation:

(D) May we use a term x without presupposing, by that same fact, the *existence* of the entity (object) named by x?

In other words, what worries him is the possibility that a speaker uses non-denoting or general terms just

---

[3]   See for example the book by Alex Orenstein, in which the author argues that existence is not a matter of logical quantification (Orenstein, 1978, cf. also Rescher, 1978, pp. 57–66).

believing that there is something real named by them. But – we may ask – are those really *ontological* problems? It seems to me that they are, instead, logical and linguistic ones. For example, I may find someone believing in the existence of winged horses. If they tell me that Pegasus exists, in order to show them that this statement is incorrect I will not use quantification theory but, rather, I invite them to pursue an empirical recognition. It may turn out, at some point, that they believe in the existence of mental entities, thus rendering a direct empirical recognition quite hard. Even in that case, though, we may agree on the fact that mythological texts report many stories about Pegasus and winged horses. Provided I am ready to accept an extended ontology including all kinds of mythological objects, I may also concede that the sentence 'Pegasus is the winged horse of Bellerophon' is true, while the sentence 'Pegasus is the winged horse of Hercules' is false. I may subsequently formalize those two sentences using first order logic, but this move will neither solve nor add anything to the question whether there *really* are winged horses or not. The solution, in fact, depends on two facts:

(1) The interlocutor's ability to find winged horses in the world; and
(2) Their (and my) background ontological assumptions; if they are empiricists, they will make one claim, and if they are mentalists they will make yet another claim.

The fact of the matter is that mathematical logic allows us to formalize the two sentences in a clear manner but, on the other hand, it offers no solution to the philosophical problem we are interested in, since the existential quantifier (or particular, if we adopt a substitutional interpretation of the quantifiers) is a purely formal tool and not an ontological one. The same applies to scientific reasoning: certainly first order logic does not tell us whether non-observable entities really exist or not (that is, the fact that we talk about them is no guarantee of their existence).

Going back to Quine's theses, it is difficult to find in his writings a clear distinction between what is logical (linguistic) and what is empirical. He certainly did write a lot about what there is, but never gives us a chance to find out whether, in his opinion, there really is a world independent of the language we use for *talking about* the world (and we will see later that sometimes he seems to endorse, in this regard, rather incompatible positions). Language, thus, assumes an ontological dimension which is not acceptable if we take language to be not an a priori element, but rather a socially, historically and culturally determined instrument which merely refers to reality. I think that if we follow Quine's style of reasoning we are not in the domain of ontology (whose boundaries are given by the search for what there is), but rather in the domain of formal logic, and the two domains, notwithstanding the opinion of many important analytic philosophers, are in my opinion by no means identical. If we pose the previous questions in a Quinean style, all we can do is to find out that non-denoting singular terms like 'Pegasus' or general terms like 'centaur' do not work – in language – as usual names do. No doubt this is an important result, but its consequences regard formal logic and the philosophical analysis of ordinary language, and not ontology.

It is thus difficult to understand how one may determine the existence (or the non-existence) of certain objects by adopting Quine's point of view. We can find a possible solution to this puzzling problem if – and only if – the existence of an external reality independent of any knowing subject is questioned. It would therefore be necessary to adopt a *different* notion of reality, inextricably connected with language and such that its meaningfulness coincides with our capacity to express it at the linguistic level. And in fact he gives, here and there, hints in this direction: sometimes he claims that 'ontology is *internal to* language'. But at this point we must underline a very important fact: Quine does not even seem to be conscious of the just mentioned implication which logically follows from his treatment of the ontological problems. Indeed we find, here and there in his essays, scattered remarks on the relationship between language and the world. None of these remarks, however, is clear and precise enough to offer a sound foundation for the existential questions. Quine looks satisfied with his logical formalizations and does not try to go deeper in the purely philosophical background of his theses.

Let us note, by the way, that our philosopher always claims that he is a convinced empiricist, and this is the reason why he is so often prisoner of two alternatives which seem incompatible:

(1) On the one side he supports a strong version of empiricism, according to which reality is simply (and *only*) what we can have experience of from the sensory viewpoint; but,

(2) On the other, he supports a sort of logical and linguistic realism, according to which reality is simply

(and *only*) what we are able to express within our language adequately modified by recourse to logical formalization (first order logic).

Quine never succeeds in clarifying this important issue: he does not even try to, probably because he does not have a clear perception of the difficulty of putting together the two alternatives just mentioned. His neopositivist legacy takes him to a form of radical empiricism, while his logical realism brings him in quite a different direction. As we said previously, much the same can be said about many representatives of logical positivism itself: despite their official anti-metaphysical attitude, logical positivists created one of the most fascinating metaphysics of our century.[4]

In any event, only by taking this inner tension into account is it possible to make sense of Quine's claim that Pegasus does not exist because the term 'Pegasus' does not work as a real name when it is encapsulated in a sentence. It follows – in his opinion – that we must resist the temptation to adopt an 'overcrowded' ontology. But I must stress that the attempt to base ontology on this sort of *linguistic/aesthetic* preference looks very strange: if reality were truly overcrowded from the ontological viewpoint, would it follow – according to Quine – that we should give priority to his (or even our) linguistic/aesthetic preferences rather than to the ontological structure of reality itself? Maybe Ockham's razor, after all, is not such a good ontological criterion: why should we decide to simplify, following our personal taste and opinions, a reality which is itself complex?

What objects, then, are we allowed to admit into our

---

[4] The reference work in this case is still Bergmann, 1967.

ontology? It is clear, in fact, that at least some objects do exist. Since according to Quine we cannot admit possible objects, meanings, intensional and abstract entities, what remains to be done is to determine the scope of our *ontological commitment*. Quine's answer is the following: the existence of any object is *relative to* the language we speak, and is therefore *based on* such a language. If this is the situation, it would seem to follow that there are no objects independent of the language we use to talk about them and that, furthermore, there are no objects independent of the linguistic terms which denote them (although, as we shall see later, in many occasions Quine seems to hold a different position). Physical objects, thus, become 'postulated entities' that help us organize the flux of experience. The solution to all these problems might be found, perhaps, by substituting the word 'ontology' for the expression 'logical universe of discourse', but Quine never makes such a move, and so we are back once again to the alternative previously mentioned. Either:

(E) Language and reality are the same thing,

or

(F) Language and reality, even though they do not coincide completely, are so inextricably connected that it is impossible to distinguish one from the other.

No wonder, then, that when Quine writes or talks about ontology, he always refers to language. Since the existence of objects is determined by the language one speaks, any decision concerning ontological problems implies the clarification of which ontological commitments are embedded in a particular language, and this, in turn, means that speakers of different languages assume (or may assume) *different* ontological commitments, so that ontology is internal to language as we said before. Note, by the way, that at this point we begin to identify the roots of Quine's influence on the current scientific anti-realism and, more generally, the roots of the great influence that philosophy of language today exerts on philosophy of science. The alleged incommensurability of scientific theories, in fact, stems also (and it may be said even 'mainly') from such ideas.

Ontology, thus, can be adopted according to our particular preferences. Reality poses no burdens and no limits, and any ontic decision is a linguistic one (that is, linguistic in character). It is not an alleged objective reality that tells us what ontology to adopt, but it is instead the language we speak that plays this funda-mental role. True: Quine claims that the adoption of an ontology obeys pragmatic requirements but, still, it is *language* that takes us in this direction. Let us now go back to our previous remarks on the language/world relationship according to Quine, because it is a fact that the situation depicted in his works is not as clear as I have thus far decribed it. Despite his deep interest in ontological problems, in fact, Quine's works sometimes present statements that do not seem easily reconcilable. In an important essay entitled 'Existence', our author makes the following claims:

> Which ontology to ascribe to a man depends on what he does or intends with his variables and quantifiers. This second appeal to language is no more to be wondered at than the first; *for what is in question in both cases is not just what there really is, but what someone says or implies that there is. Nowhere in all this should there be any suggestion that what there is*

depends on language. (Quine, 1970, p. 94, emphasis mine)

It should be noted that, according to Quine, formal logic determines ontology: there is no other way of making sense of his statement that: 'Which ontology to ascribe to a man depends on what he does or intends with his variables and quantifiers'. And this confirms, once again, that in his view ontology is relative to language. Subsequently, however, I emphasized the last two sentences of the quotation because I think that, in this case, the distinction between reality and language is pretty clear or, at least, it is clear that Quine is *not* – in this context – identifying reality and language. This means however that, if we adopt his strategy (which, as we said earlier, is based on standard quantification theory), we remain at the linguistic level without touching the properly ontological one, in the sense that we just cannot step outside the barrier posed by our language; and, in fact, Quine's ontological commitment is not about what there is, but about what a true theory *claims* that there is. Quine, in the essay mentioned above, recognizes – although confusedly – that *there is* an ontological level which cannot be identified with the linguistic (logical) one. This is confirmed by what he claims soon afterwards:

> What are we to say of the ontic commitment of a New Guinea aborigine – what are the purported values of his variables? I hold that there is in general no unique translation, not even unique in respect to ontic commitment, let alone logical style. I hold that our distinctively referential apparatus... belongs in an essential respect to the theoretical part of our language: namely, it is underdetermined by all

possible sensory stimulation. A result, or really another way of stating the point, is that our referential apparatus is subject to indeterminacy of translation. That is, translations not equivalent to each other could be reconciled with all behavior... It may in this sense be said that ontological questions are parochial to our culture. This is not to say that a thing may exist for one culture and be non-existent for another. *Existence is absolute, and those who talk of existence can say so.* What is parochial is the talking of it. (Quine, 1970, pp. 93–4, emphasis mine)

So – I think we may conclude – there is, after all, an external reality which does not depend on language. Let us see, then, if it is possible to detect a definition of it in Quine's works. We can find there two different concepts of reality; neither of them, however, is defined in clear terms.

(1) In a first sense, reality is composed by objects which, although not well defined, are similar to common sense objects that we perceive through our sensory apparatus. The task of language is to *differentiate* reality into particular objects, and from this it follows that, whenever talking about reality, we always do so *relative to* language.

(2) In a second sense, however, reality appears less determined and more confused, since it may be assimilated to a sort of *raw material* that produces the flux of experience or, to put it in another way, a sort of *substratum* that supports the sensible qualities of material things.

In both cases the notion of 'ontology' is by no means clear. Should we adopt notion (1) or notion (2), or maybe both, but how? In Quine's view (or at least the first one, reported in the aforementioned quotation) ontological talk rises when the human mind – which cannot be clearly distinguished from language – gives an order to the disordered fragments of raw experience which, in turn, are given to us by the just mentioned 'substratum'. This notion closely recalls a concept of 'non-differentiated reality' similar to the Kantian one. We know, however, that Quine rejects any distinction between a priori and a posteriori: he believes that any kind of ordering whatsoever cannot be separated by the act of theorizing (which, in his view, is tantamount to talking). In fact, he claims in 'On What There Is':

> Our acceptance of an ontology is, I think, similar in principle to our acceptance of a scientific theory, say a system of physics: we adopt, at least insofar as we are reasonable, the simplest conceptual scheme into which the disordered fragments of raw experience can be fitted and arranged. (Quine, 1963, pp. 16–17)

The Quinean 'ontological relativity', then, stems precisely from considerations of this sort. But it must not be forgotten that the roots of the problems we have met thus far lie in Quine's acceptance of Frege's views. According to Frege, existence is a property than can be expressed only in terms of logical quantification (and, more precisely, in terms of existential quantification). It is a property pertaining to concepts, and not to objects. Given this fact, the Fregean treatment of existence is a true turning point if compared to what the preceding philosophical traditions – and, in particular, the Aristotelian one – had claimed.

As I remarked before, I deem it correct to claim that the famed metaphor of the 'conceptual ship' introduced by Otto Neurath plays an absolutely fundamental role in Quine's thought.   Let us verify what the American philosopher claims in an essay which first appeared in 1950 in *The Journal of Philosophy*:

> The fundamental-seeming philosophical question, How much of our science is merely contributed by language and how much is a genuine reflection of reality? is perhaps a spurious question which itself arises wholly from a certain type of language. Certainly we are in a predicament if we try to answer the question; for to answer the question we must talk about the world as well as about language, and to talk about the world we must already impose upon the world some conceptual scheme peculiar to our own special language.   Yet we must not leap to the fatalistic conclusion that we are stuck with the conceptual scheme that we grew up in.   We can change it bit by bit, plank by plank, though meanwhile there is nothing to carry us along but the evolving conceptual scheme itself.   The philosopher's task was well compared by Neurath to that of a mariner who must rebuild his ship on the open sea. We can improve our conceptual scheme, our philosophy, bit by bit while continuing to depend on it for support; but we cannot detach ourselves from it and compare it objectively with an unconceptualized reality. (Quine, 1963, pp. 78–9)

Furthermore, it is worth stressing that Neurath's metaphor plays a central role not only in Quine's thought, but in the entire speculation of the logical positivists and of most analytic philosophers as well. There is a clear Kantian heritage here: we can never know reality-in-itself (ie., more or less, the *noumena*), but can nonetheless know reality as we *say* it is (ie., the *phenomena*). This sort of Kantian dualism is precisely the source of many of the problems with which Quine, logical positivists and analytic thinkers cope. Because if we assume that we can never reach reality-in-itself, it is obvious that our conceptual schemes are only bound to determine what reality is *for us*, and it is clear, too, that the language we speak becomes something much more important than a simple instrument for *referring to* a reality which is non-linguistic in character. The problem is twofold:

(A) Do we really need to assume that there is an unbridgeable gap between reality as it is and reality as we know and talk about it ?; and

(B) How justified is it to claim that we can never reach reality-in-itself?

Obviously priority must be given to question (a), since question (b) disappears as long as we stop answering in the affirmative to question (a). Thus, even analytic philosophers and, in general, linguistically oriented thinkers must face the Kantian heritage. The problem in this case, as I already hinted at before, is that most of them depict themselves as empiricists, while a careful scrutiny of their theses clearly shows that they are what I define 'linguistic idealists'.

IV

Linguistic Idealism
I would like to make clear, at this point, that I do not attach an intrinsically negative meaning to the term 'idealism'; such a move, besides being philosophically improper, is bound to disregard the important fact that idealism is a philosophical doctrine that can be

reasonably argued for. My claim is, instead, that no one should be allowed to declare officially that he is an empiricist, while his theses show that he is actually giving an idealistic picture of reality. Unfortunately such is the case with many important analytic thinkers nowadays, and I have already argued in this work that this is true even of an author like Willard V. Quine, who is commonly regarded as the champion of empiricism within today's philosophy.

This fact can be better understood if we remember that both logical positivism and the analytic tradition have always been tremendously ambiguous on the real nature of the relationship between *language* on the one side and the *world* (reality) on the other. The standard interpretation of logical positivism and of the analytic tradition claims that linguistic analysis is the best way we have at our disposal for getting rid of both metaphysics and any non-empiricist interpretation of reality. *If* it were so, it would be correct to say that linguistic analysis is the most effective anti-idealistic method devised by twentieth-century philosophy. But this picture, although still widespread and successful nowadays, is both inaccurate and misleading. For it does not take into account the essential fact that the linguistic turn, despite the strong empiricist and anti-metaphysical commitments of its founding fathers, has increasingly viewed language as an a priori element which, in turn, determines and even *builds up* reality. Many analytic thinkers – especially in the last few decades – have taken an even bolder stance, proclaiming that reality *is* language, so that, for instance, it is our conceptual schemes that determine reality.

At this point the shadow of Immanuel Kant comes on

the stage once again. According to the main representatives of logical positivism, the philosophers' task is to
find out what the nature and the extension of any
meaningful discourse are and, in so doing, they set the
limits of scientific inquiry itself. As we said before
speaking of the metaphysical tenets of logical
positivism, the philosopher thus becomes a sort of
'super-scientist' who determines the bounds of sense,
and practising scientists must rely on philosophical
opinion to discover whether their work is meaningful
or not. Linguistic analysis, therefore, becomes a sort of
prima philosophia, that is to say a super-discipline that
determines the conditions which regulate our
knowledge. But we must also recall that, according to
Kant, no pure perception of reality is possible without
the mediation of our ability to conceptualize; the
categories are always needed in order to know the
world. It follows that no absolute knowledge of reality
is ever possible, the only knowledge at our disposal
being the one relative to the conceptual apparatus. And
while Kant believed that the conceptual apparatus
filtering experience is located in human intellect, the
analytically-oriented thinkers locate it in language.
Both, in sum, speak of *preconditions* regulating human
knowledge, be they a priori categories or language. In
both cases, it is philosophy that answers the basic
questions, and this fact gives further ground to the
thesis I previously stated: the anti-metaphysical stance
of logical positivism and of the analytic tradition is
more theoretical than real. It looks more like a philosophical slogan than an effective accomplishment.

Just as Kant thought that our knowledge of the world
makes sense only with reference to a system of a priori
categories, so the analytically oriented philosophers

deem it correct to say that our discourse about the world may be meaningful only as long as it is regarded as a system of linguistic representation. But what is 'language' if we start from these premises? Certainly it is neither a part of the world nor a tool devised by mankind for accomplishing communicative – ie., social – purposes. Language becomes, rather, an a priori factor which categorizes reality. It makes no sense to ask where it comes from, because its connection to reality is something inexplicable. And, taking that path, sooner or later one is bound to conclude that language and reality are exactly the same thing, a position that many representatives of the analytic tradition are actually endorsing in the present day. They are simply developing the Kantian position in a consistent manner – as the classical idealists did in the nineteenth century – shifting the attention from episte-mology to philosophy of language and the theory of meaning. All this is confirmed by the following – and very interesting – remarks put forward by David Pears:

> Wittgenstein's leading idea was that we can see further than we can say. We can see all the way to the edge of language, but the most distant things that we see cannot be expressed in sentences because they are the preconditions of saying anything. (Pears, 1987, pp. 146–7)

Note how close this notion of 'preconditions' is to the Kantian one. We may wonder, however, why it is necessary to suppose that there is such an unbridgeable gap between what can be said and what can be seen. And, furthermore, why should we assume the notion of the *edge of language* to be real and correct? It seems to me that many of the analytic tradition's basic theses rest, once again, on a notion of language conceived of as a super-natural (ie., a priori) factor. If we reject this notion, sense-conditions are no longer 'ineffable', because they must be traced back to reality conceived of as a whole of which man is just a small part. And this means that the doctrine of the *limits of language* is likely to take us up a blind alley (although it is fascinating from a purely philosophical viewpoint).

It is well known that the question of linguistic idealism has been addressed already by several analytic authors who dealt with Wittgenstein's thought.[5] In their writings, however, the term 'idealism' is used in a non-standard sense, which has little to do with what we have said thus far. They, in fact, somehow connect idealism with solipsism, but why should we think that solipsism and idealism are connected, or that solipsism is a probable (or even necessary) outcome of an idealist outlook on reality? It seems to me, thus, that many representatives of the analytic tradition do not use the term 'idealism' in its classical meaning. To me, all this looks rather strange, because I do not see how, say, Hegel's or Gentile's idealism may be found to be equivalent to some kind of solipsism. For this reason, the articles mentioned in footnote 5 are not taken into account in this context.

V

Epilogue
The logical positivists cleverly realized that modern science has pushed philosophy into a corner from

---

[5] Let us only mention three articles. Those by Gertrude Elizabeth Anscombe (Canfield, 1986, pp. 188–215), Norman Malcom (Canfield, 1986, pp. 339–57), and Bernard Williams (Canfield, 1986, pp. 318–37).

which it is difficult to come out safely. So, they reacted by finding a job specifically devised for philosophers, ie., analysis of language, and afterwards they proceeded to transform linguistic analysis into a sort of new metaphysics which is supposed to provide philosophers with *normative* rules (obviously set forth by the logical positivists themselves). At this point philosophy was certainly saved from extinction, but quite a high price – at least from a purely neopositivist viewpoint – had to be paid: that of adopting an unconscious, although very fascinating, new metaphysics.

We already noted before that there is a strict parallelism between a large part of contemporary linguistically oriented philosophy and idealism, and now I want to say something more on this topic. The idealist claims:

(A) We cannot step out of *thought*: if we admit that there is an external reality which transcends thought, then, by the same act of thinking it, this alleged external reality is no longer transcendental. It follows that we can never overcome the cognitive identity between being on the one side, and thought on the other.

But most analytic philosophers would paraphrase (a) in the following manner:

(B) We cannot step out of *language*: if we admit that there is an external reality which transcends language, then, by the same act of talking about it, this alleged external reality is no longer transcendental. It follows that we can never overcome the cognitive identity between being on the one side, and language on the other.

We might say, thus, that for classical idealism whatever is foreign to thought is unknowable, while for the analytic tradition whatever is foreign to language is unknowable as well. But how can we make sense of the idea that there is something uncreated by thought but, at the same time, necessarily connected with it? And just how – we may wonder – can we understand the idea that there is something foreign to language but, at the same time, necessarily connected with it?

As was mentioned previously, we have to bear in mind that language is in the analytic tradition something much more important than the ordinary language we use daily to communicate with other people and to refer to an external reality. Language becomes, more or less, the logical structure of the world, an extremely powerful and a priori factor which – borrowing a distinction introduced by Wilfrid Sellars – includes both overt (linguistic) and covert (mental) semantic categories; in this sense language just becomes a variant – although with some original characters – of classical idealism's thought (Sellars, 1969, pp. 506–27, cf. also Sellars, 1963, chap. 5). We can trace the development of this view back to the classics of analytic philosophy, ie., Gottlob Frege, the Ludwig Wittgenstein of the *Tractatus Logico-Philosophicus*, Rudolf Carnap and many others. Philip Kitcher has recently claimed in this regard:

Frege's investigations are commonly viewed as a decisive turn, one that dethroned epistemology from its central position among the philosophical disciplines and that set the philosophy of language in its place. In retrospect, we can trace a great lineage from Frege, leading through Russell, Wittgenstein, and Carnap to the professional philosophy practised in

Britain, North America, Australasia and Scandinavia in the postwar years... Frege's opposition to what he perceived as intrusions from psychology or biology is evident from celebrated passages in the *Grundlagen*. The methodological stance he inspired becomes explicit in propositions of the *Tractatus*... Anglo-American philosophers have explored a wide range of disciplines, using ideas from psychology, biology, political science, economics, and the arts to reformulate traditional questions in epistemology and metaphysics. Some of their endeavors mark the return of epistemological naturalism, scorned by Frege and labelled as illicit philosophy by Wittgenstein. (Kitcher, 1992, pp. 53–5)

But let us note that even the later Wittgenstein, notwithstanding the opinion of many authoritative scholars, is not that distant from this conception. Think of his linguistic games, a notion through which reality is bound to the very limits of our language. This conception is exactly what Gustav Bergmann has named the 'metaphysics of logical positivism', a metaphysics which is basically shared by the analysts of ordinary language.

We live in a century in which philosophy has been largely dominated by preoccupation with language and linguistic analysis. Not only logical empiricism and analytic philosophy of ordinary language took this stance, but also hermeneutics, whose representatives think that the only job philosophy can perform is interpreting cultural texts. And Wittgenstein himself is not that distant from this trend of thought, particularly when he claims that his philosophical method switches all questions on truth into questions of meaning. This explains well enough why Michael Dummett states that 'the theory of meaning is the foundation of all philosophy, and not epistemology as Descartes led us into believing' (Dummett, 1973, p. 699).

So it seems to me that most of contemporary philosophy became just 'obsessed' with language (which is different from being seriously interested in it), forgetting that linguistic analysis is just one philosophical method out of many. Even man himself has been identified with language, just leaving aside the fact that man came first and language later. Language is in fact recent, as science shows us, and many parts of our personality are guided by non-linguistic criteria.

All this has important consequences on (i) the philosophy of science, (ii) philosophy itself, and (iii) the entire philosophical vision of the world that surrounds us. As language is a relatively new entry in the history of reality, it cannot have any sort of ontological supremacy. Not only is this so: it is likely to hide the non-linguistic dimensions of our human nature while, being restricted to mankind, it cannot explain a very large number of the features of reality as such. Let us then stress that science, instead, always tries to enlarge (and to deepen) as much as possible our vision of reality and, in order to do this, we must push our sight both toward the past – when mankind did not yet exist – and the future – when mankind perhaps will no longer be there. This in turn means trying to gain a good comprehension of *reality as a whole*: human and non-human, mental and non-mental, linguistic and non-linguistic. Certainly language has a role in this enterprise, although not a unique one. By trying to reduce an extremely complex reality to something much simpler, this approach cannot even explain *why* language was born and *for what purposes*. Language becomes a sort of divinity which is supposed to explain everything while, since it is a rather mundane and imperfect product of the human mind, it needs indeed to be explained by tracing its origins which, as we said, are both social and practical. So the authors who – like Quine – mean to replace any argument on reality with arguments on human language that talks about reality are bound to miss the richness of reality itself: this is the reason why we need a *semantic descent* replacing Quine's semantic ascent.

REFERENCES

Gustav Bergmann, *The Metaphysics of Logical Positivism*, 2nd edn (Madison: University of Wisconsin Press, 1967).

John V. Canfield (ed.), *The Philosophy of Wittgenstein*, vol. 8: Knowing, Naming, Certainty and Idealism (New York-London, Garland: 1986).

Rudolf Carnap, *Meaning and Necessity* (Chicago: University of Chicago Press, 1947).

Michael Dummett, *Frege. Philosophy of Language* (London: Duckworth, 1973).

Philip Kitcher, 'The Naturalists Return', *The Philosophical Review*, vol. 101, no. 1 (1992), pp. 53–114.

Otto Neurath, 'Protokollsatze', *Erkenntnis*, vol. 3 (1932), pp. 204–14.

Alex Orenstein, *Existence and the Particular Quantifier* (Philadelphia: Temple University Press, 1978).

David Pears, *The False Prison* (Oxford: Clarendon Press, 1987).

Alvin Plantinga, *The Nature of Necessity* (Oxford: Clarendon Press, 1974).

Willard V. Quine, *From a Logical Point of View* (New York: Harper & Row, 1963).

————— , 'Existence', in Wolfgang Yourgrau and Allen D. Breck (eds.), *Physics, Logic, and History* (New York, London: Plenum Press, 1970).

Nicholas Rescher, 'The Equivocality of Existence', in *Studies in Ontology*, American Philosophical Quarterly Monograph Series, no. 12 (Oxford: Blackwell, 1978).

Richard Rorty, 'Wittgenstein, Heidegger, and the Reification of Language', in Charles Guignon (ed.), *The Cambridge Companion to Heidegger* (Cambridge: Cambridge University Press, 1993).

Wilfrid Sellars, 'Empiricism and the Philosophy of Mind', in Wilfrid Sellars, *Science, Perception and Reality* (London: Routledge and Kegan Paul, 1963).

————— , 'Language as Thought and as Communication', *Philosophy and Phenomenological Research*, vol. 29 (1969), pp. 506–27.

Peter F. Strawson, *Analysis and Metaphysics* (Oxford: Oxford University Press, 1992).

Ludwig Wittgenstein, *Tractatus Logico-Philosophicus*, ed. Alfred J. Ayer (London: Routledge and Kegan Paul, 1961).

WAS THE LATER WITTGENSTEIN
A TRANSCENDENTAL IDEALIST?

Daniel D. Hutto

I

Introduction
In his paper 'Wittgenstein and Idealism' Professor
Bernard Williams proposed a 'model' for reading
Wittgenstein's later philosophy which he claimed
exposed its transcendental idealist character.[1] By this he
roughly meant that Wittgenstein's later position was
idealistic to the extent that it disallowed the possibility
of there being any independent reality that was not
contaminated by our view of things.[2] And he thought it
was transcendental in the sense that 'our view of things'
is not something that we can explain or can locate *in*
the world.[3]

---

[1] It is important to note that Williams was only ever offering a way of
making sense of the later writings and not a definitive interpretation of
those writings. As he wrote: 'We have here, in a vague sketch, the outline
of a view – I am not going to claim anything as strong as that
[Wittgenstein] held it – I offer this model and its implied connection with
the earlier work as a way of looking at and assessing [the] later material'
(Williams, 1974, p. 85).

[2] This reading fits nicely with Wright's description of the idealist as one
who 'challenge[s] the whole idea that [discourse] is properly seen as geared
to the expression of thoughts whose aim is to reflect an *independent*
reality' (Wright, 1993, p. 3).

[3] Williams sums up his views on this matter in this passage: 'The fact that
in this way *everything can be expressed only via human interests and
concerns*, things which are expressions of mind, and which themselves

I will be arguing that even if we accept Williams' interpretation of Wittgenstein it does not follow that the latter sponsored any form of transcendental idealism. I will make this case in several stages and on two different platforms. Firstly, I shall give a brief description of the underlying basis of Williams' interpretation. Secondly, I shall defend the general thrust of it against a critique which issued from Malcolm. Finally, I will argue that the views ascribed to Wittgenstein by Williams do not make him a transcendental idealist. On the one hand, this case is made by showing that there is a non-trivial resemblance between Williams' Wittgenstein and Donald Davidson who is a self-styled realist. On the other hand, I set out exegetical reasons for thinking that if the continuity that Williams sees between the *Tractatus* and the later writings actually exists then it provides reason in itself not to regard Wittgenstein as an idealist.

II

Williams' Wittgenstein
What kind of interpretation might lead us to think that the later Wittgenstein was a transcendental idealist of sorts? Williams' train of thought made these initial mainline stops:

(A) There is evidence that Wittgenstein was a transcendental idealist in the *Tractatus* (actually he follows Hacker, by and large, and calls him a Transcendental Solipsist).

cannot be explained in any further terms: that provides grounds, I suggest, for calling such a view a kind of idealism' (Williams, 1974, p. 85, emphasis mine).

(B) In Wittgenstein's later writings the transition from the solipsistic 'I' to an all-embracing 'we' still 'contains an important element of idealism' (Williams, 1974, p. 79).

Let us consider the evidence in support of (A). Williams sets out three tenets of the *Tractatus* which he sees as making the position described therein essentially a form of 'transcendental idealism' (Williams, 1974, pp. 78–9). Here is a paraphrase of those tenets:

(1) The limits of my language are the limits of my world.
(2) The limits of language must be staked out from the 'inside'.
(3) The 'I' which forms the limit is not something in the world – and hence cannot be itself investigated.

I will not dally here to assess this reading – I will return to that business later – my concern at this stage is simply to describe it. Clearly, as Williams sees it, (1) and (2) establish the idealistic nature of the Tractarian position while (3) secures its transcendental character. Having *prima facie* established (A) by appeal to these well-known Tractarian doctrines Williams goes on to suggest that there is a continuity between the later writings and the *Tractatus* with respect to these tenets.[4] In fact he claims that the only important change to Wittgenstein's position as it concerns the issue of

---

[4] What makes Williams' interpretation so interesting is that it challenges more orthodox readings, like Hacker's, which see the later work as embodying a 'detailed refutation of solipsism and of idealism' (Hacker, 1986, p. 81, p. 106). It is odd, however, that Williams tells us he is 'substantially in agreement with Mr. P. M. S. Hacker...' (Williams, 1974, p. 77).

transcendental idealism is a shift in his use of pronouns – a move from the first person singular 'I' to the first person plural 'we'.

Of course he notes that Wittgenstein changed his views with respect to the possibility of a 'private language' but, as far as he is concerned, this change is simply the prime motivator of the pronoun shift and not a move away from idealism. It would seem then, by Williams' lights, that the important shift in the later works was really only a transition from the Tractarian postulation of a lonely solipsistic subject forming the limits of the world to a thorough-going anti-individualism – a move from solipsism to an 'aggregate solipsism' (cf. Williams, 1974, pp. 82–3).

By adopting this reading, Williams hopes to explain the vague and indefinite use of 'we' in Wittgenstein's later writings (cf. Williams, 1974, pp. 79, 90, 92). His proposal is that Wittgenstein's use of 'we' shifts from referring to particular human groups, which are the objects of attention or comparison, to referring to *the* human group which is always doing the observation. Such that it is actually present in the later work this kind of referential confusion reminds us of the difficulties that arise when one tries to 'make sense' of solipsism (ie., to give it expression in ordinary language). The problem is that the ordinary use of 'I' is a poor guide to its metaphysical use. When one attempts to *express* solipsism as a position the mixing of these two notions becomes acute. Normally, one mistakenly attempts to describe the solipsist 'I' while keeping the 'psychological' subject in mind instead of focusing only on the 'metaphysical' subject. This is why solipsism can be shown to be correct but remains unstateable.

Crucial to Williams' interpretation is that we accept a transcendental reading of the 'we' of Wittgenstein's later writings, at least in some instances. Bearing this in mind, the main questions which direct my inquiries in the sections to come are as follows: (i) Is Williams' interpretation of Wittgenstein's later work even *plausible*? and (ii) If we accept Williams' interpretation are we committed to regarding the later Wittgenstein as a transcendental idealist of a linguistic sort? I shall attempt to answer these questions with a 'yes' and a 'no' respectively.

III

Malcolm's Critique

Malcolm attempts to dismiss the charge that Wittgenstein was a transcendental idealist by directly striking out against the plausibility of Williams' interpretation. He does this by challenging the claim that Wittgenstein's use of 'we' is 'vague or indefinite' – the idea that its reference vacillates (Malcolm, 1982, p. 251). He writes:

> In Wittgenstein's writings the reference of 'we' is precise. The reference is always to some actual human group or society, in contrast with another real or imagined one. I do not find 'a we which is not one group rather than another in the world' but is instead 'the plural descendant of that idealist I of the *Tractatus*'. (Malcolm, 1982, p. 254)

Malcolm's point is that because the 'we' – or more precisely 'we's' – of the later work always designate some particular human group *in the world* there can be no sense in thinking of them as being of the same order as the metaphysical subject denoted by the 'I' of the *Tractatus*. In this way he tries to discredit Williams' interpretation by attacking it at its root: that is, the idea that there is a simple continuity between the two periods of Wittgenstein's thought on the matter of, what we might call, transcendental subjectivity. For without that continuity the Williams' interpretation fails to be even *plausible* as a way of approaching the later works.

Malcolm wants us to recognize that Wittgenstein always has some individual group in mind, whether it be real or imagined. He wants us to realize that most references to 'we' occur only when Wittgenstein is making a comparison between ourselves and another human group for the *very purpose* of helping us to see that the way we use concepts is not the only way they might be used (Malcolm, 1982, p. 261). In contrast to Williams who sees Wittgenstein as helping us to move around 'within our form of life', Malcolm insists that the whole point of the cross-tribal comparisons is precisely to give us a means of stepping *outside* our own form of life. This is to enable us to get a clearer, more objective view of it. Such comparisons are thus made for reflective purposes.[5]

Support for this position is provided by a wealth of examples drawn from *On Certainty*, *Philosophical Investigations* and *Zettel*. For example, Malcolm recounts one extreme case of cross-tribal comparison found in *Zettel* (§ 380). Therein Wittgenstein conjures up a tribe which employs two different concepts of pain

---

[5]   This is how he puts the point: 'In describing forms of life, world-pictures, language-games, real or imaginary, that differ from our own, we are enabled to *reflect* on our own concepts and to see them *objectively*; we distance ourselves from our concepts and view them from *outside*; as it were' (Malcolm, 1982, p. 262, emphasis mine).

– 'one is applied where there is visible damage and is linked with tending, pity etc. The other is used for stomach-ache, for example, and is tied up with mockery of anyone who complains' (Wittgenstein, 1967, § 380). Malcolm holds that, in effect, such a tribe does not allow for the idea of 'an invisible cause of pain' (Malcolm, 1982, p. 255). Accordingly, unless members of this tribe can locate some kind of outer bodily damage, they will not regard the person as experiencing what-we-would-call-'pain'. Their notion of what counts as pain cuts much more finely than would ours. Or as Wittgenstein puts it they 'have concepts which cut across ours' (Wittgenstein, 1967, § 379).

Malcolm makes much of this case since it is the kind of example which, he thinks, serves to refute Williams' interpretation. It is allegedly evidence that there can be cases where our understanding of another 'form of life' isn't 'non-trivially' conditioned by our own way of seeing things. It provides a paradigm case of our having to step 'outside' our own form of life. For, if Malcolm is correct, the narrow notion of pain used by this imaginary tribe is remarkably dissimilar to our own so much so that he claims their attitude toward pain 'would seem *incomprehensible* to us' (Malcolm, 1982, p. 255, emphasis mine).

What should we make of this talk of incomprehensibility? Malcolm's way of coming to terms with it is to draw two sorts of distinction: one between 'description' and 'understanding' – and another, in parallel fashion, between 'language games' and 'world pictures'. He allows that other language games can be compared since we can 'objectively' *describe* them but that it is possible for other world pictures to be incomprehensible to us – since we can fail to *understand* them. The possibility of such failure is allegedly due to the fact that alien world pictures may be 'based on different instinctive responses'.

It will be useful to draw some distinctions of our own here. For I believe we must regard Malcolm as supporting either a strong or weak reading of incomprehensibility on this score. On a weak reading the claim that another is 'incomprehensible' has the same kind of force as in everyday phrases like 'I can't make sense of you at all' or 'I don't understand you'. We use such language – not when we are completely baffled by the other person – but when some aspect of what they are doing confuses us. It is only against the background of a general understanding that we could find another's actions odd or puzzling. For, to employ a variant of an oft-quoted Davidsonian moral, the ascription of *too much* incomprehensibility will leave us with nothing to be confused about.

However, it is vital to note that so long as we read 'lack of understanding' or 'incomprehensibility' *weakly* then we won't have undermined the basis for Williams' interpretation of Wittgenstein.[6] Namely, on a weak reading of 'incomprehensibility', it is still *possible* to see the later works as an exploration of 'our' concepts and their potential limits (to avoid confusion we might speak rather of the limits of concepts and give up the quibbles concerning ownership). On this reading,

[6] It is interesting to note that Michael Root also reads Wittgenstein as allowing for the existence of 'people who are engaged in ritual actions that are so different from our own actions that we may not be able to understand them' – '[actions] that we cannot see – as resembling any of our own –' (Root, 1986, p. 304). Yet even though Root seemingly agrees with Malcolm on this issue of Wittgensteinian exegesis he also makes it clear that, by his lights, 'Wittgenstein too discounts the idea of the radical other' (Root, 1986, p. 304).

although consideration of 'alien concepts' will enable us to take up a reflective stance with respect to our *usual use* of concepts, adopting such a stance does not require us (or even allow us) to 'step outside our own form of life'. At least not in any dramatic sense.

For example, the 'narrow' concept of pain used by the tribe in *Zettel* can be seen as a deviation or restrictive version of our usual concept of pain (even if it *is* heading in an 'unusual direction'). And Wittgenstein himself admits such deviations cannot be too great in the remark which follows the passage referred to by Malcolm. He writes:

> But in that case isn't this man just overlooking something that is there? – He takes no notice of it and why should he? – But in that case his concept just is fundamentally different from ours. – *Fundamentally* different? Different. (Wittgenstein, 1967, § 381).

By reading Wittgenstein in this moderate way one *could* reconcile Malcolm's claim about incomprehensibility (read weakly) with Williams' method for interpreting Wittgenstein. Hence, a weak reading of 'incomprehensible' will not do for the purpose of discrediting the plausibility of Williams' proposal for it makes the gap between us and the others too small to be of interest.

A strong reading of 'incomprehensibility', however, would serve to contradict Williams' interpretation. To make this point vividly – we might consider the Wittgenstein-inspired project of Rodney Needham who hoped to expose the fact that many translators and anthropologists, who are accustomed to using themselves as a model, can be too quick to ascribe their own psychological states to others (cf. Needham, 1972, pp. 8–9).

Needham hoped to make us aware of this kind of bias by focusing on the common ascription of 'beliefs' to certain exotic peoples. By enjoining us to examine the history of the concept 'belief' he intended to graphically illustrate why we would be ill-advised to attribute *this* type of psychological attitude to people who have not shared in the same intellectual background as English-speakers. For instance, he claimed that the Chinese word *hsin* does not easily translate into 'the modern sense of "belief" which the concept came to have under Greek and Latin influences' (Needham, 1972, p. 23). The reason for our inability to translate the word, he suggests, is due to the fact that the Chinese concept 'belongs to an autonomous psychology that in some regards appears to frame a *radically* distinct view of human capacities and their relationship to the nature of things' (Needham, 1972, p. 37, emphasis mine).

If we take Needham at his word the Chinese operate with a set of 'strongly incomprehensible' psychological concepts since he is unable even to 'describe' this difference in the way Wittgenstein managed to describe the practice of the tribe with the 'narrow concept of pain'. To endorse this kind of strong reading of 'incomprehensibility' would be, in effect, to sponsor some form of 'cultural relativism'. Nevertheless, I'm inclined to agree with Root that this kind of incautious 'rhetorically extravagant' talk of 'radically distinct views' smacks of hyperbole (Root, 1986, p. 299). On the one hand if the others are so radically different that we cannot describe their 'perspective on things' in any coherent way then we have designated nothing worth calling a perspective. On the other hand, as Root nicely puts the moral of Davidson's 'The Very Idea of a Conceptual Scheme': 'One cannot show that a mind is indescribable by proceeding to describe it' (Root, 1986, p. 300). If this is right then the very idea of strong incomprehensibility is, indeed, incoherent.

Malcolm's critique of Williams is caught on the horns of this dilemma. If he hopes to discredit Williams' interpretation by suggesting that Wittgenstein endorsed the possibility of 'incomprehensible world pictures' *in the weak sense* (which is what I think he intends) then he won't have done enough to expose the implausibility of that interpretation. For such a view is consistent with Williams' position that the comparisons between ourselves and others in the later works are not really comparisons between different human groups, rather they are explorations of *our one and only set of* concepts – even if the boundaries of those concepts are loose-fitting.

However, if Malcolm is seeking to sabotage Williams by suggesting that Wittgenstein endorsed the possibility of 'incomprehensible world pictures' *in the strong sense,* then one could argue that he is ascribing to Wittgenstein a naive and unworkable position. And, in that case, as Williams was only ever claiming to provide a useful method for approaching the later works, it is clear, on charitable grounds, that his interpretation would serve us better than one that makes Wittgenstein's position incoherent.

But we may wish to take the Williams interpretation seriously for another reason as well. For, it, unlike Malcolm's, enables us to make sense of the reflective activity which is the basis of the cross-tribal comparisons themselves. This is important since even Malcolm is prepared to admit that Wittgenstein's project is a reflective one in this respect. The problem for Malcolm is that it is natural to think that such reflective activity must take place from a vantage point which can encompass both the foreign and the domestic use of concepts. For how else, we might ask, is it possible to consider and compare them both?

Moreover, this will lead us to ask the further question: *Who* is it that compares 'our' concepts with those of others? For such comparisons must be made by someone who, at the very least, is not themselves an object of scrutiny at the time of making such comparisons. If *we* are describing 'ourselves' we must always leave out of the picture the 'synthesizing subject' who does the describing. Any attempt to turn *that* subject into an object of attention presents us with an immediate infinite regress of subjects. Certainly one possible way around this, available to supporters of the Williams' interpretation, is to say that it is the transcendental subject who performs the synthesis. This frees us from the infinite regress 'problem' because in taking this line we can abandon the idea that it ever was a genuine problem. Rather, we must simply come to understand and accept that, at bottom, the 'subject' which describes cannot, at the same time, be described.[7]

Of course, I am not suggesting that the later Wittgenstein would have wanted to give such an answer. As Jonathan Lear points out 'Wittgenstein was of course trying to deny the possibility of a transcendent perspective from which one can view our form of life'

---

[7] Lear sees that the only way to avoid this quandary is to realize that 'the anthropological stance is not what it pretends to be. It is not genuinely an observational stance, it is rather an artefact of philosophical inquiry – we take up the anthropological stance not when we actually go out an observe other tribes, but when, in philosophical reflection, we construct various tribal practices and locate rule-following activity within them – we discover that the anthropological stance is not at war with transcendental inquiry, it is of a piece with it' (Lear, 1986, p. 289). Because of this he says 'What we are confronted with is not the limit of the world, but the limit of the anthropological stance' (Lear, 1986, p. 292).

(Lear, 1986, p. 279). And it does appear as if in the later writings he no longer felt the force of the problem which had once brought him to confess that the *Tractatus* propositions were, because of their transcendental a priori nature, necessarily nonsensical.

Nevertheless, it isn't clear that this lack of concern on his part is any kind of reliable indicator that the later work is completely free from a similar transcendental tendency – one which generates similar difficulties. For example, as I have just argued, the very act of comparing different language games with our own seems to require us to take up a transcendental perspective – even if it is only temporal in character.[8] The evident lack of attention given by Wittgenstein to this sort of question is, according to thinkers such as Lear, one of the main failings of the later works. In fact Lear suggests it is recognition of this very lacuna that caused Wittgenstein to regard his later work as 'unfinished'.[9] And it is because Lear himself wishes to 'finish' that philosophical project – to develop a more coherent 'transcendental anthropology' – that he is concerned to answer the question: 'How are we to understand reflective philosophical activity when it goes on within a form of life?' (Lear, 1986, p. 282).

---

[8] Perhaps this was what Wittgenstein was driving at in saying 'One might think: if philosophy speaks of the use of the word "philosophy" there must be a second-order philosophy. But it is not so: it is, rather, like the case of orthography, which deals with the word "orthography" among others without then being second-order' (Wittgenstein, 1953, § 121). This is, of course, a very different approach than the one presented by the Tractarian doctrine of showing.

[9] He even goes so far to write: 'Even a sympathetic reader of Wittgenstein's later philosophy must, I think, conclude that it represents an unfinished work' (Lear, 1986, pp. 267, 283). He goes on to support this view by considering some of Wittgenstein's remarks in the preface of the *Investigations* concerning his inability to 'weld his thoughts together'.

I repeat: obviously one way of doing this is to read Wittgenstein by Williams' lights. We can see the later works as supporting a 'no-we' solipsism that does not refer to an individual group of people in the world but rather gestures at the perspective from which we take up the reflective stance. Such a 'we' cannot be employed in the 'ordinary sense' and hence resembles the Tractarian 'I' used to designate the metaphysical subject – the one which could only be shown not stated.

I say again, the point is not that Wittgenstein held such views but that the Williams' interpretation offers a coherent and not implausible way of reading the later writings. Finally, it is worth emphasizing that if we adopt a Williams-type interpretation, as Lear does, then, *contra* Malcolm, the pronoun 'we' *is* ambiguous in just the way Williams suggests. That is to say, it becomes intelligible to ask: Are we the observers or the observed? The ambiguity arises because coherency demands that, in some sense, we are both.[10]

The important question to ask now is what should we make of all this? If we follow Williams' lead and use his model to read Wittgenstein's later works are we thereby committed to seeing the later Wittgenstein as subscribing to a linguistic form of transcendental idealism? I think not. To show this I will initially consider the work of Donald Davidson – whose position on these matters, I suggest, fits Williams' interpretation of the later Wittgenstein quite snugly. Only then will I give attention to Wittgenstein's own remarks on these matters.

[10] Lear is right to say 'Perhaps...Wittgenstein should have distinguished between we and a form of life in much the same way Kant should have distinguished the "I" from the "I think". "Form of life" is a predicate which may be predicated of various objects – We should eventually come to appreciate that when we talk philosophically about "our form of life" what we are trying to describe is not an object' (Lear, 1986, p. 291).

IV

A Davidsonian Reading
If we accept, for the sake of argument, that the Williams interpretation is at least a plausible way of reading the later Wittgenstein we are still left with the question: Is the transcendental side of Wittgenstein's philosophy necessarily idealistic in character? One way of approaching the question is to consider the work of Donald Davidson. For there seems to be a non-trivial resemblance between his position and that of Wittgenstein on all of the issues which, according to Williams, add up to make the latter an idealist. For example, we find Davidson endorsing the idea that our language is the best guide to metaphysics, that ultimately our way of seeing things is the *only* way of seeing things, and that the basis of language cannot itself be explained since it is a transcendental condition of 'experience' (broadly construed).[11]

It certainly looks as if Davidson is a philosopher who supports the kind of 'aggregate idealism' which Williams attributes to Wittgenstein. The big question, however, is whether or not Davidson's position is idealist. And here it is interesting to note that although he sponsors the trio of tenets that Williams regards as

---

[11] As he puts it: 'in making manifest the large features of our language, we make manifest the large features of reality' (Davidson, 1984, p. 199). He writes 'A community of minds is the basis of knowledge; it provides the measure of all things. It makes no sense to question that standard or to seek a more ultimate one' (Davidson, 1991, p. 264). He tells us: 'It would be good if we could say how language came into existence in the first place, or at least give an account of how an individual learns his first language, given that others in his environment are already linguistically accomplished. These matters are, however, beyond the bounds of reasonable philosophic speculation' (Davidson, 1991, p. 157). As Maker say 'Our general ability to know and describe what there is – at this juncture – is taken for granted' (Maker, 1991, p. 356).

embodying Wittgenstein's idealism, Davidson is a self-styled realist. How can that be?

Davidson has tried to make clear the modesty of his 'realism' in a number of places (cf. Davidson, 1986a, 1986b, 1990b). His commitment to realism is directly connected to his views on radical interpretation. For he has argued that we learn to interpret others in a social environment on the basis of what the world provides us. We may see the situation more clearly if we consider the position of the radical interpreter who has nothing but his observations and principles of charity to go on when interpreting others. As Davidson stresses in such a situation, 'what can be observed, of course, is speech behaviour in relation to the environment, and from this certain attitudes toward sentences can be fairly directly inferred, just as preferences can be inferred from choices – From such acts it is possible to infer that the speaker is *caused by* certain kinds of events to hold a sentence true' (Davidson, 1990b, p. 318, emphasis mine).

In light of this remark, it is perhaps worth digressing at this point to make clear what role causality plays in the process of interpreting speech acts. This is important because some philosophers may be misled into thinking that an invocation of causality at this juncture is at odds with the overall transcendental, non-reductive nature of the account. For instance, Evnine thinks that Davidson's invocation of 'causal talk' is at odds with his 'interpretative hermeneutic project [which] goes with an idealist theory of content' (Evnine, 1991, p. 175).[12] For to engage in such talk is surely to

---

[12] As Evnine says, 'Causation – is a non-holistic relation between a belief and an object or event. If we hold that what a belief is about is determined by what causes it, we allow the possibility of a gap between what a belief is

open up a necessary *gap* between what causes my thought and what my thought is about – a split between what is given and how I interpret it.

But the worry that a Davidsonian approach to interpretation will go the way of 'crude causal theories', and revitalize the scheme/content distinction, is unwarranted. It is certainly true that in his talk of causation and correspondence, he wants to maintain the idea that there is a mind-independent world that we 'confront' and, *prima facie*, Evnine is right to think that this opens up a gap between what causes a speaker's utterances and what the speaker means by those utterances. Nevertheless, Davidson holds that, viewed as a divide between a *lone* subject and the world, such a gap is unintelligible. What is required to make sense of such a gap is an inter-subjective standard upon which to generate a notion of an objective world independent of ourselves. The subject/object split (or scheme/content distinction) is generated *only* when we have access to an inter-subjective standard; a social world. It is only in such a space that we can employ the normative criteria needed for treating utterances as truth-bearing or not.

Truth, and our notion of an objective world, would seem to develop in the process of learning from, and interpreting the utterances of, others. We might say the concept of truth (ie., objectivity), in some sense, *emerges* when communicators establish public criteria for the assessment of reports made by others. And, since 'truth' emerges in this way it must be regarded as

about, and what else is believed about that thing' (Evnine, 1991, p. 150). Evnine sees Davidson's programme as threatening to endorse a causal variant of the scheme/content distinction, the third dogma of empiricism, which Davidson himself denounces.

transcendent. It must be taken as a basic concept.[13] Or to put the point in the context of concerns about Davidson's use of 'causation', we must realize that we can only make sense of a 'gap' between the subject and some object as a 'gap' found *within* the world – within experience.[14] It is during interpretation, by 'triangulating', that we are able to determine what *causes* another to use their words as they do (and whether they use them correctly or not).[15]

[13] Davidson himself strongly cautions us in several places not to try to further explain truth. 'We should not say that truth is correspondence, coherence, warranted assertability, ideally justified assertability, what is accepted in the conversation of the right people, what science will end up maintaining, what explains convergence on single theories in science, or the success of our ordinary beliefs. To the extent that realism and antirealism depend on one or another of these views of truth we should refuse to endorse either' (Davidson, 1990b, p. 309). Elsewhere he writes, 'Truth is as clear and as basic a concept we have. Tarski has given us an idea how to *apply* the general concept (or try to apply it) to particular languages on the assumption that we already understand it; but of course he didn't show how to define it in general (he proved, rather, that this couldn't be done). Any further attempt to explain, define, analyse or explicate the concept will be empty or wrong: correspondence theories, coherence theories, pragmatist theories, theories that identify truth with warranted assertability (perhaps under "ideal" or "optimum" conditions), theories that ask truth to explain the success of science or serve as the ultimate outcome of science or the conversations of some elite, all such theories either add nothing to our understanding of truth or have obvious counter-examples' (Davidson, 1990a, pp. 135–6).

[14] Lear makes this point well by saying: 'The Metaphysical Subject need not be conceived, as Kant thought, as lying outside the world, nor, as the early Wittgenstein thought, as its limit: it is we who live in the world. What we are confronted with is not the limit of the world, but the limit of the anthropological stance' (Lear, 1986, p. 292).

[15] Davidson illustrates what he means here rather nicely: 'If I were bolted to the earth I would have no way of determining the distance from me of many objects. I would only know they were on some line drawn from me toward them. I might interact successfully with objects, but I could have no way of giving content to the question where they were. Not being bolted down I am free to triangulate. Our sense of objectivity is the consequence of another sort of triangulation, one that requires two creatures. Each interacts with an object, but what gives each the concept of the way things are objectively is the base line formed between the creatures by language' (Davidson, 1985, p. 480).

In a sense, therefore, the *causes* of which Davidson speaks in the above quotation are already incorporated, non-reductively, into the social context of interpretation. But this is not to say they are 'constructed' by society. Therefore, although Davidson does speak of causality, objectivity and correspondence, it is vital to notice that the role these concepts play in his work is nothing like that which they play in traditional correspondence theories of truth and reference which he, himself, considers *absurd* (Davidson, 1986b, p. 307). In other words since the notions of objective truth and error arise only in the context of interpretation and against the background of an inter-subjective norm, we can expect *subjectivity* and *objectivity* to emerge, as it were, simultaneously. His way of expressing this is to say, 'the foundations of knowledge must be subjective and objective at once' (Davidson, 1986b, p. 327). We might make use of Heidegger's term here and say they are *equiprimordial* (Heidegger, 1962, sect. 43, p. 200).

I take this also to be what Heidegger means when he says, 'the world is disclosed essentially along with the Being of Dasein' (Heidegger, 1962, sect. 43, p. 203). The choice of words is important here. Notice Heidegger says the world is 'disclosed' to us and not simply 'constructed' or 'created' by us. Likewise his student, Gadamer, makes this quite explicit by telling us: 'The agreement about things that takes place in language means neither a priority of things nor a priority of the human mind' (Gadamer, 1960, p. 78). This is what frees Davidson from idealism. For he too thinks it would be a mistake to think that reality was *dependent upon us* even though ours are the only standards for interpreting reality (cf. Putnam, 1987, p. 12).[16]

[16] As Rorty puts it 'if one follows Davidson, one will not know what to

I hope it is now clear why it would be wrong to tar Davidson with an idealist brush simply because he supports many of the doctrines that Williams attributes to the early (and later) Wittgenstein. I further hope this reveals that, at the very least, it is possible to hold such views without committing oneself to 'idealism' *per se*. In the final section of this paper I will consider some remarks from Wittgenstein himself – found in both the later works and the *Tractatus* – which should lead us to doubt whether we ought to regard him as sponsoring a form of transcendental idealism.

V

A Wittgensteinian Exegesis

Wittgenstein's later position substantially agrees with Davidson's in the respect that both philosophers regard contact with the world and its objects as crucial to the mastery of 'language' (cf. Wittgenstein, 1967, § 455). This is the case even though the former's view of language mastery is far less 'intellectualist' than is Davidson's.[17]   For, whereas Davidson regards the coming to recognize the conditions under which another's utterance will be *true* as being all-important to interpretation, it is clear that Wittgenstein wished to consign any and all attachment to correspondence

make of the issues between realist and anti-realist. For one will feel in touch with reality *all the time*' (Rorty, 1986, p. 145).

[17] He says such things as: 'Giving grounds, however, justifying the evidence, comes to an end; – but the end is not certain propositions striking immediately as true, ie., it is not a kind of seeing on our part; *it is our acting, which lies at the bottom of the language-game*' (Wittgenstein, 1969, § 205, emphasis mine). And also: 'I want to regard man here as an animal; as a primitive being to which one grants instinct but not ratiocination. As a creature in a primitive state. Any logic good enough for a primitive means of communication needs no apology from us. Language did not emerge from some kind of ratiocination' (Wittgenstein, 1969, § 475)

theories of truth 'traditional' or otherwise to his past.[18] Consider this remark:

> Children do not learn that books exist, that armchairs exist, etc., etc., – they learn to fetch books, sit in armchairs, etc., etc.
>
> Later questions about the existence of things do of course arise. 'Is there such a thing as a unicorn?' and so on. But such a question is possible only because as a rule no corresponding question presents itself.... (Wittgenstein, 1969a, § 476)

Although it may be that Davidson and Wittgenstein have different attitudes about precisely *how* it is that we are related to the world (or perhaps Davidson encompasses something of both Wittgenstein's earlier and later selves in this regard) it is quite clear that, as concerns transcendental realism and idealism, they stand together. Like Davidson, Wittgenstein is continually trying to steer clear of positions occupied by philosophers of both these camps. In a remark from *The Blue Book* he openly tells us that, 'the common-sense man...is as far from realism as from idealism' (Wittgenstein, 1958, p. 48).[19] And in *Zettel* he remarks:

> One man is a convinced realist, another a convinced idealist and teaches his children accordingly. In such

---

[18] Smart provides us with an excellent comparison between these two thinkers on just this issue (cf. Smart, 1986, pp. 98–100).

[19] In the surrounds of this remark Wittgenstein is careful to distinguish between the common-sense man and the common-sense philosopher. As Hacker points out this is because the commonsense philosopher is likely to be some kind of naive realist of a Johnsonian sort – and hence they will have no power to settle the debate since they are a participant in it (cf. Hacker, 1986, pp. 226–7). I believe this is connected with Wittgenstein's view that one cannot give a commonsense answer to a philosophical problem (Wittgenstein, 1958, pp. 58–9).

an important matter as the existence or non-existence of the external world they don't want to teach their children anything wrong.

What will the children be taught? To include in what they say: 'There are physical objects' or the opposite?...

But the idealist will teach his children the word 'chair' after all, for of course he wants to teach them to do this and that, eg., to fetch a chair. Then where will be the difference between the idealist-educated children and the realist ones? Won't the difference only be one of battle cry? (Wittgenstein, 1967, §§ 413 and 414; see also Wittgenstein, 1980, §§ 338–9).

Wittgenstein's point in these extended passages is that the divide between these two positions is, *practically speaking*, uninteresting.[20] Both stances are effectively indistinguishable when we consider them in the realm of the ordinary. He is drawing our attention to the fact that addenda such as 'and there are mind-independent objects' or 'and there are no mind-independent objects' are paradigm examples of how philosophical language idles. Arthur Fine also recognizes this use of language as a symptom of the diseases of metaphysical realism

---

[20] In the *Investigations* he makes this explicit by saying: 'the solipsist [does] not want any practical advantage when he advances his view' (Wittgenstein, 1953, § 403, see also Wittgenstein, 1958, p. 59). This follows swift on the heels of remarks which echo points made in *The Blue Book*: 'when...we disapprove of the expressions of ordinary language (which are after all performing their office), we have got a picture in our heads which conflicts with the picture of our ordinary way of speaking. Whereas we are tempted to say that our way of speaking does not describe the facts as they really are... For this is what disputes between Idealists, Solipsists and Realists look like. The one party attacks the normal form of expression as if they were attacking a statement; the others defend it, as if they were stating facts recognised by every reasonable human being' (Wittgenstein, 1953, § 402). This is why 'A philosophical problem has the form: "I don't know my way about"' (Wittgenstein, 1953, § 123).

and idealism. As he says, all 'the realist adds on [to a core acceptance of ordinary claims] is a desk-thumping, foot-stamping shout of 'Really!' (Fine, 1984, p. 97). Likewise, the idealist (or anti-realist) only contributes to 'the core position a particular analysis of the concept of truth' (Fine, 1984, p. 97). But Fine points out it is possible to take our ordinary claims at face value – without such addenda. He says of such a position that it describes the 'natural ontological attitude' and I think Wittgenstein subscribed to it (cf. Fine, 1984, p. 98).

The point is that to be unimpressed by the posturing of the metaphysical realist is not the same as endorsing, in any ordinary sense, the view that there are 'no mind-independent objects in the world'. It is to hold that talk about mind-independent objects is simply to talk about the familiar items of our quotidian world – such as tables, armchairs, etc. That is why such a position is of a piece with the verdicts of commonsense even if it is at odds with commonsense *philosophy* of a realist character.

So where does this leave us? How can we make sense of Wittgenstein's blatant dismissal of idealism and square this with the Williams' interpretation? I think it forces us to re-examine the allegedly idealistic character of the *Tractatus*. For, I maintain that Williams' key exegetical mistake is to be found precisely when he focuses on the idea that 'limits of language are the limits of the world and that they cannot be staked out from both sides' (cf. Williams, 1974, p. 78).[21] Right there he

---

[21] Naturally this way of expressing the view is encouraged by Wittgenstein's talk of 'limits' in the *Tractatus* (cf. Wittgenstein, 1922, 4.114, 5.6 – 5.62, and 6.45). It is certainly true that this image of being 'inside', which is suggested in the *Tractatus*, is directly linked with Wittgenstein's vision of reality as a 'bounded whole'. But since there is no getting outside of language there is thus nothing to the idea of being inside it. According to Rorty, this idea was lost when the later Wittgenstein 'became reconciled

makes it seem as if it makes good sense to talk of there being two sides – an inside and an outside. And it is important to note that he even describes Wittgenstein's *later* understanding of our position in the world with reference to this metaphor of being 'inside'. He talks of our 'moving around reflectively *inside* our view of things' (Williams, 1974, p. 85, emphasis mine). But, again, the picture of our exploring language from the inside presupposes that it makes sense to speak of an outside. And I think it is this figurative usage that generates confusion and makes Wittgenstein's position appear to be transcendentally 'idealistic'.

It may help to distance ourselves from Wittgenstein's writing for a moment so as to see this confusion over metaphors from a slightly different angle. In an recent article concerning Davidson's transcendental arguments, Maker sets out the story of philosophical development with respect to the issue of transcendental subjectivity rather nicely by employing this very same inside/outside metaphor (cf. Maker, 1991, pp. 348–52). Naturally, the tale begins with the original postulated dichotomy between the realms of the subjective and the objective – that to which we have access and that to which we hope it corresponds. But, as he points out, the age-old epistemic problem generated by this picture is that nothing we can have subjective access to could ever count as *evidence* for what is objective. That is, anything we have access to is, by definition, only ever subjective and hence cannot provide evidence of an

---

to the notion that there was nothing ineffable, and that philosophy, like language, was just a set of indefinitely expandable social practices, *not a bounded whole* whose periphery might be "shown"' (Rorty, 1991, p. 57, emphasis mine). On the later view each move is always a move within language. A better metaphor would be to see language as simply moving forward rather than outward.

'objective' standard. This is how the very idea of an objective realm breeds an irrefutable scepticism.

It is here 'transcendental' thinkers come in to save the day – for they attempt to 'get us to rethink the idea that subjectivity can be properly understood as something we are trapped within, forever cut off from an objectivity lying beyond' (Maker, 1991, p. 349). Such philosophers reject the very idea of a subject/object split (conceived as being outside of, or prior to, experience) as a myth. The subjective and objective need no 'bridge' to link since they are not separated in the way the original picture suggests.

What is interesting is *how* Maker describes the next stage in the development of these ideas: 'Transcendental thinkers ask us to *interiorize objectivity*' (Maker, 1991, p. 349, emphasis mine). And, of course, that is the natural way to express the situation *if* one still has in mind the picture of a subject/object split. From *that* starting point it looks as if the proper way to describe transcendental arguments is as trying to force the 'objective' world into the subjective realm. But, of course, when we draw this picture clearly it becomes evident that such a description is inappropriate. Having dragged the world *fully* into the subjective realm we are left with nothing that can any longer be called 'subjective' or 'objective' in the philosophically dramatic sense presupposed by the original picture.[22]

---

[22] Jonathan Rée recognizes this when he says: 'It makes no sense to say either that subjectivity exists, or that the world exists: subjectivity and the world together create the environment in which questions of existence arise' (Rée, 1994, pp. 6–7). And again the reply to those who would cast Wittgenstein in idealist garb is identical to the reply that one could make on Davidson's behalf. It is that: 'Idealism as philosophically interesting and shocking presupposes the intelligibility of a radical, unbridgeable gulf between mind or language and the world in order then to deny it. It presupposes the intelligibility of the radical other inaccessible to language which Davidson has deconstructed' (Maker, 1991, p. 360).

As Maker makes clear, once we have understood that the subjective/objective split dissolves when we follow out the programme of 'radical subjectivism' we completely lose the sense that we are somehow 'trapped' within our view of things (Maker, 1991, p. 356). As he writes, it is 'a radical or thorough-going subjectivism – a subjectivism without limits – that leads to a satisfactory objectivism' (Maker, 1991, p. 356). The echoes are unmistakable. I believe that this is the precise manoeuvre which Wittgenstein was gesturing at by speaking of 'following solipsism out *strictly*'. What I have tried to do, using Maker, is to graphically illustrate the claim that 'solipsism, when its implications are followed out strictly, coincides with pure realism' (Wittgenstein, 1922, 5.64).[23] That is to say, once the subjective (whether in singular or plural form) and the objective merge on equal footing there can be no more sense to be had from the old inside/outside metaphor of our relation to reality.

It helps to see this if we also note that while it is common to take notice of Wittgenstein's diminishing of the subject by focusing on the solipsistic passages of the *Tractatus*, it is equally important to recognize that he also cut the world down to size in precisely the same fashion. Rée is one of the few authors to draw explicit attention to this issue.[24] For, as he points out, not only is *the self* not encounterable in experience, *the world* is also absent when we go looking for it. To use the

---

[23] This is also expressed in Wittgenstein's notebooks with direct reference to idealism: 'In this way idealism leads to realism if it is strictly thought out' (Wittgenstein, 1969b, p. 85).

[24] As he writes: 'The point only becomes clear when one notices the topic announced by the first words of the book: *the world*. "The world is all that is the case", according to the opening sentence; but as Wittgenstein develops the theme, it turns out that the world must also include possibilities – everything, that is to say, that might have been the case but

language of the *Tractatus* all we ever deal with are the 'facts' which are pictured in language – 'The world is the totality of facts' (Wittgenstein, 1922, 1.1). Just as the world shrinks so 'The self of solipsism shrinks to a point without extension and there remains the reality co-ordinated with it' (Wittgenstein, 1922, 5.64).

To sum up, in drawing a connection between Wittgenstein's earlier and later self I don't think Williams has quite grasped how 'radical' the early Wittgensteinian project really was with respect to the issue of idealism. What I see as a rather big change in the later writings is not a dismissal of *these* kinds of Tractarian conclusion but rather a following through the advice of the *Tractatus* with respect to them. In the later material Wittgenstein begins to practise what he had been preaching. The transcendental twaddle is cut out because it *really* can't be spoken of. Once cured of our philosophical tendency to bump our heads against the limits of language and the desire to use metaphysical language where we ought only to employ everyday language, we won't be plagued by questions or worries about realism or idealism. It is this that brings about 'The real discovery – the one that gives philosophy *peace*, so that it is no longer tormented by questions which bring itself in question' (Wittgenstein, 1953, § 133, emphasis mine).[25]

happens not to be. It is only against the background of these unactualized possibilities that actual facts take shape. But if this is what the world is, then, unlike the facts of which it is the "totality" *the world cannot be pictured*' (Rée, 1994, p. 6).

[25] It lends credence to this interpretation to note, as Hacker does, that the 'archetypal fly in the original flybottle was the solipsist' (Hacker, 1986, p. 215). He provides this quotation of Wittgenstein's from his 'Notes for Lectures on "Private Experience" and "Sense Data"': 'The solipsist flutters and flutters in the flyglass, strikes against the walls, flutters further. How can he be brought to rest?' (Rhees, 1968, p. 300). It would seem that when, even in doing philosophy, one *does* refrain from the use of 'super-

It is the philosophical free and easy use of 'super-concepts' that is the cause of our going awry. To think that we can withdraw from our ordinary use of words – to *get outside* our ordinary practice and correct it. If we could do this we might be able to classify our account as either idealistic or realistic – but these notions have no place in our everyday use of language.

VI

Conclusion
The upshot of all this is that it is implausible that Wittgenstein's later position was transcendentally 'idealistic' even if we follow Williams in thinking that certain Tractarian doctrines found their way into the later writings. For once we understand those doctrines correctly we see that there really is nothing at stake between the realist and the idealist. If one accepts the account of our position in the world as described by Wittgenstein's later writings then we find that we are indeed always speaking of and interacting with 'mind-independent things' – a world not 'composed' by us nor obedient to our concerns. But, at the same time, we never make the impossible step outside our own form of life – because there is no such place to step. Unless we imagine ourselves in the position of a Philosophical God there is no sense in our sponsoring either transcendental realism or idealism.

___

concepts' the fly can escape his bottle and philosophy can find peace. We can escape our 'puzzlement' and 'mental discomfort' once we realize that what we are striving for isn't at odds with commonsense – what we crave is just a different way of looking at facts of which we are already quite well aware (cf. Wittgenstein, 1958, p. 59).

REFERENCES

Donald Davidson, *Inquiries into Truth and Interpretation* (Oxford: Clarendon Press, 1984).

——— , 'Rational Animals', in Lepore and MacLaughlin (eds.), *Actions and Events: Perspectives on the Philosophy of Donald Davidson* (Oxford: Basil Blackwell, 1985).

——— , 'A Coherence Theory of Truth and Knowledge', in Lepore (ed.), *Truth and Interpretation: Perspectives on the Philosophy of Donald Davidson* (Oxford: Basil Blackwell, 1986a).

——— , 'Empirical Content', in Lepore (ed.), *Truth and Interpretation: Perspectives on the Philosophy of Donald Davidson* (Oxford: Basil Blackwell, 1986b)

——— , 'Afterthoughts, 1987', in Lepore (ed.), *Reading Rorty: Critical Responses to Philosophy and the Mirror of Nature (and Beyond)* (Oxford: Blackwell, 1990a).

——— , 'The Structure and Content of Truth', *Journal of Philosophy*, vol. 87, no. 6 (June 1990b), pp. 279–328.

——— , 'Three Varieties of Knowledge', in A. Phillips Griffiths (ed.), *A. J. Ayer: Memorial Essays*

(Cambridge: Cambridge University Press, 1991). Reprinted in the present volume as 'Subjective, Intersubjective, Objective'.

Simon Evnine, *Donald Davidson* (Cambridge: Polity Press, 1991).

Arthur Fine, 'The Natural Ontological Attitude', in Leplin (ed.), *Scientific Realism* (Berkeley: University of California Press, 1984).

Hans-Georg Gadamer, 'The Nature of Things and the Language of Things', *Philosophical Hermeneutics* (Berkeley: University of California Press, 1976).

Peter M. S. Hacker, *Insight and Illusion* (Oxford. Oxford University Press, 1986).

Martin Heidegger, *Being and Time*, trans. Macquarrie and Robinson (New York: Harper & Row, 1962).

J. Daniel D. Hutto, 'Minding our Language: The Role of Simulation in Linguistic Interpretation', *Inside/Out*, vol. 9 (Spring 1994), pp. 12–15.

Jonathan Lear, 'Transcendental Anthropology', in P. Pettit and J. McDowell (eds.), *Subject, Thought and Context* (Oxford: Clarendon Press, 1986).

William Maker, 'Davidson's Transcendental Arguments', *Philosophy and Phenomenological Research*, vol. 51, no. 2 (June 1991), pp. 345–60.

Norman Malcolm, 'Wittgenstein and Idealism', in G.

Vesey (ed.), *Idealism: Past and Present* (Cambridge: Cambridge University Press, 1982).

Hilary Putnam, *Realism with a Human Face* (Cambridge, Mass: Harvard University Press, 1990).

————— , *Renewing Philosophy* (Cambridge, Mass: Harvard University Press, 1993).

Bjorn T. Ramberg, *Donald Davidson's Philosophy of Language: An Introduction* (Oxford: Basil Blackwell, 1989).

Jonathan Rée, 'Subjectivity in the Twentieth Century', unpublished manuscript – read at Linguistic Representations of the Subject Conference, Liverpool, 4 July 1994.

Rush Rhees (ed.), 'Wittgenstein's Notes for Lectures on "Private Experience" and "Sense Data"', *The Philosophical Review*, vol. 77, no. 3 (1968), pp. 271–4.

Michael Root, 'Davidson and Social Science', in Lepore (ed.), *Truth and Interpretation: Perspectives on the Philosophy of Donald Davidson* (Oxford: Blackwell, 1986).

Richard Rorty, 'Pragmatism, Davidson and Truth', *Objectivity, Relativism and Truth: Philosophical Papers I* (Cambridge: Cambridge University Press, 1986).

————— , 'Wittgenstein, Heidegger and the Reification of Language', *Essays on Heidegger and Others· Philosophical Papers II* (Cambridge: Cambridge University Press, 1991).

J. C. C. Smart, 'How to turn the *Tractatus* Wittgenstein into (almost) Donald Davidson', in Lepore (ed.), *Truth and Interpretation: Perspectives on the Philosophy of Donald Davidson* (Oxford: Basil Blackwell, 1986).

Charles Taylor, *Sources of the Self* (Cambridge: Cambridge University Press, 1989).

Bernard Williams, 'Wittgenstein and Idealism', *Understanding Wittgenstein* (Cambridge: Cambridge University Press, 1974).

Ludwig Wittgenstein, *Tractatus Logico-Philosophicus*, trans. D. Pears and B. McGuinness (London: Routledge, 1922).

——————, *Philosophical Investigations* (Oxford: Basil Blackwell, 1953).

——————, *The Blue and Brown Books* (Oxford: Basil Blackwell, 1958).

——————, *Zettel* (Oxford: Basil Blackwell, 1967).

——————, *On Certainty* (Oxford: Basil Blackwell, 1969a).

——————, *Notebooks 1914–1916*, eds. G. H. Von Wright and G. E. M. Anscombe; trans. Anscombe (Oxford: Blackwell, 1969b).

——————, *Remarks on the Philosophy of Psychology* Vol. II (Oxford: Blackwell, 1980).

Crispin Wright, *Truth and Objectivity* (Cambridge, Mass: Harvard University Press, 1993).

SUBJECTIVE, INTERSUBJECTIVE, OBJECTIVE[1]

Donald Davidson

It is typical in contemporary philosophy to take up problems one by one, to avoid the dangers of striving for an overview. This has been my own habit. But occasionally one may be excused for yielding to the urge to take a broader look at the philosophical terrain; and that is what I do in this paper. I plan to discuss three large topics: our knowledge of our own minds (the subjective), our knowledge of other minds (the intersubjective), and our knowledge of nature (the objective). What particularly concerns me here is the relations among these three varieties of knowledge.

Having chosen so large a canvas, I cannot hope to give detailed arguments for my views. Where I know of such arguments, I have spelled them out elsewhere. My aim here is to sketch the way I think the three sorts of knowledge form interdependent aspects of the epistemic situation in which we all find ourselves.

I know, for the most part, what I think, want, and intend, and what my sensations are. In addition, I know a great deal about the world around me, the locations and sizes and causal properties of the objects

---

[1] An earlier version of this essay, entitled 'Three Varieties of Knowledge', appeared in A. Phillips Griffiths (ed), A. J. Ayer. Memorial Essays (Cambridge: Cambridge University Press, 1991).

in it. I also sometimes know what goes on in other people's minds.

Each of these three kinds of empirical knowledge has its distinctive characteristics. What I know about the contents of my own mind I generally know without appeal to evidence or investigation. There are exceptions, but the primacy of unmediated self-knowledge is attested by the fact that we distrust the exceptions until they can be reconciled with the unmediated. Our knowledge of the world outside of ourselves, on the other hand, depends on the functioning of our sense organs, and this causal dependence on the senses makes our beliefs about the world of nature open to a sort of uncertainty that arises only rarely in the case of beliefs about our own states of mind. Many of our simple perceptions of what is going on in the world are not based on further evidence; our perceptual beliefs are simply caused directly by the events and objects around us. But our knowledge of the propositional contents of other minds is never immediate in this sense; we would have no access to what others think and value if we could not note their behaviour.

Of course all three varieties of knowledge are concerned with aspects of the same reality; where they differ is in the mode of access to reality.

The relations among the three sorts of empirical knowledge, particularly questions of conceptual priority, have long headed the list of philosopher's epistemological concerns, and they are my subject here. Most familiar approaches to the question how the three sorts of knowledge are related take self-knowledge as primary, perhaps because of its directness and relative certainty, and then attempt to derive knowledge of the 'external world' from it; as a final step, they try to base knowledge of other minds on observations of behaviour. This is not, needless to say, the only direction the derivation can take: one may instead accept knowledge of the external world, at least in some of its manifestations, as basic, and try to relate or reduce the other forms of knowledge to it. The failure of the many reductive proposals constitutes much of the history of philosophy from Descartes to the present. If many philosophers have turned away from these problems in recent years, it is not because the problems are thought to have been solved, but because the problems seem intractable. There is also, of course, the wistful hope that the problems themselves are illusory.

This cannot be the case. There are compelling reasons for accepting the view that none of the three forms of knowledge is reducible to one or both of the others. Before I am finished I shall give my own reasons for believing this; but I take the hopelessness of finding effective modes of reduction to be apparent from the almost universal rejection of standard reductionist programs. Scepticism in various of its familiar guises is our grudging tribute to the apparent impossibility of unifying the three varieties of knowledge: one form of scepticism springs from the difficulty of accounting for our knowledge of the external world on the basis of our knowledge of our own minds; another recognizes that our knowledge of other minds cannot consist only in what we can observe from the outside. The intractability of the mind-body problem is another such tribute.

It is striking the extent to which philosophers, even those who have been sceptics about the possibility of justifying beliefs about the external world, have put aside these doubts when they have come to consider the problem of other minds; striking, since the latter problem can arise only if knowledge of behaviour, and hence of the external world, is possible. Holding the problems apart has the unfortunate effect of obscuring the fact that the two problems rest on a common assumption. The assumption is that the truth concerning what a person believes about the world is logically independent of the truth of those beliefs. This certainly seems to be the case, for surely the totality of a person's beliefs and subjective experiences is logically consistent with the falsity of any of those beliefs. So no amount of knowledge of the contents of one's own mind insures the truth of a belief about the external world. The logical independence of the mental works equally in the other direction: no amount of knowledge of the external world entails the truth about the workings of a mind. If there is a logical or epistemic barrier between the mind and nature, it not only prevents us from seeing out; it also blocks a view from outside in.

It is sometimes thought that if we separate the problem of knowing what is in a mind from the problem of knowing about anything whatever outside of ourselves, then the problem of knowledge of other minds is solved when we recognize that it is part of the concept of a mental state or event that certain forms of behaviour, or other outward signs, count as evidence for the existence of that mental state or event. There are two difficulties with this answer. The first is that it offers no explanation of the asymmetry between the indirect knowledge we have of other minds and the direct knowledge we have of our own mind. The proffered solution insists that behavioural evidence can suffice for the justified attribution of mental states to others, while it recognizes that such evidence is generally irrelevant to self-ascriptions of the same states. But if we are given no explanation of this striking asymmetry, we ought to conclude that there are really two kinds of concepts: mental concepts that apply to others, and mental concepts that apply to ourselves. If the mental states of others are known only through their behavioural and other outward manifestations, while this is not true of our own mental states, why should we think our own mental states are anything like those of others? The other difficulty is, at this point, only suggestive: why, if this answer to the problem of knowledge of other minds is satisfactory, should we not accept an analogous solution to the problem of our knowledge of the external world? Yet it is widely recognized that this answer to general scepticism is unacceptable. Do we distinguish between the problems because we suppose that while we have no access to the outside world except through experience, we nevertheless can intelligibly extrapolate to the experiences of others, since we have access to experience in our own case? But this supposition begs the question, since it assumes, without explaining, that what we call the mental states of others are similar to what we identify as mental states in ourselves.

I have been rehearsing these well worn problems and perplexities for several reasons. I want, first of all, to stress the apparent oddity of the fact that we have three irreducibly different varieties of empirical knowledge. We need an overall picture which not only accommodates all three modes of knowing, but makes sense of their relations to one another. Without such a general picture we should be deeply puzzled that the same world is known to us in three such different ways. And, second, it is essential to appreciate the extent to which problems that have usually been taken one at a time are interrelated. There are three basic problems: how a mind can know the world of nature, how it is possible for one mind to know another, and how knowledge of nature, especially behaviour, can yield knowledge of other minds. It is a mistake, I shall urge, to suppose that these questions can be collapsed into two, or taken in isolation.

In trying to form a picture of the relations among the three kinds of knowledge we must do much more than show that they are mutually irreducible; we must see why they are irreducible. This in turn will involve bringing out the respective conceptual roles played by each of the forms of knowledge, and why each of these roles is indispensable – why we could not get along without all of them. Of course, in saying this I set myself firmly against scepticism. For the Cartesian or Humean sceptic about the external world holds that it is all too obvious that we can get along without knowledge of the world of nature – what we know of our own mind is self-sufficient, and may be all the knowledge we have. The sceptic about other minds is equally convinced we can get along without knowledge of other minds – this must be possible if we are forever uncertain whether we have it.

It may seem at first that we could rather easily get along without a form of words to express our beliefs about the mental states of others or of ourselves. I think this is imaginable; but the issue with which I am concerned is primarily epistemic, not linguistic. It is whether we could get along without knowledge of minds, both our own and those of others. I shall argue that we could not. What we could not do is get along without a way of expressing, and thus communicating, our thoughts about the natural world. But if we can do this, the transition to also being able to attribute thoughts is relatively simple, and it would be astonishing if this step were not taken. With respect to our own thoughts, it is no more than the difference between saying assertively 'Snow is white' and saying assertively 'I believe that snow is white'. The truth conditions of these assertions is not the same, but anyone who understands the first assertion knows the truth conditions of the second, even if he does not command a sentence with those truth conditions. This is because anyone who understands speech can recognize assertions, and knows that someone who makes an assertion represents himself as believing what he says. Similarly, someone who says to Jones that snow is white knows the truth conditions of 'Jones believes that snow is white' (even if he does not know English nor have a way of expressing belief).

Belief is a condition of knowledge. But to have a belief it is not enough to discriminate among aspects of the world, to behave in different ways in different circumstances; an earthworm or a sunflower does this. Having a belief demands in addition appreciating the contrast between true belief and false, between appearance and reality, mere seeming and being. We can, of course, say that a sunflower has made a mistake if it turns toward an artificial light as if it were the sun, but we do not suppose the sunflower can think it has made a mistake, and so we do not attribute a belief to the sunflower. Someone who has a belief about the world – or anything else – must grasp the concept of objective truth, of what is the case independent of what he or she thinks. We must ask, therefore, after the source of the concept of truth.

Wittgenstein put us on the track of the only possible answer to this question, whether or not his problem was as broad as ours, and whether or not he believed in answers to philosophical problems. The source of the concept of objective truth is interpersonal communication. Thought depends on communication. This follows at once if we suppose that language is essential to thought and we agree with Wittgenstein that there cannot be a private language.[2] The central argument against private languages is that unless a language is shared there is no way to distinguish between using the language correctly and using it incorrectly; only communication with another can supply an objective check. If only communication can provide a check on the correct use of words, only communication can supply a standard of objectivity in other domains, as we shall see. We have no grounds for crediting a creature with the distinction between what is thought to be the case and what is the case unless the creature has the standard provided by a shared language; and without this distinction there is nothing that can clearly be called thought.

In communication, what a speaker and the speaker's interpreter must share is an understanding of what the speaker means by what he says. How is this possible?

---

[2] I make no claims about how broadly Wittgenstein intended his thesis about private languages to be interpreted; perhaps he intended his argument to apply only to those concepts which are necessarily private. But I, like Saul Kripke, think the argument applies to language quite generally and so (I would say) to all propositional thought (cf. Kripke, 1982). I should add that while I accept the idea that communication is the source of objectivity, I do not think it depends on speakers using the same words to express the same thoughts. The use to which I put the Wittgensteinian insight will emerge presently.

It would be good if we could say how language came into existence in the first place, or at least give an account of how an individual learns his first language, given that others in his environment are already linguistically accomplished. These matters are, however, beyond the bounds of reasonable philosophic speculation. What we can do instead is ask how a competent interpreter (one with adequate conceptual resources and a language of his own) can come to understand the speaker of an alien tongue. This can reveal essential features of communication, and will throw indirect light on what makes possible entry into language *de novo*.

The practised interpreter seeks to assign a propositional content to the utterances of a speaker. In effect he assigns a sentence of his own to each of the sentences of the speaker. To the extent that he gets things right, the interpreter's sentences provide the truth conditions of the speaker's sentences, and hence supply the basis for the interpretation of the speaker's utterances. The result can be thought of as a recursive characterization of truth, by the interpreter, of the sentences, and hence potential utterances, of the speaker.

An interpreter cannot directly observe another person's propositional attitudes; beliefs, desires, intentions, including the intentions which partly determine the meanings of utterances, are invisible to the naked eye. He can, however, attend to the utterances themselves, and we can assume without circularity that it is possible to detect one or another attitude a speaker has toward her own utterances, and from this we may infer attitudes to sentences. The sort of attitudes I have in mind are holding a sentence true at a time, or wanting a sentence to be true, or preferring that one sentence rather than another be true. The assumption that we can detect such an attitude does not beg the question of how we endow the attitudes with content, since a relation between a speaker and an utterance such as holding true is an extensional relation which can be known to hold without knowing what the sentence means. I call such attitudes non-individuative, for though they are psychological in nature, they do not bestow individual propositional contents on the attitudes.

In *Word and Object* Quine appealed to the non-individuative attitude of prompted assent. Since someone assents to an utterance, or holds a sentence true, in part because of what he believes and in part because of what the utterance or sentence means in his language, Quine's problem was to separate out these two elements on the basis of evidence that combined their influence. If the separation succeeds, the result is a theory of both belief and meaning for the speaker, for it must yield an interpretation of the speaker's utterances, and if one knows both that the speaker assents to the utterance, and what it means in his mouth, one also knows what he believes.

The process of separating meaning and opinion invokes two key principles which must be applicable if a speaker is interpretable: the Principle of Coherence and the Principle of Correspondence. The Principle of Coherence prompts the interpreter to discover a degree of logical consistency in the thought of the speaker; the Principle of Correspondence prompts the interpreter to take the speaker to be responding to the same features of the world that he (the interpreter) would be responding to under similar circumstances. Both principles can be (and have been) called principles of charity: one principle endows the speaker with a modicum of logical truth, the other endows him with a degree of true belief about the world. Successful interpretation necessarily invests the person interpreted with basic rationality. It follows from the nature of correct interpretation that an interpersonal standard of consistency and correspondence to the facts applies to both the speaker and the speaker's interpreter, to their utterances and to their beliefs.

Two questions now obtrude. The first is: why should an interpersonal standard be an objective standard, that is, why should what people agree on be true? The second is: even if it is the case that communication assumes an objective standard of truth, why should this be the only way such a standard can be established?

Here is a way of answering these questions. All of us find certain aspects of the world salient: we react in relevantly similar ways to the assorted sensory proddings that come our way. Evolution and subsequent learning no doubt explain these conditionings. But what makes us say various reactions are similar? To say, or see, that things are similar requires a concept, a conscious grouping; mere conditioning falls far short of this. It is only when we describe conditioning that we consciously pool stimuli and responses as similar, and correlate the groupings. As would be interpreters of the verbal behaviour of the speaker of an alien language, we group certain patterns of speaker's verbal behaviour together: 'Mutter', 'Schnee', 'Tisch', when repeated as one word sentences, sound similar if we are appropriately attuned. If we discover classes of objects or events in the world that seem similar to us, and that we can correlate with the utterances of a speaker, we are on the way to interpreting the simplest linguistic behaviour.

If we are teaching someone a language, the situation becomes more complex, but more clearly interpersonal. What seems basic is this: an observer (or teacher) finds (or instils) a regularity in the verbal behaviour of the informant (or learner) which he can correlate with events and objects in the environment. This much can take place without developed thought on the part of the observed, of course, but it is the necessary basis for attributing thoughts and meanings to the person observed. For until the triangle is completed connecting two creatures, and each creature with common features of the world, there can be no answer to the question whether a creature, in discriminating between stimuli, is discriminating between stimuli at the sensory surfaces or somewhere further out, or further in. Without this sharing of reactions to common stimuli, thought and speech would have no particular content – that is, no content at all. It takes two points of view to give a location to the cause of a thought, and thus to define its content. We may think of it as a form of triangulation: each of two people is reacting differentially to sensory stimuli streaming in from a certain direction. Where the incoming lines intersect is the common cause. If the two people now note each other's reactions (in the case of language, verbal reactions), they can each correlate these observed reactions with their stimuli from the world. A common cause has been determined. The triangle which gives content to thought and speech is complete. But it takes two to triangulate. Two, or, of course, more.

Until a base line has been established by communication with someone else, there is no point in saying his thoughts or his words have a propositional content. If this is so, then it is clear that knowledge of another mind is essential to all thought and all knowledge. Knowledge of another mind is possible, however, only if one has knowledge of the world, for the triangulation which is essential to thought requires that those in communication recognize that they occupy positions in a shared world. So knowledge of other minds and knowledge of the world are mutually dependent; neither is possible without the other. Ayer was surely right when he said, '... it is only with the use of language that truth and error, certainty and uncertainty, come fully upon the scene' (Ayer, 1956, p. 54).

Knowledge of the propositional contents of our own minds is not possible without the other forms of knowledge since without communication propositional thought is impossible. But we are not in a position to attribute thoughts to others unless we have our own thoughts, and know what they are, for the attribution of thought to others is a matter of matching the verbal and further behaviour of others to our own propositions or meaningful sentences.

It should now be clear what ensures that our view of the world is, in its plainest features, largely correct. The reason is that the stimuli that cause our most basic verbal responses also determine what those verbal responses mean, and the content of the beliefs that accompany them. The nature of correct interpretation guarantees both that a large number of our simplest beliefs are true, and that the nature of these beliefs is known to others. Of course many beliefs are given content by their relations to other beliefs, or are caused by misleading sensations; any particular belief or set of beliefs about the world around us may be false. What cannot be the case is that our general picture of the world and our place in it is mistaken, for it is this picture which informs the rest of our beliefs, whether they be true or false, and makes them intelligible.

The assumption that the truth about what we believe is logically independent of the truth of what we believe is revealed as ambiguous. Any particular belief may indeed be false; but enough in the framework and fabric of our beliefs must be true to give content to the rest. The conceptual connections between our knowledge of our own minds and our knowledge of the world of nature are not definitional but holistic. The same is true of the conceptual connections between our knowledge of behaviour and our knowledge of other minds.

There are, then, no 'barriers', logical or epistemic, between the varieties of knowledge. On the other hand, the very way in which each depends on the others shows why none can be eliminated, or reduced to the others.

As noted above, we may think of an interpreter who aims to understand a speaker as matching up sentences of his own with the utterances and states of mind of the speaker. The totality of evidence available to the interpreter determines no unique theory of truth for a given speaker, not just because actually available evidence is finite while the theory has an infinity of testable consequences, but because all possible evidence cannot limit acceptable theories to one. Given the richness of the structure represented by the set of one's own sentences, and the nature of the connections between the members of this set and the world, we should not be surprised if there are many ways of assigning our own sentences to the sentences and thoughts of someone else that capture everything of relevant significance.

The situation is analogous to the measurement of weight or temperature by assigning numbers to objects.

Even supposing there are no errors of measurement, and that all possible observations have been made, an assignment of numbers to objects that correctly registers their weights is not unique: given one such assignment, another can be produced by multiplying all the numbers by any positive constant. In the case of ordinary temperature (not absolute temperature), any correct assignment of numbers can be converted to another by a linear transformation. So we can say, if we please, that interpretation or translation is indeterminate, or that there is no fact of the matter as to what someone means by his or her words. In the same vein, we could speak of the indeterminacy of weight or temperature. But we normally accentuate the positive by being clear about what is invariant from one assignment of numbers to the next, for it is what is invariant that is empirically significant. The invariant is the fact of the matter. We can afford to look at translation and the content of mental states in the same light.[3]

I once thought that the indeterminacy of translation supplied a reason for supposing there are no strict laws connecting mental and physical concepts, and so supported the claim that mental concepts are not even nomologically reducible to physical concepts. I was wrong: indeterminacy turns up in both domains. But one source of indeterminacy in the case of the mental is that the line between empirical truth and truth due to meaning can not in general be clearly defined on behavioural grounds; and behavioural grounds are all we have for determining what speakers mean. It is here

---

[3] Here I accept Quine's thesis of the indeterminacy of translation, and extend it to the interpretation of thought generally. The analogy with measurement is my own.

that the irreducible difference between mental concepts and physical concepts begins to emerge: the former, at least in so far as they are intentional in nature, require the interpreter to consider how best to render the creature being interpreted intelligible, that is, as a creature endowed with reason. As a consequence, an interpreter must separate meaning from opinion in part on normative grounds, by deciding what, from his point of view, maximizes intelligibility. In this endeavour, the interpreter has, of course, no other standards of rationality to fall back on than his own. When we try to understand the world as physicists, we necessarily employ our own norms, but we do not aim to discover rationality in the phenomena.

How does the normative element in mental concepts prevent their reduction to physical concepts? Perhaps it is obvious that definitional reduction is out of the question; but why can't there be laws – strict laws – that connect each mental event or state with events or states described in the vocabulary of an advanced physics? When writing about this twenty years ago I said, in effect, that one can hope for strict connecting laws only when the concepts connected by the laws are based on criteria of the same sort, and so a strict law could not combine normative with non-normative concepts (cf. Davidson, 1980). This answer still seems to me right as far as it goes, but it has understandably failed to persuade critics. I now want to add some further considerations.

One further consideration is this: strict laws do not employ causal concepts, while most, if not all, mental concepts are irreducibly causal. An action, for example, must be intentional under some description, but an action is intentional only if it is caused by mental factors such as beliefs and desires. Beliefs and desires are identified in part by the sorts of action they are prone to cause, given the right conditions. Most of the concepts that feature in common sense explanations are causal in this way. An accident was caused by the fact that the road was slippery; something is slippery if it causes appropriate objects to slip under appropriate circumstances. We explain why the wing of an aeroplane does not break when it bends by noting that it is made of partially elastic materials; a material is elastic if there is something about it that causes it, under appropriate conditions, to return to its original shape after deformation. Such explanations do not lend themselves to precision for two reasons: we cannot spell out in detail when the circumstances are appropriate, and the appeal to causality finesses part of what a full-scale explanation would make manifest. Descriptions of objects, states and events that are needed to instantiate strict, exceptionless laws do not contain causal concepts.

In the case of causal properties like elasticity, slipperiness, malleability, or solubility we tend to think, rightly or wrongly, that what they leave unexplained can be (or already has been) explained by the advance of science. We would not be changing the subject if we were to drop the concept of elasticity in favour of a specification of the micro-structure of the materials in the aeroplane wing that cause it to return to its original shape when exposed to certain forces. Mental concepts and explanations are not like this. They appeal to causality because they are designed, like the concept of causality itself, to single out from the totality of circumstances which conspire to cause a given event just those factors that satisfy some particular explanatory interest.

When we want to explain an action, for example, we want to know the agent's reasons, so we can see for ourselves what it was about the action that appealed to the agent. But it would be foolish to suppose there are strict laws which stipulate that whenever an agent has certain reasons he will perform a given action.

The normative and the causal properties of mental concepts are related. If we were to drop the normative aspect from psychological explanations, they would no longer serve the purposes they do. We have such a keen interest in the reasons for actions and other psychological phenomena that we are willing to settle for explanations that cannot be made to fit perfectly with the laws of physics. Physics, on the other hand, has as an aim laws that are as complete and precise as we can make them; a different aim. The causal element in mental concepts helps make up for the precision they lack; it is part of the concept of an intentional action that it is caused and explained by beliefs and desires; it is part of the concept of a belief or a desire that it tends to cause and so explain actions of certain sorts.

Much of what I have said about what distinguishes mental concepts from the concepts of a developed physics could also be said to distinguish the concepts of many of the special sciences such as biology, geology, and meteorology. So even if I am right that the normative and causal character of mental concepts divide them definitionally and nomologically from the concepts of a developed physics, it may seem that there must be something more basic or foundational that accounts for this division. I think there is.

Knowledge of the contents of our own minds must, in most cases, be trivial. The reason is that, apart from special cases, the problem of interpretation cannot arise.

When I am asked about the propositional contents of my mind, I must use my own sentences. The answer is usually absurdly obvious: my sentence 'Snow is white', like my thought that snow is white, is true if and only if snow is white. My knowledge of the contents of another mind, like my knowledge of my own mind – like all knowledge, in fact, is possible, I have argued, only in the context of a generally correct, and shared, view of the world. But such knowledge differs from the knowledge I have of my own mind since it is necessarily inferential, and depends, among other things, on observed correlations between the speech and other behaviour of the person and events in our communal environment.

The fundamental difference between my knowledge of another mind and of the shared physical world has a different source. Communication, and the knowledge of other minds that it presupposes, is the basis of our concept of objectivity, our recognition of a distinction between false and true belief. There is no going outside this standard to check whether we have things right, any more than we can check whether the platinum-iridium standard kept at the International Bureau of Weights and Standards in Sévres, France, weighs a kilogram (this comparison was valid when the standard in Sévres defined the kilogram). We can, of course, turn to a third party and a fourth to broaden and secure the interpersonal standard of the real, but this leads not to something intrinsically different, just to more of the same.

I spoke before of an analogy between how we assign numbers to keep track of the relations among objects with respect to temperature or weight and how we use our own sentences to identify the contents of the thoughts and utterances of others. But the analogy is incomplete. We depend on our linguistic interactions with others to yield agreement on the properties of numbers and the sort of structures in nature that allow us to represent those structures in the numbers. We can't in the same way agree on the structure of sentences or thoughts we use to chart the thoughts and meanings of others, for the attempt to reach such an agreement simply sends us back to the very process of interpretation on which all agreement depends.

It is here, I suggest, that we come to the ultimate springs of the difference between understanding minds and understanding the world as physical. A community of minds is the basis of knowledge; it provides the measure of all things. It makes no sense to question the adequacy of this measure, or to seek a more ultimate standard.

We have dwelt at length on the inescapability of the objective aspect of all thought. What remains of the subjective aspect? We have not, clearly, obliterated the difference between self-knowledge and knowledge of other minds: the first remains direct and the second inferential. And objectivity itself we have traced to the intersections of points of view; for each person, the relation between his own reactions to the world and those of others. These differences are real. Our thoughts are 'inner' and 'subjective' in that we know what they are in a way no one else can. But though possession of a thought is necessarily individual, its content is not. The thoughts we form and entertain are located conceptually in the world we inhabit, and know we inhabit, with others. Even our thoughts about our own mental states occupy the same conceptual space and are located on the same public map.

The philosophical conception of subjectivity is burdened with a history and a set of assumptions about the nature of mind and meaning that sever the meaning of an utterance or the content of a thought from questions about external reality, 'my' world from the world as it appears to others. It holds that the subjective is prior to the objective, that there is a subjective world prior to knowledge of external reality. The picture of thought and meaning I have sketched here leaves no room for such priority since it predicates self-knowledge on knowledge of other minds and of the world. The objective and the inter-subjective are thus essential to anything we can call subjectivity, and constitute the context in which it takes form. Collingwood put it succinctly:

> The child's discovery of itself as a person is also its discovery of itself as a member of a world of persons... The discovery of myself as a person is the discovery that I can speak, and am thus a persona or speaker; in speaking I am both speaker and hearer; and since the discovery of myself as a person is also the discovery of other persons around me, it is the discovery of speakers and hearers other than myself. (Collingwood, 1938, p. 248).

It may seem that if sharing a general view of the world is a condition of thought, the differences in intellectual and imaginative character among minds and cultures will be lost to sight. If I have given this impression it is because I have wanted to concentrate on what seems to me primary, and so apt to go unnoticed: the necessary degree of communality essential to understanding another individual, and the extent to which such understanding provides the foundation of the concept of truth and reality upon which all thought depends. But I do not want to suggest that we cannot understand those with whom we differ on vast tracts of physical and moral opinion. It is also the case that understanding is a matter of degree: others may know things we do not, or even perhaps cannot. What is certain is that the clarity and effectiveness of our concepts grow with the growth of our understanding of others. There are no definite limits to how far dialogue can or will take us. The question whether the concepts that could develop through intercourse with others perhaps more different from ourselves than we can now imagine should be called further refinements on our present concepts, or radically new concepts, seems to me a distinction without a difference.

Some worry that if all our knowledge, at least our propositional knowledge, is objective, we will lose touch with an essential aspect of reality: our personal, private outlook. I think this worry is groundless. If I am right, our propositional knowledge has its basis not in the impersonal but in the interpersonal. Thus when we look at the natural world we share with others we do not lose contact with ourselves, but rather acknowledge membership in a society of minds. If I did not know what others think I would have no thoughts of my own and so would not know what I think. If I did not know what I think, I would lack the ability to gauge the thought of others. Gauging the thoughts of others requires that I live in the same world with them, sharing many reactions to its major features, including its values. So there is no danger that in viewing the world objectively we will lose touch with ourselves. The three sorts of knowledge form a tripod: if any leg were lost, no part would stand.

REFERENCES

A. J. Ayer, *The Problem of Knowledge* (London: Macmillan, 1956).

R. G. Collingwood, *The Principles of Art* (Oxford: Oxford University Press, 1938).

Donald Davidson, 'Mental Events', reprinted in *Essays on Actions and Events* (Oxford: Oxford University Press, 1980).

Saul Kripke, *Wittgenstein on Rules and Private Language* (Oxford: Blackwell, 1982).

Willard Van Orman Quine, *Word and Object* (Cambridge, Mass: MIT Press, 1969).

THE PLURALITY OF WORLDS, HISTORICAL TIME, AND UNIQUENESS

Guy Stock

I want to examine the notion of a world as distinct from that of reality. The notion of reality I take to be fundamental for metaphysics. The metaphysician's aim, I take it, is to give in very general terms a characterization of reality as it is in its ultimate nature. I shall follow F. H. Bradley in drawing a distinction between the real world and reality.

The main point of contemporary relevance that I make is a claim with respect to the limits that can be set to historical and cultural relativism. However, at the same time I hope to sketch a view that takes the the natural sciences to have a special place within the spectrum of human knowledge without taking fundamental physics, or cosmology, or genetics, or whatever, to have any special significance for a metaphysical characterization of the ultimate nature of reality.[1]

---

[1] As a physicalist metaphysician might put it: the ultimately subvenient reality. Wittgenstein (in his early work at least) saw the necessity for distinguishing between the real world and reality, but in a way which ruled out empirical science as a means for gaining knowledge of the essential nature of the latter. Wittgenstein's way made the notion of determinate propositional sense the central object of study. Bradley rejected that very conception of a proposition as incoherent (cf. eg., Wittgenstein, 1961b, p. 39, dated 22/1/15).

In the final section I will raise a metaphysically, and epistemologically, significant question with respect to the source of uniqueness in our thinking and experience. I will indicate where, on Bradley's view, that source cannot be taken to lie. That view, it seems to me, has considerable force and will underpin what I say about the plurality of worlds and the distinction to be drawn between the real world and reality.

According to the usage of the word 'world' that I adopt it would not be straightforwardly wrong but it would be misleading to say that the metaphysician seeks to give an account of the world as it is in its ultimate nature. It would be misleading because on the view I propose there is no such thing as the world. Or, at least, there is no such thing as the world if, in that context, 'the' is parsed as implying uniqueness.

However, on the view I am proposing the sense in which there is a plurality of worlds is not to be confused with that adapted from Leibniz and employed, for their own purposes, by certain contemporary modal logicians. Or, at least, it is not to be confused with it in so far as that view involves the claim that reality in its ultimate nature consists of a plurality of possible worlds a unique one of which is contingently existent, and is perceptible by us, in contrast to an unlimited plurality of merely possible worlds which are contingently non-existent, are in principle not perceptible by us, yet are capable of being objects for our thoughts.

The notion of a world that I am advocating is closer to that employed by Nelson Goodman:

> In what important and often neglected sense are there many worlds? Let it be clear that the question here is not of the possible worlds that many of my contemporaries, especially those near Disneyland, are busy

making and manipulating. We are not speaking of multiple possible alternatives to a single actual world but of multiple actual worlds. (Goodman, 1978, p. 2)

Goodman is a radical pluralist with respect to worlds. No human activity, science or art, theoretical or practical, in the context of which a world is (as Goodman puts it) 'made and manipulated' is to be singled out as metaphysically privileged. In this he differs from Quine (cf. for example Quine, 1981, pp. 97–8). Quine, in his review of Goodman's book, is in complete sympathy with the short shrift Goodman gives to Leibnizian merely possible worlds. Moreover, Quine rejects a reductionist physicalism of a semantic kind. As he puts it: '...not...everything worth saying can be translated into the technical vocabulary of physics; not even...all good science can be translated into that vocabulary' (Quine, 1981, p. 98).

He argues that the physicist cannot allow anything to happen in the world (and here I assume he intends 'the' to imply uniqueness), '...not the flutter of an eyelid, not the flicker of a thought...' (Quine, 1981, p. 98), without positing some, admittedly in detail unknowable, redistribution of states at the microphysical level. Hence, Quine argues that anybody who is willing to allow that 'physics is all very well in its place' (Quine, 1981, p 98) (and surely we all must) is thereby, with respect to metaphysics, a physicalist in that he will be committed to holding that nothing happens or exists, in the unique system of existence, outside the scope of the fundamental laws of physics.

However, this argument, as stated, does little more than beg the question against the radical world pluralist. I might, if only for purposes of argument, allow that the physicist, when doing his physics and thinking in terms of the ideas internal to some fundamental physical theory, must take everything that happens in the world thus identified to be subject to a set of fundamental laws which are strictly universal in scope with respect to that world.[2] But the crucial question, for the world pluralist, then is: in what sense, or with what right, is the world thus identified (the world of microphysical states) to be taken as identical with, say, the world I can think of, here and now, as containing my body together with these flickering eyelids of mine, and my present fleeting thoughts about Quine? For familiar reasons it is not possible simply by pointing to indicate unambiguously the world meant.

Although, contra Quine I wish to advocate a fairly radical world pluralism, there is, I shall argue, a particular world which, although it is not to be regarded in Leibnizian fashion as uniquely existent, must be treated by the metaphysician with special deference. It is, I hardly need emphasize, not the world of fundamental physics, or of cosmology, or any system of objects that can be thought of in terms of the concepts internal to such theories. It is what I shall refer to as the world of human history. This is, it seems to me, the system of existence that people like ourselves would in most conversational contexts have uppermost in mind when employing the expression 'the real world' as a referring expression.

However, at this point, I must stress that, although the world of human history must be seen as having a special status, I am not claiming that the framework of thought by means of which it is to be identified yields

---

[2] See Nancy Cartwright, 1994 pp. 279–92, for a view of scientific laws which conflcts with the Quinian picture; see also Horgan, 1993 eg., pp. 560–66, for the view that physicalism requires the causal 'completeness' of physics.

anything like a metaphysically adequate conception of reality as it is in its ultimate nature. On the contrary, application of the framework of thought in question can be seen as the fundamental source of the most profound philosophical problems rather than their solution. On the slightest reflection our application of the framework can be seen to generate, and be shot through with, disparate, incommensurable elements and inconsistencies. For instance our problems in relation to the nature of time, the existence of – and our knowledge of – the past and future, the problem of other minds, the identity of the self, the problems of linguistic meaning and identifying reference themselves, and so on, are all generated by an exercise of the framework in question. Therefore as such it cannot, within the context of metaphysics, be taken as capable of yielding knowledge of reality as it is in its ultimate nature.

In the language of metaphysics the framework of thought in question must be seen as yielding us, through its exercise, at best only a more or less adequate appearance of reality. However, in practice, in our daily lives, we have no option but to apply the framework of thought in question. We can entertain no real doubt, as opposed to contrived doubt of a hyperbolic Cartesian kind, with respect to its fundamental principles (cf. Wittgenstein, 1969, § 308, and also §§ 21, 401, 403). Moreover, it seems to me that it cannot be taken to be a mere theory of reality (as it were, a folk theory), at least, if by 'theory' is meant a framework of belief which human beings could conceivably at some time, through an advance in scientific knowledge, discover to be false and which, as a result, they could decide to abandon. This would be so if only because the justification of such an abandonment would require reference back to the contents of specific practices and beliefs of particular people in the past and thus require an exercise of the very framework in question.

What, then, in more detail, do I mean by the expression 'the world of human history' and what are some of the main structural features of that world?

The best way, I suggest, to get a reasonably clear conception of those features is to think of the world of human history as the arena, or system of existence, within which those events take place which historians, current affairs commentators, biographers, sports reporters, and so on, make the objects of their studies and reports.

The events that the historian, in this sense, is concerned with are at a fundamental level the 'deeds and sufferings' of individual human beings (cf. Collingwood, 1973, pp. 213–17). The historian must, at least as a necessary condition of fulfilling his aim, trace the antecedents and consequences, intended and unintended, of individual human beings' actions in so far as those actions have proved to have some wider significance in the lives of subsequent human beings. Even the Marxist, or neo-Marxist, theoretician of history, who sees the ultimately significant forces in history as operating through class conflicts, or through the exercise of power by one social group over another historically exploited group, must construe the effects of these forces to be realized in, and to be traceable through the – perhaps – largely false consciousness of individual human beings.

Identification and description of an individual human being's actions will in general require the historian to have the capacity not merely to locate the particular dates and places of those actions, with a fair degree of accuracy, but also to penetrate to the agent's motives and intentions and thus, at the same time, penetrate to his beliefs (true or false, reasonable or bizarre, familiar or culturally alien) in so far as they were relevant to the circumstances of his action.

It will be possible to articulate the main structural features of the world of human history by reflecting on the central presuppositions of the possibility of historical knowledge thus construed. This will amount to reflecting on what must be the case if particular descriptions of individuals' deeds and sufferings, of the kinds typically given by historians, are to be capable of being either true or false, and on what must be the case if particular explanations of the kinds typically constructed by historians are to be capable of being either sound or unsound. In other words it will amount to an attempt to articulate in propositional form what, in Wittgenstein's usage of the term, are grammatical features of the language in which history is written. These features are, therefore, to be seen as features of a world, or (we could equally well say) features of human life, with which anybody who understands the historian's use of language, and is in a position to understand the sense of particular historical claims, irrespective of whether or not he is in a position to assess the truth-values, or soundness of those claims, must thereby be already acquainted.

The following, it seems to me, are seven central presuppositions, or conditions of the possibility of, history. These will constitute a set of structural principles which can be known to apply a priori to the world of human history. As such they will be principles the application of which could not be intelligibly placed in question by the historian in the context of his activities as a historian or by us in understanding the historical reports we read or see on television and so on.

In the context of this list, when I use the expression 'the world' I shall mean the world of human history as contrasted with, and differentiated more or less radically from, for instance, the worlds of the contemporary physicist, chemist, cosmologist, or from the worlds of William Faulkner's novels, or of my dreams, or of myth, or of Catholic doctrine and so on.

(i) The world is a single spatio-temporally extended system of existence in which the acts of any genuinely historical human being (as opposed to those of merely fictional, or imagined, or dreamt of, or supposed, or falsely believed in, human beings) will one and all occur.

(ii) Any genuinely historical human being's acts, bodily or otherwise, will occur at successive moments of his waking life and will be ordered in a determinate time order throughout that life. Moreover all the acts of numerically different individuals, in so far as they are genuinely historical, will be ordered in relation to one another in one and the same linear time series. Thus relative to the time of an arbitrarily chosen event (eg., the time of the birth of Christ) the time of any genuinely historical act will either be simultaneous with it, or locatable at a time a determinate amount of time earlier than it, or locatable at a time a determinate amount of time later than it.

(iii) At each successive instant of a human being's life he will occupy a determinate three dimensional region of space on, or more or less near to, the earth's surface. Since no two human bodies can occupy the same region of space at the same instant of time each human being will, in living his life, trace a unique and continuous track through space. Hence the claim made with respect to any human being that he was at a given moment of time at a determinate position in space relative to the earth's surface must be either true or false, even though in many cases it will be absolutely impossible to know which.

(iv) Each human being will have in sense perception a unique perspectival viewpoint at each instant of his waking life and will at each instant have various direct modes of practical and cognitive access, through the agency of his body, to things currently located in space more or less close to his body. He will not have these direct modes of cognitive and practical access to things past, or things future, or things at the present moment spatially too remote for him to grasp, or see, or speak to, or hear and so on.

(v) The world is a nexus of happenings causally connected in a thoroughgoing way so that those events will be capable of ramifying in their consequences, with more or less historical significance, throughout space and future time. Hence the lives of human beings at any given time in history, in any given region of the world, will be able to be affected, for better or worse, to a greater or lesser extent, by the past actions of themselves and other human beings no matter when or where they occurred.[3]

(vi) The world is a system in which individual human beings are amongst the fundamental causes of what happens. They are efficient causes in Aristotle's sense,

---

[3] For instance we cannot doubt that the actions of the Nazis in Germany in the 1930s and 1940s have profoundly affected the lives and attitudes of many people today and the consequences of their actions, which are still being realized in the actions of people today (eg., in Steven Spielberg's making of the film *Schindler's List*), will continue in that way to ramify without foreseeable limit of time.

or free causes in Kant's sense of the term. Individuals are capable of intervening in the course of events, both in human affairs and in the natural world, and of making things turn out, intentionally or unintentionally, differently from how they would have in the absence of that intervention.[4]

(vii) The world is a non-deterministic system of events. It will contain at any given juncture an open future (cf. Braine, 1988, chap. 11). Human beings are in a large part responsible for the character of their own lives (with the proviso that their consciousness might be more or less false) and, to some extent, for the condition of the physical environment in which they live. At any given juncture the alternatives open will be more or less constrained by given circumstances and laws, but there will always be genuine alternatives. Hence the course of human history is not determined by anything outside itself (cf. Collingwood, 1973, pp. 224–6).[5]

I now want to reflect on the essential singularity of the world of human history and the way in which, and the extent to which, it allows for the generation of a plurality of worlds.

---

[4] We exercise this way of thinking, in particular, (i) when thinking of the scientific and technological knowledge that the human race now possesses, through the work of natural scientists in the past, as having enabled us to transform the lives we lead, and (ii) when thinking of the scientist's role in controlled experiments as one of intervening in the natural course of events.

[5] On Collingwood's view the historical process cannot be driven, or animated, in the present independently of agents who have learned, adapted, rejected, and developed ideas from the past. And what is thus gained from the past, and thus lives on in the historical process via the actions by which individuals are, at each waking moment, constantly in the process of making their own lives and natures, could not have been acquired by them without the exercise of a mode of understanding of others (and, for that matter, of themselves) which is in essence identical with that used by the professional historian.

The world of human history is (as just noted) essentially a single spatio-temporally extended and causally interconnected system of individual agents and events. The historian must regard any genuinely historical being – as opposed to fictional, or merely imaginary, or mythical human beings – as having occupied at each instant of his life, some position in space relative to his own present position, and to have perceived things in, and operated causally in, the very same causal nexus as he himself presently does.

Moreover, the contemporary historian will be, or at least ought to be, true to his time and thus true to the natural sciences in so far as they indubitably constitute well established bodies of knowledge with respect to certain aspects of the world (Bradley, 1993, pp. ii and 32). The contemporary historian must take even pre-historic human beings to possess fundamentally the same anatomy, biology, physiology, neurophysiology, and so on, as ourselves and as being subject (with more or less well-known local variations) to fundamentally the same physical, chemical, astronomical, geological, climatic and geographical environments. In so far as our contemporary sciences undeniably give us pan-historical knowledge of certain essential aspects of ourselves and of our physical environments, the historian cannot but take the individuals whose deeds and sufferings he is concerned with, no matter how remotely past or alien in belief and culture the societies in which they lived might have been, as having to confront in their lives fundamentally the same biological and physical conditions as we do.

Now the idea of the world of human history thus articulated is, of course, itself in one way a historically and culturally relative one. But it cannot be regarded,

it seems to me, as merely such an idea. It is a historically and culturally relative idea in the sense that it has
not, we know as a matter of historical fact, been
available to human beings of all historical ages or, even
today, to human beings in all societies that presently
exist in the world.

However, in a sense which is philosophically significant, it cannot be regarded as an idea which is merely
historically or culturally relative. It is not a merely
historically or culturally relative idea of the sort the
objectivity of which can be undermined by our
realization that there have been human beings at other
times and in other cultures who have seen things very
differently from the way we do and for whom in consequence this world, in the experiences constitutive of
their lives, must have been a very different place. It is
not such an idea since it must be possessed and
exercised in any society the members of which are to be
in a position to investigate, and appreciate, in a
thoroughgoing comprehensive fashion, the extent and
disparateness of the historically and culturally diverse
beliefs and practices that have at past times existed,
and do presently exist, in this world.

However, this reflection leads us to a sense in which
we must regard the world of human history itself as
radically plural.

As a result of the work of historians, archaeologists,
and anthropologists we know that people in different
historical ages, and in different parts of the world in the
present age, have come to hold radically disparate
systems of belief from our own and to adopt moral
practices in their lives indefinitely diverse in their
contents from our own – often to the very limits of
intelligibility for us.

For instance, we know that at the limits of historical time which divided historic human beings from prehistoric ones there must have been human beings who lacked the conceptual capacities required to think about time and space systematically in anything like the way we do. Such individuals could not conceivably have had anything like the conception that is available to us of the world in which they lived. Our capacities to think comprehensively, and precisely, about times indefinitely remote in the past and future, and about things indefinitely distant in space, in different directions, could only have developed gradually, throughout human history, with the development of written languages.[6] In particular they could not have developed without the development of the vocabularies of arithmetic and geometry, and the vocabularies involved in our use of instruments for the more or less accurate measurement of the passage of time, of velocities, and distances and directions in space. Before the development of such dating and placing vocabularies (ones in principle translatable into those which we presently employ) human beings could not conceivably have had anything like our comprehensive conception of the world in which, as a matter of indubitable historical fact, they one and all lived. They could not, that is, have thought of the world in which they lived as being a single spatio-temporally extended, causally interconnected, nexus of events, that was the very same world in which all actual human beings, past, present and future, would of necessity exist and live their lives.

It follows that the world in which such human beings in fact lived must, within the contents of their conscious

---

[6] This is something which, as a historical matter of fact, surely could not be doubted by historians.

experiences, ie., in the contents of the dateable
thoughts, perceptions, emotions, desires and actions
constitutive of their daily lives, have presented itself in
a totally disparate way from that in which it presents
itself to us in our lives here and now. It is clear, then,
that the world in which such human beings lived, and
which was (we cannot intelligibly doubt) the very same
world as that in which we now live, must have been for
them, in the contents of their conscious experiences, a
very different world from what it is for us – a world
into which we can have scarcely any insight whatsoever.

Moreover, even if we confine our reflection to historic
times, as opposed to pre-historic ones, many human
beings who will have shared explicitly our comprehensive conception of the world of human history as a
uniquely actual, causally interconnected, system of
existence, will nevertheless have had radically different
systems of belief, metaphysical and otherwise, with
respect both to the kinds of thing existing within time,
and within space, and to the existence of the spatio-
temporally extended world as a whole.

And it is a platitude that we need not make reference
to the experiences of individuals living outside our own
times and cultures to make substantially the same point.
If we take a devout present-day Catholic and a militant
atheist of a physicalist persuasion, the world will be
present as a very different world within the experiences
constitutive of their respective lives.[7] This would be so
even though (as we might suppose) the Catholic and the
atheist by vocation happened both to be historians, or
both to be physicists, who were in total agreement,
within the contexts of their disciplines, with respect to
the objects of their professional investigations.

---

[7] In this context, and earlier, I could equally as well have used the word
'reality'.

In this final section I want to consider the metaphysically and epistemologically significant notion of uniqueness and enquire how it can be taken to relate to what I have called the singularity of the world of human history. In order to do so I want to distinguish two different, and inconsistent, ways in which we apply the spatio-temporal frame of thought internal to our historical thinking. There is a sense, I shall argue, in which one of these applications must be taken to be, in a metaphysically significant way, fundamental.

We may apply it to reality either from what I shall call a theoretical or objective standpoint, or alternatively from what I shall call a practical or egocentric standpoint.[8]

The theoretical application highlights the way of thinking about time involved in what McTaggart called the B-series. It involves thinking of every event in time as being orderable in relation to a particular arbitrarily chosen time (eg., to the time regarded as the time of the birth of Christ, which is conventionally taken as the arbitrary origin of our dating system) either as simultaneous with it, or as being at a determinate amount of time earlier than it, or as being at a determinate amount of time later than it.

---

[8] Leibniz's epistemology accounts for this aspect of our experience of time and space (and for the sensibility of finite subjects in general) in terms of the degree of imperfection, and consequent confusion, which attends the exercise of our active representative faculty. This faculty was for Leibniz (unlike for Kant) in essence identical with God's and, hence, in perfected form would yield omniscience with respect to all that contingently exists, or could have existed instead. The unique degree of confusion (= imperfection = passivity) which attends S's exercise of the faculty, accounts for the uniqueness of S's viewpoint on, or position in, the world and hence for his identity as a finite substance (cf. eg., L. E. Loemker (ed.), 1976, sect. 67 'Monadology' (1714) sect. 60 for the point about confusion and perspective).

Thus, for instance, in a theoretical application of the spatio-temporal frame of thought internal to historical thinking I will be able to think of each act in the whole series of my waking acts, bodily and otherwise, from birth to death, as locatable in a succession by reference to determinate instants of time in the earlier/later series constitutive of historical time, and as occurring when I am at determinate positions in space in relation to the earth's surface. However, in thinking of time and of my life in this way no act in my life will be marked out uniquely as occurring at the present time: each and every one will be present at some time. Hence, in making a merely theoretical application of the temporal frame internal to historical thinking, there will be no room, for instance, for the thought that the time of my death, or the turn of the century, is closer now (ie., closer to the present time) than it was, say, yesterday (ie., when yesterday was present).[9] The time of my death in the earlier/later series is eternally fixed and therefore, if I think simply in terms of the earlier/later series, its time cannot be thought of as coming closer to any other time. Hence if I make a theoretical application not only of the temporal frame internal to historical thinking, but also analogously of the spatial frame, I will think of myself, like Wittgenstein's metaphysical subject, as a limit to the world of human history with nothing in the world able to be any closer to me, either in time or in space, than anything else (Wittgenstein, 1961, 5.641).[10] And since nothing in

[9] Although each of these applications results in a different conception of time I do not want to suggest that the capacities to make these applications could as a matter of psychological fact be possessed in separation from one another.

[10] Wittgenstein also says, elsewhere, 'For the consideration of willing makes it look as if one part of the world were closer to me than another (which would be intolerable)' (Wittgenstein, 1961b, p. 88)

particular in the world, as distinct from anything else, will be marked out in a special way as being presently given to me there will be no room for the idea of my exercising causal agency in the world.

The alternative practical or egocentric way of applying the spatio-temporal frame internal to historical thinking, on the other hand, highlights the way we have of thinking about time that corresponds with McTaggart's A-series. In thinking about time in this way we think of any other time in the time series of historical time as lying, relative to the present instant of time, a determinate amount of time either in the past or in the future.

The present, therefore, plays within the practical application of the temporal frame internal to my historical thinking an irreducible role. It acts as a radically non-conventional, guaranteed unique, source-point for my application of that temporal frame and by reference to which I can in my current thinking identify unambiguously determinate times and periods of time, without limit of remoteness, both in the past and in the future.

Of course, I will be able to wonder at any moment, what the present time, or date and time, is. Any present perception will be able to take its position in the earlier/later series of human history. However, any answer to the question 'What is the time now?' would have to be expressed in terms of some dating system (eg., midnight, 31st December, 1999) and my understanding of such a description as unambiguously specifying a time in the earlier/later series would require me to be able to think of the arbitrary origin for the application of that system as being fixed by reference to an event conventionally taken to have occurred 2000 years ago, to the day, or hour, or minute, or second (eg., 2000 years to the second before the uniquely present chime of Big Ben).

An analogous point can be made with respect to my understanding, at any moment, of a specification of a position in space by, for example, the use of a spatial co-ordinate system like that of latitude and longitude. If, at some time, I do not know where on earth I am, then a numerical specification of my latitude and longitude can tell me. But in order for that specification to be intelligible to me I need to be able to think of my body, and the objects I can presently perceive around me, as being at a determinate distance in a determinate direction from the arbitrary origin of the system. My body, and my perceptions of the objects presently around it, will thus constitute a non-conventional source point for my application of the spatial frame internal to my historical thinking.

There is a sense, therefore, in which I must take my practical, or egocentric, application of the spatio-temporal frame internal to historical thinking as fundamental. My present experiences, for example, my perceptions and actions, bodily and otherwise, here and now, provide me with a unique point of contact with reality from which, given the kind of conceptual powers that human beings like ourselves acquire in mastering our natural languages, I can at any moment think precisely of individuals and events in the world of human history no matter how remote in time and space. Without this ability I could not, of course, speculate metaphysically about the nature of the spatio-temporally extended system of existence as a whole.

Now I can ask what seems to me to be an epistemologically and metaphysically significant question: What makes what I have referred to as my unique point of contact with reality in my present experience – in the perceptions, actions, desires, emotions I enjoy here and now – unique?

It seems to me that I cannot (at least in a metaphysically adequate way) construe my point of contact with reality in present experience to be unique in virtue of its occurring at a unique position in a particular, uniquely real, spatio-temporally extended world. As Bradley put it: the idea that time and space are principles of individuation must be rejected (Bradley, 1967, pp. 63–4; cf. also p. 98). The point, simply put, is this: The idea of a spatio-temporal series, like any linguistically communicable content, is simply an idea. It is as such a universal and intrinsically general content.[11] No matter how much descriptive content I might write into my idea of a spatio-temporal system, if I had to remain within my thinking simply at the level of generality intrinsic to ideas, I could not on any occasion have a guarantee that there was not a plurality of spatio-temporally unrelated spatio-temporal systems meeting my description.

Hence, although the uniqueness of my present experiences must be taken to give me a handle on this present moment of time, and this position in space, and these together provide the non-conventional source-point essential to my practical application of the spatio-temporal frame internal to historical thinking, it seems to me that the uniqueness of my experiences must be taken in metaphysics as underivative. It must be taken as given prior to the ideal contents in terms of which I

[11] Bradley here is rejecting Kant's 'solution' to the problem, namely that of taking time and space to be given to sentient subjects non-conceptually via a mode of pure intuition. Kant's solution was unsatisfactory, Bradley maintained, because it involved reference to unknowable things-in-themselves (cf. Bradley, 1968, chap. 12, esp. p. 111).

am compelled, in the context of my thinking, to describe those experiences as particular kinds of experience.[12]

In particular the uniqueness of my present experiences cannot satisfactorily be construed within metaphysics as something I know in knowing the experiences to have the merely thinkable, and therefore intrinsically general, character of occurring at a particular position in a particular spatio-temporally extended, and causally interconnected, series of events. On the metaphysical view in question (which I take to be Bradley's) I will inevitably – and for historical purposes without doubt quite correctly – think of the immediate experiences here and now enjoyed in my perceptions, actions, and so on, in terms of their linguistically communicable contents and intentional objects, and thus as dateable and placeable in the earlier/later time series of a particular world – namely that of, to use Bradley's expression, 'my real world'. However, if I am seeking metaphysical adequacy in my thought, my immediate experiences cannot be construed as unique in virtue of being an array of dateable, causal and cognitive, relations between a particular human being (namely, Guy Stock) and particular objects, known as occupying determinate positions within a particular spatio-temporally extended world. Even less could I think satisfactorily of my immediate experiences now as epiphenomena supervenient on events which are unique in virtue of their unique positions in the causal nexus of a particular brain (this one here just beneath my skull) describable in terms of the highly general concepts

---

[12] As Bradley says: 'It is not by its quality as a temporal event or phenomenon of space, that the given is unique. It is unique not because it has a certain character, but because it is given' (Bradley, 1967, p. 64).

internal to the contemporary neurophysiologist's theories.[13]

Hence, on the metaphysical view in question, these experiences (my deeds and sufferings now), not in their communicable characters as locatable in the time and space of human history, but as immediately enjoyed felt contents within an indefinitely complex centre of experience, are to be construed as providing an irreducible non-discursive knowing-and-being-in-one-with (and thus identity with) – in the metaphysically strict sense of the term – reality, that is, with that which is genuinely individual and unique.[14]

[13] Kripke's causal theory of proper names like 'Guy Stock' provides a plausible enough account of their use within the world of human history. However, Russell's concerns in his Theory of Descriptions were deeper and nearer to Bradley's. His account of ordinary names as disguised descriptions was formulated in the context of his account of logically proper names which he posited as required to designate genuine particulars (individuals) which were capable of acting as (i) ultimate, immediately known, subjects of predication in atomic propositions expressing perceptions, and as (ii) source-points for the egocentric application of the spatio-temporal framework internal to historical thinking and without which unambiguous reference to logical constructions, like Guy Stock, by means of existentially quantified propositions, would be impossible. Bradley rejected the possibility of propositions meeting the requirements of Russell's posited atomic propositions but retained something like Russell's disguised description account of proper names (cf. eg., Bradley 1967, vol. 1, pp. 60–61 and pp. 124–5).

[14] I thank the members of the Philosophy Departments of Trinity College, Dublin, Aberdeen University, and Dundee University, for their discussions of earlier versions of this.

REFERENCES

Francis H. Bradley, *The Presuppositions of Critical History* (Reprinted Bristol: Thoemmes Press, 1993; 1st edn 1874).

————, *Principles of Logic*, vol. 1 (Oxford: Oxford University Press, 1967; 1st edn 1883).

————, *Appearance and Reality* (Oxford: Clarendon Press, 1968; 1st edn 1893).

David Braine, *The Reality of Time and the Existence of God* (Oxford: Clarendon Press, 1988).

Nancy Cartwright, 'Functionalism vs. the Patchwork Theory of Laws', *Proceedings of the Aristotelian Society*, vol. 94 (1994), pp. 279–92.

Robin G. Collingwood, *The Idea of History* (Oxford: Oxford University Press, 1973).

Nelson Goodman, *Ways of Worldmaking* (Indianapolis: Hackett Publishing, 1978).

Terence Horgan, 'From Supervenience to Superdupervenience', *Mind*, vol. 102, no. 408 (1993), pp. 555–86.

Leroy Loemker, *Leibniz's Philosophical Papers and Letters* (Dordrecht: D. Reidel, 1976).

Willard V. O. Quine, *Theories and Things* (Cambridge, Mass: Harvard University Press, 1981).

Ludwig Wittgenstein, *Tractatus Logico-Philosophicus*, trans. D. Pears and B. F. McGuinness (London: Routledge and Kegan Paul, 1961a).

———— , *Notebooks 1914–1916* (Oxford: Basil Blackwell, 1961b).

———— , *On Certainty* (Oxford: Basil Blackwell, 1969).

THE SUMMUM BONUM AND IDEALIST ONTOLOGY

Leslie Armour

The idealist ethics of the end of the last century and the beginning of this one tried to establish the unity of the moral life. The problem was the reconciliation of happiness and duty – the reconciliation of the notion that any moral agent has a claim to have his or her interests attended to with a principle of responsibility to others which places limits on this claim.[1] In what later seemed a state of innocence, it was widely taken for granted that men and women had a right to seek happiness and a duty to attend to the welfare of others.

The end to this innocence had something to do with the puzzling way in which some philosophers, above all, perhaps, F. H. Bradley, conceptualized both the problem and its possible solutions. Bradley asked 'Why should I be moral?' and he claimed that morality had to be transcended – a position which gave weight to H. A. Prichard's contention that perhaps moral philosophy

---

[1] The idealists were not of course alone. From Kant to Sidgwick the reconciliation of happiness and duty seemed the most difficult and often the most important of problems. For Kant the necessity of this reconciliation was the basis of his best (if inconclusive) argument for the existence of God. Sidgwick believed, too, that only a metaphysical solution which provided for the kind of necessary unity could solve the problem. But he despaired of being able to demonstrate the metaphysics (cf. Sidgwick, 1902, pp. 496–509, especially pp. 501–502).

rested on a mistake (cf. Bradley, 1927, Essay 2, and Prichard, 1912, pp. 21–37).[2]

Still, I shall argue that the problem of the reconciliation of duty and happiness is basic *and* that the only possible solution involves some elements of an idealist ontology – though it also gives us reason to be cautious about how we use and understand those elements.

Bradley wrote two biting chapters in *Ethical Studies* entitled 'Pleasure for Pleasure's Sake' and 'Duty for Duty's Sake'. And he was at least right to think that, if one uses 'duty' in a large sense which includes 'the pursuit of virtue', and 'happiness' in a sense which includes the range of things which would normally be called 'self-interest' or at least long-range self-interest, the concepts must figure in any practical moral discussion.

I

The Claims of Autonomy, Factual and Moral

Our sense of autonomy arises out of experiences which provide necessary conditions for moral discourse. McTaggart argued that the simplest notion is that each of us is an irreducible centre of experience. Russell, though he had his doubts about what he liked to call 'ego-centric particulars', insisted that each of us goes through life with a fixed left and right. Each of us is constantly at the centre of a field of experience (cf. also Armour, 1979).[3] But this centre of experience has no

---

[2] Prichard's most important claim is that there is a logical gap between the claim that x is good and the claim that x ought to be brought into being or that x ought to be done. The separation of 'good' and 'ought' becomes conceivable as soon as one asks 'Why should I be moral?'.

[3] But the discussion here takes a different direction. I rely on Russell (Russell, 1948, chap. 4.). And, of course, one should not ignore the relevant parts of McTaggart (McTaggart, 1921, 1927, chap. 36).

necessary content. In a curious sense it *is* 'the self' in the sense of the unique entity which gives rise to claims of moral autonomy. Yet its connection to the contents of the field of experience is arbitrary. In principle any human being can, directly or vicariously, have any human experience. This fact figures in the basis for the claims to moral equality, for it enables one to argue that there are no experiences which are the special preserve of classes, races or genders. It may be certain that we cannot in practice all have the same experiences, but we are talking animals and we can make a fair stab at imagining one another's experiences.

Statements about our fields of experience cannot be reduced to statements about anything else, for there are properties of them which are not properties of anything else. These properties are associated with having a fixed left and right while being at the centre of a particular experience.

One cannot instantly infer from this that something is named by the first person singular pronoun. For, as D. H. Mellor says, the facts which make statements, sentences, and propositions with 'I' in them true have to be the same facts which make such expressions with 'Leslie Armour' in them true if, in fact, I am Leslie Armour and there is no distinction intended (cf. Mellor, 1991, chap. 1). I might claim that there is a peculiar duality in this. But, unless one is very careful, admitting this duality would ultimately lead to seeming contradictions of the form 'Leslie Armour and I are the same person but what is true of Leslie Armour is not true of the being referred to by the first person pronoun'.

Professor Mellor believes such dualities are an absurd feature of our Cartesian heritage. 'If there are first person facts then the fact that I am Hugh Mellor must be one of them.' Part of the confusion, he thinks, is caused by a failure to notice the difference between sentence types and sentence tokens. 'I live in Ottawa' is true of hundreds of thousands of people. It is a 'sentence type'. A particular utterance of it is a 'sentence token' and such a token is true, of course, if and only if a particular person utters it. The belief is true depending on who holds it, and this makes it seem eerily subjective. Nevertheless, any serious attempt, Mellor says, to drive a wedge between the facts which make sentences with 'I' in them express true propositions and those which make sentences with 'Leslie Armour' in them express true propositions will produce contradictions.

But there remain serious difficulties with attempts to dispose of this subjective entity. I am not necessarily the person with the best claim to know whether I am Leslie Armour or not. I may think that I am Napoleon or God, and may lack, for psychological reasons, the necessary abilities for finding out that I am not.

Part of the problem has to do with the easy shift between the notion of a centre of experience and the notion of a curiously occult entity referred to by the pronoun 'I'. The best way of explaining the situation is that what the 'I' refers to is the constant centre of experience – something Russell conceded that he could not get rid of despite his assaults on egocentric particulars in general. Quite differently, what is meant by being 'Leslie Armour' is having a certain *filling* to the field of experience. Leslie Armour is a person with a certain history, some friends, some family, some entries in his curriculum vitae and so on. It is logically possible that I could have an attack of amnesia and forget all this and that my habits might well change so that I thought of myself as Hermann Schmidt, a Heidelberg Sanskrit lecturer who suffered from a tragic (but romantic) inability to reconstruct his past before the moment at which he began the study of exotic languages. There is a real sense in which the centre of experience now filled with Schmidt experiences is the same one which was once filled with Armour experiences. (There will be a continuous chain of experiences, though not of memories.) And so I might, if the memory chain should be repaired, one day say that I am both Schmidt and Armour. But it makes little sense to say that 'Schmidt is *really* Leslie Armour'. For Armour could not have performed Schmidt's role in the world.

One can still see why Professor Mellor finds such talk irritating. It does seem as though this centre of experience has no description beyond its existence as a mere centre, for it cannot by definition be any part of what I was calling the 'filling' to the field. The centre appears to exist as a kind of necessary feature of experience but not to have any necessary content, and, indeed, it does not necessarily have any content at all.[4]

What we seem to have here is a synthetic a priori proposition. No one can imagine not being in the centre of a pool of experience, though this centre has no literal neurophysiological existence (the centre of the brain is the *corpus callosum*, which surely does not function literally as a physical centre of co-ordination). The proposition that one is always at such a centre does not seem to be a logically necessary truth. But it does seem to be a proposition necessary to the possibility of moral discourse. For moral discourse is about what

---

[4] Compare this with Wittgenstein's remark in the *Tractatus* 5.632: 'The subject does not belong to the world: rather, it is a limit of the world' (Wittgenstein, 1972, p. 117).

choices we ought to make, and it centres on the notion that there are unique individuals who are in some intelligible sense both continuous and autonomous. If one denies that each of us is such a centre then the whole notion of moral continuity and responsibility seems to break down, and there is no longer any sense in assigning responsibilities or imagining choices.

To deny that this kind of autonomy entitles us to moral consideration is to deny that it is important to morality that the conditions for its possibility should exist and be maintained or that it is better that morality should exist than that it should not. But if it does not then, surely, 'better' and 'worse' will have no meanings. Yet they do have meanings precisely because there are autonomous individuals with choices to make and because it is evident that no one would want to substitute a random pick among the choices for his or her own decisions. This kind of autonomy gives us moral claims which, in certain circumstances, become rights.

II

The Claims of Duty

I know that I am a moral agent because I know that I am a centre of experience and my experience is precisely of the kind which gives rise to autonomy. But what about the moral agency of others? The correspondingly simple answer is that I know that you are a moral agent if I know that you are a proper user of the first person pronoun.

How do I know this? Suppose the telephone company builds into my telephone a programme which speaks to you using the first person pronoun. Now it happens, if it is just a programme or a programme combined with a randomizing device (thus giving it a footing in the world of the machines which are now said to learn and sometimes even to think), that I can substitute the machine's description for the personal pronoun. In so far as I can make this substitution, it is not using the first person pronoun as you and I do. For in human cases one can never make the substitution. The behaviour of the machine can always be traced to some object – some element of its programme or some consequence of its randomizing devices understood in terms of the correct understanding of the probabilities built into the machine. These probabilities are structures in the world, the logical equivalent of the 'filling' which belongs to our own centres of experience. But in human cases the 'I' refers to no part of the 'filling' of the field of experience but to the centre of its structure. There will therefore be things which we say and do which cannot be traced back to any 'object'. And since the computer (or any machine) is an object in the world, there are propositions which it must accept. If it rejects *all* the propositions put to it, it rejects its own programme and even the bases from which programmes might be generated, and it goes black. But human beings (if they suffer from no special handicap) can reject any and every proposition. We can believe nothing whatever if we choose – unless there is some blockage in our experience.[5]

---

[5] This claim involves further suppositions about belief. Believing may well be a propensity to act in certain ways, and we must, of course, act; but not every propensity to act is a belief, and persons without beliefs may still act well enough. They need only act, for instance, on propositions which they doubt less strongly than others. Machines have no corresponding propositional attitudes. Of course, our bodily behaviour may be programmed by propositions which never reach consciousness, but in this case we would not say that the actions are 'ours'.

Though we can train ourselves and our machines to manipulate discourse through combinations of mechanical rules and randomizing devices, the fact remains that our discourse is always built on the limitation of an infinity. Without even drawing on the grammatical arguments which thinkers like Terence Langendoen and Paul Postal have used to show that natural languages require not just the infinity of aleph-null but much larger uncountable infinities for their understanding, we can see that language confronts us with infinity (Langendoen and Postal, 1984). The exchange of meanings requires a potentially unlimited discourse. Each use of a word changes its meaning in the way that each conviction adds or subtracts something from the law of larceny. The language must always be indefinitely malleable and beyond any limit and the recognition of meanings must always outrun any programme.

When our experience becomes locked in, we become diminished moral agents or not moral agents at all. Such blockages seem always to turn out to have natural explanations in the physical world. Experiences can become frozen through drugs, malfunctioning of the central nervous system, or other physical impediments. The kinds of debilitating mental disease which diminish responsibility turn out on sufficient examination to have physiological causes. The accumulating evidence suggests that the causes of the disease are in our physi-ologies and in our social organizations and not literally in our psyches. People with diminished responsibility remain moral agents with respect to their rights to comfort and happiness. It is their duties which are diminished. So it is with animals.

The 'I' is *nothing* in terms of objects in the world, but

it is nothing in a very special sense in which 'nothing' means openness to everything. One can surely argue that only a fully-open being could be a moral agent in the full and unqualified sense because it is precisely this openness to the whole of reality which makes responsibility in any absolute sense possible. If we were structured in a way which would impose limits that could never be overcome, then our picture of reality would inevitably be distorted and all our information would be coloured in a way which would always make responsibility problematic.

Anything whatever can be reflected within our being. It is this absolute openness which enables us to be linked to one another.[6] Yet it is this very openness which *necessitates* our ties to one another. The intelligible use of the first person pronoun implies a distinction. There could be no first person pronouns if there were not at least second person pronouns. For the first person implies a distinction. And the 'I' is not to be contrasted with the things in the world – for all the things in the world are reflected or capable of being reflected *within* individual experience.

The very fact that our expressions are linguistic forges us into communities. We acquire practical identities within communities of meaning and we take our places in the world by reason of the fact that we share a language which no single person could, by its logical nature, invent. It is this which involves us constantly in duties.

---

[6] Compare – from a different line of argument – the exposition of Lévinas (Lévinas, 1971).

III

Looking for a Principle
And so we have both duties and claims to happiness. But just why do we think that they conflict? Have we forgotten something? A hundred years before Kant, Henry More, writing in the university which was to produce Henry Sidgwick and G. E. Moore, could claim with great confidence to have a solution to these problems. Ethics, he said, was a matter of living 'well and happily' (More, 1668, p. 1). Living well meant doing one's duty, and responsibility and happiness went together as comfortably as pie and cheese.

One might think that More's confidence that the conflicting bits could be reconciled was falsely bolstered by his invention of the expression 'boniform faculty'. But Ralph Cudworth hints at a way of making good sense of this curious expression.[7] Cudworth says that, just as light and sight are both 'Soliform' things without being the sun itself, so pleasure, truth and knowledge are boniform things without being the good itself.

In fact the sun *is* revealed to us in our analysis of light and sight, neither of which we might at first glance associate with it in the way which our knowledge of

---

[7] The reference is to Latin editions of More's *Enchiridion Ethicum* (More, 1669, p. 5; Southwell translation, 1690, p. 6). The idea has something in common with Aristotle's phronesis and Newman's 'illative sense'. But it is worked out as a special function of the *intellect*. In terms of More's Platonism, to call the boniform capacity a 'faculty' does not imply its ultimate separation, but only that it is a distinct expression of the intellect, one which has unique properties which add something to the world. *The Oxford English Dictionary* ascribes the expression to More, but it was used in the period by Gale, Cudworth and Norris as well. Cudworth explains his position in *The True Intellectual System of the Universe* (Cudworth, 1678, p. 204). The book was published ten years after More's *Enchiridion,* but Cudworth had been working on it for a long time.

astronomy and physiology now suggests to us. Indeed it is the recognition of the way in which light and sight go together which enables us to assess the evidence we have about the nature of the sun. If we saw by projecting some mental beam outward on the world – as many ancients thought – we would be unlikely to get straight about the sun. What is more, since light seems to pass instantly from point to point, if it were not for its involvement with our perceptual processes, we might have missed understanding its origin.

So good may well be revealed in the ways in which knowledge, truth, and pleasure go together. Pleasure is not, as Cudworth says, the good in itself. For no sensible person thinks that pleasure can be good except in reference beyond itself. If the only pleasures we knew were derived from enjoying the destruction of others and resulted in our own self-destruction, no one would say pleasure was good. And yet it would be very puzzling, for pleasure would still have the form of something to which we were naturally attracted. Its absence would leave us all unsatisfied.

There is an analogy between the ways in which the sensation of pleasure gives us clues about how we are tied to the world and how the good can be understood, and the ways in which seeing gives us clues about how light and its source are to be understood. Since pleasure is often good, but clearly not *the* good itself, we are forced to seek for the source of the good beyond our immediate sensations, just as, seeing involves illumination but is not the source of the light, we are forced to seek for a source beyond ourselves, and so we try to understand the function of the sun.

Admittedly, there is a conceptual ambiguity about pleasure which Cudworth's analogy seriously obscures.

In one sense, what we mean by pleasure is some feeling or other but in another sense what we mean by it is something which gives us satisfaction. When I say that I 'take pleasure in trying to get Descartes right' I don't quite mean the same thing by 'pleasure' as when I say that 'a glass of Scotch gives me pleasure'. By the second statement I may sometimes be referring to a sensation, by the first I am surely not. Throughout this discussion I have tried to keep in sight two sets of concepts which include happiness, pleasure, and self-interest on one side, and duty and something like the public good on the other. The members of the first set surely do play roles in our 'inner lives'. But so do the second. One can have a 'sense of duty' and the public good can be something one imagines. By the same token one's pleasures can be publicly expressed.

Just as we cannot prise our concept of seeing apart from our understanding of light and its source, so we cannot quite shake pleasure loose from some idea of goodness – some idea which explains why it would be so very odd to denounce it as worthless or bad.[8] There would be something quite absurd about urging everyone to live a life of pain, and if the mere absence of pain were all that counted, we would be as well off dead.

In Cudworth's lexicon, truth and knowledge, like pleasure, are 'boniform qualities'. For they, too, are something the absence of which must leave us unsatisfied and something to which we are naturally

---

[8] Of course, there are ascetics who seem to do so, but they seem invariably to imagine great joy in heaven, blissful unity with the deity, or at least a very nasty hell which they might escape by eschewing sin. Buddhists may seem to go far in this direction, but they ultimately deny that Nirvana is a purely negative notion even if it is derived from a Sanskrit word meaning 'running out of fuel'.

attracted. They are central ingredients in our claims to be human. But they are not *the* good. Indeed knowledge and truth seem to be related to one another much as light and sight are related. We say that we have the truth when we recognize that certain criteria are met, and the meeting of these criteria is (in one sense) knowledge. But what is it that gives them their form in the way that the sun gives form to light and sight? They are related to 'good' because if all states of affairs were of equal value – if there was no 'good' – it would not matter what we claimed to be true *or* good. Cudworth might have argued that truth and knowledge do matter for the different reason that moral judgements on particular cases always involve one or more factual premises. It is good in general to give water to thirsty dogs, but if the dog one confronts has just been given medicine which, when combined with water, will kill it, it is not.

This argument – which Cudworth does not advance but which seems implicit in all that he says about these matters – can be extended to tie pleasure together with truth and knowledge, for it is obvious at least that there are factual judgements about what produces pleasure and that these are objective in the sense that they are not always merely internal personal states. It is obvious, too, that, if truth and knowledge really are 'boniform' qualities, this commitment to a truth which outruns simple subjectivity also tells against egoistic hedonism, for the good is not simply my pleasure. Truth and knowledge are in principle the same for all of us and the obligation to have regard for them is one of the bases of communal interest and responsibility.

The idea of the 'boniform' emerges as we begin to see the good as something which shows itself in truth, knowledge, and pleasure, but is not any or all of them. More's expression 'boniform faculty' need mean no more than this capacity to discover and delineate the good. What is being said by More and Cudworth is essentially that the good is not to be confused with the properties through which it is expressed. This suggests part of the claim which G. E. Moore made two and a half centuries later – goodness is in a way a unique characteristic which cannot be 'dissolved' into any other characteristics, but any Cambridge Platonist would deny the further claim that goodness cannot be effectively *associated with* any other properties. On the contrary, their doctrine enables us to say that some of what Moore called 'natural qualities' are 'boniform'.

Thus we may see how goodness gets to be associated with both subjective states like pleasure and objective concerns like truth and knowledge which lead us out into a community, and this is how duty and happiness come to be bound up with one another. But we will recreate our problems in a new way if we come to think of goodness as manifesting itself through different characteristics, and we may come to ask puzzling questions: How much pleasure would we trade for how much truth or knowledge?[9]

---

[9] Philosophers rarely speak of the temptation not to seek one's proper pleasures. But the notion is not absurd. Indeed Cudworth's daughter Damaris (Lady Masham) explores the subject in her *Occasional Thoughts in reference to a Vertuous Christian LIFE* – I have kept the capitals as they are in the original (Cudworth, 1705). She says: 'It is true that the love of happiness (which consists in pleasure) is the earliest, and strongest principle of humane Nature' (Cudworth, 1705, p. 71). And she adds that the Law of Reason suggests that it is also our duty to pursue this principle. 'Thus our duty and happiness can never be divided' (Cudworth, 1705, p. 73).

IV

The Puzzle of Sir David Ross

Such questions are odd, but enticing. Sir David Ross argued that the clusters which he called virtue and duty and those he called pleasure and happiness must be distinct. His ground was that 'we are totally unable to see how any amount of one of these could be equal in goodness to any amount of the other' (Ross, 1930, p. 154).

The notion of 'amount' is curious. Yet his assertion offers us an initial way of looking at the question. No one supposes that I could argue that I was justified in refusing to help a small child who had fallen down while crossing the street in order to enjoy two extra minutes of the pleasure of reading Kant. But might I not reasonably plead that the pleasure involved in being allowed to finish reading a poem justifies my being five minutes late in meeting a friend for coffee? The trade-off seems evident in small matters. But is not Ross right about large ones? What if there is a real chance of rescuing someone from a fire but a large chance of losing my life in the process?

Below the surface lies an apparent conflict of types of moral theory. Those who champion duty and virtue *per se* often hold the view that doing one's duty or being virtuous is simply what is right. It makes no difference what the outcome is. Those who champion happiness, pleasure and above all self-interest naturally incline to the view that what matters is what result is produced by a given action.

It is hard to say exactly what the 'happiness' of which Sir David Ross speaks actually is. At one point he suggests that one might contrast virtue with 'say, pleasure', and he suggests that pleasure, though an important example, is only an example. What he means, I think, most generally, is that a certain state of being content with oneself, of being able to accept one's own condition, is an undoubted good. For everyone, happiness will be some acceptable species, even if a rather low-level one, of what F. H. Bradley called self-realization (Bradley, 1927, pp. 214–51).

Again, there may be a problem about virtue and duty. Sir David speaks now of one, now of the other. Some people have supposed that a 'morality of virtue' is to be contrasted with a 'morality of rules'. But Alasdair MacIntyre, who has done most to raise the question of virtue in recent years, has said that the contrast is a misrepresentation of his notions, for 'any adequate morality of virtues' requires 'as its counterpart a morality of laws'. One leads to the other. For some purposes virtue and duty do need to be kept separate, but they belong together in this discussion.[10]

Nor are they necessarily so separate from happiness as one might at first think. Henry More speaks generally of happiness which implies a right ordering of our affairs rather than simply pleasure. But More was not merely trading on the ordinary distinction between pleasure and happiness. He had going for him a principle widely held by Neoplatonists and later idealists. In its simplest form, this principle has it that

---

[10] Sir David Ross offers pleasure as an example, 'say, pleasure' (Ross, 1930, p. 154). On the same page the 'Kantian' view is associated with the predominance of virtue, but shortly after it is associated with the predominance of duty and of the supreme worth of conscientious action (Ross, 1930, p. 157). Though Bradley's *Ethical Studies* is largely devoted to the question of self-realization, the topic is directly addressed late in the work (cf. Bradley, 1927, p. 214 ff). Alasdair MacIntyre's remark that the contrast of virtue and rules misrepresents his position is found in *After Virtue* (MacIntyre, 1981, p. ix, cf. MacIntyre, 1984, p. 152).

any plurality can only be understood in terms of some unity. Thus, if doing one's duty and searching for happiness are really both species of moral actions, we must somehow be able to understand them as expressions of some higher unity, and we must seek meanings for them which will accord with this principle. This is supposing, indeed, that they are somehow rival claimants for the same prize. For, on this view, every plurality is intelligible only in relation to some unity and every genuine unity must express itself through a plurality which (a) continues the principle of that unity and (b) expresses a principle of differentiation which brings out an element of that unity which would otherwise have been hidden.

Perhaps the *locus classicus* of this principle is in Proclus's *Elements of Theology* 7–13 (cf. Proclus, 1963, propositions 8–13, pp. 9–17, commentary pp. 194–202). The central Neoplatonic elements are those expressed in Plotinus's *Enneads* V, i, and Proclus's *Elements* 1–6. They suggest that any reality must be conceived as a kind of unity in diversity which produces a definite order in things. How might duty and happiness together order a human life? Perhaps they are aspects of self-realization. This would be the most direct route to an idealist ethics.

But achieving one's self-realization is not *the same as* doing one's duty, for one can imagine that people have duties other than the attainment of their own self-realization – even if that self-realization is also the realization, somehow, of the Absolute, and one can also imagine that a great deal of self-realization might be achieved while duty, even if recognized, might not get done. It is also quite possible that people sometimes or even often do their duty without recognizing it.

Equally, it does not follow that self-realization implies happiness except on a supposition which seems, quite literally, self-destructive in more than one sense. If self-realization is only achieved – as some idealist philosophers have surely implied – when the self to be realized has been expanded through reason and experience so that it is identical with the Absolute, then, in so far as unhappiness must represent some lack on the part of its victim, unhappiness is impossible for the realized self and the Absolute. But perhaps so is happiness.

V

The Roads to Dissolution
There are at least five imaginable lines of escape from the conflict of happiness and duty apart from the Neoplatonic and idealist one which I shall suggest and the obvious but unsuccessful attempt to link happiness and duty in the notion of self-realization. They fail, but their failure will reveal important clues to the solution.

The first solution is Kantian. Kant holds that God can create a situation which reconciles the principles (Kant, 1952, pp. 128–36). He can make us both happy and capable of doing our duty. To this one must say: 'Yes he can, but only by ceasing to be a Kantian.' He cannot change my duties, but he can make me happy to carry them out. This, however, changes my fundamental nature and violates Kant's end-in-itself principle. Certainly Kant envisaged that God would create a genuine Kingdom of Ends within which we would all be happy, all be treated as ends in ourselves, and all be virtuous. But this must mean transforming those who would be made unhappy by doing their duty. It is rather like solving the problem of a man who wants to be let out of a mental hospital by giving him a pill which makes him think that he is happy to stay there.[11]

The second solution – the truly classical solution – is to hold that the conflicts do not occur for virtuous people. It is sometimes suggested that this is the solution of the saints, but such a solution supposes, once again, that a significant moral act is not just some act which it is my duty to perform but something else as well, essentially something which occurs within the consciousness of one who is made happy by it. It cannot be enough just to recognize virtue when one sees it or to understand that happiness is a legitimate pursuit, for many who recognize duty and accept the legitimacy of happiness experience conflicts. How is one to be made happy by being virtuous if one recognizes the conflict? God may change one's nature, and one can call this grace. But then, again, God is tampering with moral autonomy.

The third solution depends on the claim that the conflicts don't matter unless some ultimately significant moral action is adversely affected. It supposes that trivial conflicts are inevitable but that, in the end, the beatific vision or whatever its Kantian equivalent might be is sufficient to override all such trivialities. This supposes that a significant moral act is not just any act

---

[11] Of course Kant's own Kingdom of Ends principle hints at a different resolution, for it supposes a situation in which community interest and self-interest may well come together. But Kant did not develop the principle at great length himself and indeed insisted that it was logically on all fours with his universalization principle. He believed, I think, that he needed God. But it is true that some exploration and further development of the Kingdom of Ends principle is probably needed to make Kant's philosophy consistent (cf. Armour and Singh, 1986, pp. 13–27). At any rate the Kantian resources for dealing with the questions I am dealing with here are not exhausted by what I take to be Kant's failed attempt to put God to work, and I use some Kantian ideas in a different way later in this paper.

which it is my duty to perform or some act which bears on happiness, but something else as well. If so, then there is some more important characteristic which is the explanation of this special significance. But, if that were the case, we would have yet another principle to reconcile with the original ones. We might just know by some special insight which acts were significant. We might have what Aristotle called *phronesis,* or we might have Newman's illative sense. But these, I suppose, would not do, for they are powers which enable us to draw the right conclusions from principles. For us to be able to deal in this way with the problem of triviality we would need to be able to make immediate moral judgements which would satisfy us. It is notorious that we cannot do this. For a particular act to be moral it must be shown that there is a connection between it and morality. Since morality is a universal notion and moral actions are particular, some principle must join them.

The fourth solution is to hold that the happiness or immediate self-interest principle and the principle of virtue or obligation simply belong to different levels of consciousness, and we learn, in the end, that duty has precedence over happiness as we move to the level at which 'pleasure for pleasure's sake' appears to be absurd. F. H. Bradley argues this view throughout the central chapters of *Ethical Studies.* He says we should start at the level of feeling. The expression 'feeling' denotes not merely sensations or sense data. At the very least, Bradley thought, sensations apart from relations are mere abstractions. The concept of 'feeling' was meant to denote the rich original experience from which abstractions are made. Bradley wants us to see that feelings are capable of meaningful analysis. They are not mere bearers of proper names (Bradley, 1930).

We are expected to see that feelings come organically and are internally related to their responses. One does not feel angry and averse to the object of one's anger as if one's anger and aversion are two distinct things. The two come fused together. One does not have the idea of chocolate fudge until one grasps that, in the ordinary way, it is pleasant tasting stuff. The pleasure principle is the natural principle of this level of consciousness.

But such a principle breaks down because it seems to reveal a self who has the pleasures and who can be brought into some state of equilibrium, some state of being at ease with oneself, by means of the accumulation of such pleasures. Yet feelings cannot be accumulated or saved. One may attempt to find satisfaction in pleasure, but no self emerges from such an attempt.

We are therefore given a hint of and driven to search for another level of consciousness in pursuit of the self. The self, as Hume insisted, does not reveal itself at the level of sensation even when sensation has been expanded to include everything Bradley wants to include in 'feeling'. It seems to be something which rises above the transient states of pleasure and aversion. But the self we so imagine, according to Bradley, has become an abstraction from which the Kantian moral agent emerges as an empty universal form.

We must therefore accept the actuality of community in the world, but, in Bradley's view, the actual community in which I find myself is what he calls a concrete universal – a universal in which the property is expressed through its actual instances. It is in this actual community that Bradley promises that we will find our proper 'station' and 'its duties'. This community is one in which each of us garners an identity from the others, and yet it is a community in

which each individual is perfectly distinct and so bound
by no ultimate universal rule.

As we follow the levels of consciousness, paradoxes
emerge. I am dependent on the whole, but no formal
rule binds me to it. I am distinct and unique and yet I
have only a relational and not a substantive identity.
My experience is but a facet of the whole and yet I
experience myself through it as unique and distinct.

Bradley's ultimate solution is that the paradoxes all
disappear in the Absolute, which can reconcile all of
them. But unless we can see how the trick is to be done
this recourse to an ultimate unity is of the same order as
Kant's postulate about God. It may be a necessary
postulate of practical reason, but the statement of the
need does not seem to be a justified assertion about
knowledge.

There is a fifth, more mundane solution. The
Rawlsian 'wide reflective equilibrium'. Rawls means to
deal with specific principles which fall under one or
other of the general principles I have been discussing.
He intends to deal with problems posed by our need to
decide on the relation between such principles as those
involved in the search for prosperity, freedom, and
dignity. But he does have to reconcile happiness and
duty, and he does hold that hedonism, for instance, is
not adequate by itself as a moral principle. Within his
philosophy all such conflicts seem ultimately to be
referred either to the immediate intuitions of persons in
idealized circumstances – behind the veil of ignorance
for instance – or else are left to be solved by the
principle of 'wide reflective equilibrium'. Intuitions
about happiness and duty seem to be precisely the
concepts which clash in the context which we have been
exploring. Rawls' argument for the 'wide reflective

equilibrium' is to be found in *A Theory of Justice*. This method, as Kai Nielsen has argued, is essentially one of searching for coherence (Rawls, 1971, pp. 456 ff, Nielsen, 1988, pp. 19–38). But principles must be coherent in relation to something. What? Nielsen has an answer: we start with 'Our considered judgements given in the traditions which are a part of our culture'. But this is sleight of hand. It, too, finds a new overriding principle. It might not be the one which Nielsen suggests, though the connection between Rawls and the ideology of American liberalism is strong enough to allow us to think that Rawls did start in the way that Nielsen suggests. But no matter. It might be some other principle. Then, however, the other principle would be overriding. Again, some other principle might emerge from the changing structure which resulted from the attempt at coherence. Would that not have the same result?

VI

The Principle of Proclus
Let us then turn to what I shall call the principle of Proclus. In its simplest form, this principle has it that (1) every plurality is intelligible only in relation to some unity, and (2) every genuine unity must express itself through a plurality, which (A) continues the principle of that unity and (B) expresses a principle of differentiation which brings out an element of that unity which would otherwise have been hidden. But Proclus also insists that each thing must have its good. The unity which is the good must show itself specifically in a plurality.
The discussion of wholes and parts in his *Elements of*

Theology, propositions 67–70, suggests strongly that every part of the system is determined to its place and function by the whole and that, therefore, each component has a function which, if it is a conscious function – as some will be – will be construable as its natural duty.[12]

What any component of reality naturally aims at cannot, thus, be evil in and of itself. We see that there is a track from the principle that one is entitled to one's happiness, one's natural contentedness, which comes from developing one's place in the scheme of things (and so is now clearly related to self-realization), to the pursuit of one's own pleasures, and on to the notion of one's duty. What ultimately gives one pleasure is to recognize one's place in the whole and to realize the One in a return to it. But one's pleasure does not result simply from the recognition that one has behaved virtuously. It has all the components of a rich concrete existence in one place in a universe which, if not perversely distorted, radiates the goodness of the One.

VII

The Mutual Implications of Duty and Happiness
On this view, as soon as one has analysed the nature either of duty or of happiness, one is led to the other. In a sense, it is not hard to show that this is reasonable. How are we to know that happiness and duty, or self-realization and virtue, conflict? Only because both states or both members of the pairs of states seem to us to be good. Can this be merely a verbal illusion in the

---

[12] The principle of differentiation is to be found in Proclus (1963, pp. 2–17, 59–63), as is the notion of natural duty (pp. 64–7).

sense that 'good' now has no meaning beyond the sum of happiness and virtue? If not, it is surely worth exploring.

Francis Sparshott has argued that 'good' is a word which functions only as 'a philosopher's dummy' (Sparshott, 1958, pp. 79–80). He distinguishes 'goodness' from what he calls 'real' ethical words. He does so because his thesis is that what the philosophical analysis of goodness actually is intended to achieve is the illumination of these other terms, which include such words as 'honourable', 'honest', 'heroic', 'generous' and 'hospitable'. It is these that we want to throw light upon, but we don't usually find them in central places in philosophical discourse. Is this a mistake? It is not, he says, 'for the discussion would be even more likely to mislead if it were carried on in the light of what it was supposed to illuminate'.

Such a view seems to render insoluble the kind of problem I have been discussing. For it suggests that an analysis of a single 'dummy' word, 'goodness', is what is required, but that the issues to be illuminated are themselves irreducibly pluralistic. We may, however, cast some light on the question by noticing in what sense those engaged in finding knowledge might be said to be using 'dummies'. Veterinarians are interested in problems about horses in general and so write books about 'the horse'. Whatever is in the book, however, should apply, in so far as it is general, to any horse whatsoever. The expression 'the horse' is, we might say, a veterinary textbook writer's dummy. When we come to apply it, we substitute 'Toby' or 'Flying Avenger' or 'Watering Trough' for 'horse'. Might it not be so with goodness? There are only, we might say, particular instances of goodness: Francis's generosity to his philosophical opponents, or Sam's bravery in rescuing a drowning pig.

Did Proclus confuse the fact that we must speak of 'the good' with the alleged fact that there is something called goodness? Perhaps not. One reason for thinking not is the nature of the problem of reconciling happiness and duty. The conundrum comes about in part because, almost (but not quite) tautologically, it is good to do one's duty. (Presumably the assertion would be tautological if we employed the right concepts of goodness and duty. But it may be that we cannot get them precise enough to make sure that the tautology holds.) And, intuitively, it is good to pursue one's happiness. Yet it is clear that the principles implied are distinct and can conflict. They cannot conflict if they do not give rise to rival views about what one ought to do. Now it is tautological, as well, that what one ought to do is to promote the good. If there is not something which is good in each case, no conflict can arise. If good is not a distinct property, how can two activities so different each promote the good? Yet it would seem that, here, too, there is a paradox. Nothing is just good. Goodness is always instantiated through something else. There are good men, good horses, and good arguments. But the person who says she is searching for the good but that she will not accept it in case it comes mixed with anything else is evidently doomed to failure. So is the person bent on the devil's work, who says he is out to destroy goodness itself. Nothing counts as just being good and nothing counts as destroying goodness. Must Professor Sparshott be right? How can 'good' be other than a dummy word?

The explanation takes us to the root of an ontological problem which may be discerned at the base of philosophies like those of Plotinus and Proclus. The problem is this: in general, when we look for explanations, we look for some state of affairs which is logically or temporally prior and which will explain the states of affairs which, logically or temporally, come after it. But of each such thing, person, event, or state of affairs one can ask: what caused that? This would be true even if the ultimate explanation hung on the existence of a God which one thought of as having, in any ordinary sense, what might be called an ontological condition. For to have an ontological condition is to exhibit some determinate form or mode of being, and every determinate form of being requires an explanation just because it excludes other compatible determinate forms or modes of being.

Yet not all that one can speak of is like this. The good may be manifested through this or that. But it cannot *be* this or that, or else only this or that could be good. The truth, rather, is that all things are good in some measure – in the measure that they express the good. This is so, for instance if (as seems to be the case) to be evil is always to lack something or if (as also seems to be the case), since order is one of the goods, there cannot be an orderly paradigm of evil. Evil, then, cannot be expressed in terms relative to goodness. But if this is so, goodness can neither be nothing at all nor a straightforward ontological condition. Such an argument would lead one directly to Plato's form of the good as the ultimate explanation, in some sense, of all things. Therefore, speaking of the form of the good in the traditional way as the 'sun of Plato', Aquinas says 'in our religion we call this God' (Aquinas, 1920, I, 79, 4), though it is surely God in a very special sense – a 'form' or quasi-entity beyond determinate nature and therefore in Neoplatonist language beyond being and non-being.

As such it is the One which expresses itself as the good. Only what is the One can have the unity which the idea of goodness demands and only what is the good can be what is expressed through a myriad of different things. At least symbolically, this is the connection between duty and happiness. The One represents the inner perfection, toward which everything which is manifested by this unity in successive emanations is drawn, and this is happiness *per se*: the contentment of what is good with itself. But the One is necessarily expressed through a myriad of things. What is content in and with itself must nevertheless go beyond itself, for its nature is given in its relation to the whole. This reaching out represents duty. Thus happiness or self-realization and duty or virtue are ultimately one and the same principle in two manifestations.

But let us come down to earth, for such rhetorical indulgences may seem to be evasions of the need to face real problems about risking one's life to save drowning sailors or deciding what to do when one's duties seem overwhelming and only misery is in view. It is still true, as Sir David Ross says, that we cannot imagine any quantity of duty which equals any quantity of happiness. It is just that the very thing which compels us to consider duty compels us to consider happiness. Each of us needs as much happiness as will secure our perception of our own well-being, for it is that well-being which gives each of us something to contribute and our awareness of it which enables us to know what we have to contribute. To ask what a man or a woman has to communicate by way of doing his or her duty is to ask, therefore, just how much inner goodness such a person has – the same inner goodness on which happiness might be founded. That is to say that duty and happiness are not distinct in quite the way that we had supposed.

What then of the ontology which this discussion seems to justify? If being is what the good is expressed through, good is beyond it. If what I have been saying is true, then 'goodness' is not analysable away. The world conceived as an arena for human life is ordered by 'the good'. But it is also true that the unity expresses itself through an irreducible plurality, and good is found only in the particulars.

Finding such a concept is the kind of thing which Kant describes as 'orienting oneself in thought', a process by which we start with some subjective phenomenon – like the ability to tell our right hand from our left hand – and use this to build an objective structure through which we can find out which way is east (Kant, 1900, pp. 134 ff; Kant, 1963, pp. 168 ff). There really is an east even though what it means to orient oneself is to relate some publicly available symbol systems to an individual (though hardly 'private') experience. It is more complicated to start with the attraction of pleasure, but once one recognizes the ways in which it is related to knowledge and truth, one is on the way to some success.

There really is a good as there really is an east, and good is truly a concept which informs the issues of human life. Questions about idealist ontology may begin from there.

REFERENCES

Thomas Aquinas, *Summa Theologica*, trans. English Dominican Fathers (London: Burns, Oates and Washbourne, 1920).

Leslie Armour, 'Russell, McTaggart, and "I"', *Idealistic Studies*, vol. 9 (January, 1979), pp. 66–76.

Leslie Armour and Chhatrapati Singh, 'The Kingdom of Ends in Morals and Law', *Indian Philosophical Quarterly*, vol. 13 (January–March 1986), pp. 13–28.

F. H. Bradley, *Ethical Studies* (London: H. S. King, 1870; revised London: Oxford University Press, 1911; Oxford: Clarendon Press, 1927).

————— , *Appearance and Reality* (Oxford: Clarendon Press, 1893, 1897, 9th impression, corrected, 1930).

Damaris Cudworth, *Occasional Thoughts in reference to a Vertuous Christian Life* (London: A. and J. Churchil 1705).

Ralph Cudworth, *The True Intellectual System of the Universe* (London: Richard Royston, 1678).

Immanuel Kant, *Critique of Practical Reason*, trans. L. W. Beck (Indianapolis: Liberal Arts, 1952).

—————— , *Was heisst sich im Denken orientieren?* Werke, vol. 8 (Berlin: German Academy of Sciences) trans. Gabrielle Rabel as '*What Does it Mean [or Signify] to Orient Oneself in Thought?*', in *Kant* (Oxford: Clarendon Press, 1963).

D. Terence Langendoen and Paul M. Postal, *The Vastness of Natural Languages* (Oxford: Basil Blackwell, 1984).

Emmanuel Lévinas, *Totalité et infinité* (The Hague: Martinus Nijhoff, 1971).

Alasdair MacIntyre, *Whose Justice? Which Rationality?* (London: Duckworth, 1981).

—————— , *After Virtue* (Notre Dame, Indiana: Notre Dame University Press, 1984).

J. M. E. McTaggart, *The Nature of Existence*, 2 vols (Cambridge: University Press, 1921, 1927).

D. H. Mellor, *Matters of Metaphysics* (Cambridge: Cambridge University Press, 1991).

Henry More, *Enchiridion Ethicum* (London: J. Flesher, 1668; 2nd edn with additional preface, 1669); trans. Southwell, as *An Account of Virtue* (London: Benjamin Tooke, 1690).

Kai Nielsen, 'In Defence of Wide Reflective Equilibrium', in Douglas Odegard (ed.), *Ethics and Justification* (Edmonton: Academic Printing and Publishing, 1988).

Plotinus, *Ennéades,* ed. and trans. Émile Bréhier (Paris: Belles Lettres, 1924–38).

Plotinus, *The Enneads,* ed. and trans. A. H. Armstrong (Cambridge, Mass: Harvard University Press, 1966–84).

H. A. Prichard, 'Does Moral Philosophy Rest on a Mistake?', *Mind,* vol. 21, no. 21 (1912), pp. 21–37.

Proclus, *Elements of Theology,* ed. and trans. E. R. Dodds (Oxford: Clarendon Press, 1963).

John Rawls, *A Theory of Justice* (Cambridge, Mass: Harvard University Press, 1971).

Sir David Ross, *The Right and The Good* (Oxford: Clarendon Press, 1930).

Bertrand Russell, *Human Knowledge, Its Scope and Limits* (New York: Simon and Schuster, 1948).

Henry Sidgwick, *Methods of Ethics,* 7th edn with final editing by E. E. Constance Jones (London: Macmillan, 1902).

F. E. Sparshott, *An Enquiry Into Goodness* (Toronto: University of Toronto Press; and Chicago: University of Chicago Press, 1958).

Ludwig Wittgenstein, *Tractatus Logico-Philosophicus,* revised and corrected (London: Routledge and Kegan Paul, 1972).

WHY THE IDEALIST THEORY OF INFERENCE STILL MATTERS

Phillip Ferreira

As many commentators have observed, a general lack of interest in theories of inference has been a notable feature of twentieth-century epistemology and philosophical logic. And when we ask why this has been the case we are usually told that inference is a 'subjective' process which is best treated by the psychologist (and not the philosopher or logician). We are also frequently told that the widespread interest in the process of inference that characterized the writings of the English idealists is but another indication of their hopelessly 'subjective' orientation. Modern logic and epistemology should be, we hear, concerned with what is wholly objective; and if philosophers discuss inference at all they must take care not to fall into considerations of its psychological aspects.

Characterizations of the late nineteenth and early twentieth-century idealist logic as 'subjective' and 'psychological' were, of course, frequently encountered in the writings of the early analysts. What is most interesting, though, is that the idealist logicians themselves rejected this interpretation of their views. Indeed, the idealists – I am thinking primarily of F. H. Bradley and Bernard Bosanquet here – saw their doctrine of inference as a *defence* of objectivity in logic and the theory of knowledge. And, on their view, the *real* sources of subjectivism (and ultimately irrationalism) were the doctrines of idealism's uncomprehending critics. First, was the empiricist associationism of Hume and Mill (carried on to the end of the nineteenth century by Bain and Croome Robertson); and, second, the new formalism which – despite any increased facility in the manipulation of argument forms it may have realized – did nothing, as they saw it, to advance the theory of knowledge. Indeed, Bradley and Bosanquet argued that whenever formal logic ventured into the theory of knowledge its confused conception of implication led it into errors that were as serious as those of associationism; and neither associationism nor formalism, they believed, could provide an adequate account – either normative or descriptive – of human reason. On the view of the English idealists, only a theory of material inference which saw the contents of our experience as both interpenetrating and hierarchically organized could achieve this end.

My goal in this paper, then, is to explicate this controversial claim. And, although I shall spend most of my time examining Bradley's and Bosanquet's attack on different conceptions of inference, I shall also briefly comment on their positive doctrine and its significance for recent philosophy. It will be my claim that the idealist theory of inference still provides an attractive alternative to the ossified views that have come to characterize so much of the contemporary debate.

I

While it is no longer controversial to claim that the empiricist account of inference (the theory of the association of ideas) leads to an indefensible subjectivism in the theory of knowledge, just why the idealist authors saw this as being the case is often misunderstood. Hence, I would like to begin by briefly describing the attack on associationism as made by F. H. Bradley in his *Principles of Logic* (Bradley, 1922). Bradley was, of course, the individual most responsible for relegating associationism to the back-burners of the philosophical debate during the closing decades of the last century. And in what follows I shall attempt – even if only in outline – an account of his argument.[1]

The first, and perhaps most important, point to be made by the associationist is that 'thought' is nothing more than a psychological state that differs from the given data of sense in being less 'lively' or 'forceful'. And, starting with this assumption, the theory goes on to claim that we infer one fact from another – that is, we proceed from one mental image to another – upon the basis of two closely related psychological mechanisms – the 'similarity' and 'conjunctive regularity' between impressions and ideas.

But let us begin by considering the notion of conjunctive regularity. Here the theory claims that certain ideas (ie., given sense impressions or subsequent 'thoughts' derived from sense) tend to become associated with one another through their repeated appearance in either simultaneous or successive relations of contiguity. And the strength of the associative bond that develops is, according to the theory's proponents, determined by the frequency with which we encounter the elements in these contiguous relations. The bond between associated elements

---

[1] For his complete criticism see Bradley, 1922, pp. 299–345; cf. also Bradley, 1935, pp. 205–38.

becomes, as Mill puts it, more 'rapid' and 'certain' as the number of times the contiguous relation occurs; and when two phenomena have been experienced in such conjunctive relation with *complete* regularity (ie., without exception) there develops between them what has been referred to as an 'indissoluble' or 'inseparable' association.[2]

A common example of indissoluble association might be that between the ideas (ie., images) 'fire' and 'heat'. Because of the previous regularity of their contiguous appearance within our experience, whenever we see or think of 'fire' we immediately and with great force also think of 'heat' (even when there is no impression of 'heat' presently given to sense). And it is, according to the associationist, solely upon the basis of a *psychical bond* established through such conjunctive regularity that this 'inseparable' association comes about. While there may be many associations which do not carry this degree of force, those phenomena which have become so 'riveted' (to use Mill's language again) are seen by common sense as connected – not by our own mental habits – but intrinsically and in themselves. Of course, we are told that the phenomena don't *really* exhibit this connection at the level of sense experience; but through the development of indissoluble association it *appears* as if they do. And our belief in such things as 'necessary connections' is explained (or rather explained away) through just this mechanism.

To be sure, not all cases of association are understood as 'indissoluble'. There can be on this theory differing degrees of strength to our associations; and, indeed, our entire sense of the probable (as opposed to certain) behaviour of the universe stems from associations

---

[2] What follows in the text is taken directly from Mill, 1979, pp. 177–8.

which are less than indissoluble. The important point to bear in mind, though, is that – whether we are considering indissoluble association or something weaker – the theory allows for the development of *radically different* associative bonds within the minds of different individuals regarding the same phenomena.

We must also pay close attention to the other psychological mechanism that is at work in the theory of the association of ideas; and I am here referring to 'resemblance' or 'similarity'. The theory of associationism claims that in order for there to develop psychical bonds between phenomena on the basis of contiguity, we must also have before us the natural relation of *resemblance* between a present impression (or idea) and a previous one. For example, unless my present impression of 'fire' resembles a previous one, the present contiguous appearance of 'fire' and 'heat' will not add to or strengthen what has gone before. Hence, resemblance is a crucial component in both the initial development and subsequent strengthening of the psychical bonds between all associated phenomena. However, after the psychical bonds between non-resembling phenomena (eg., 'fire' and 'heat', or 'snow' and 'cold') have been established, the relation of similarity still plays a crucial, though somewhat different, role. It is, according to the associationist, only through the relation of resemblance between a present impression and a previously experienced one that the non-resembling (but associated) idea can be called up. For example, unless there is a naturally occurring similarity between a present impression of 'fire' and one which has somehow been preserved, the non-resembling but indissolubly associated idea of 'heat' could never be revived.

Now, the theory of associationism was criticized by F. H. Bradley at a number of levels. Two of the most powerful objections – I shall refer to them as Bradley's technical complaints – I have treated at length elsewhere; hence, I shall only briefly discuss them here.[3] However, they do cast serious doubt on the ultimate coherency of the doctrine; and, given their enormous influence, they must not be ignored.

The first of these objections, then, is that while the doctrine of associationism demands that our ideas be *preserved* in some sort of mental 'storehouse' (in order that they might later be called-up or revived), no intelligible account of how this might occur can be provided (Bradley, 1922, pp. 305–308). Indeed, Bradley saw the idea of a 'storehouse' of psychical images as not only landing us in metaphysical absurdities but also as failing to appreciate the source of individuation and particularity which accrues to any psychical image. According to Bradley, it was always the *context* in which an image arose that makes it *this* particular image. And when we realize that the context in which such a 'thought' occurs can *never* be precisely the same as when it originally appeared, we are forced to acknowledge that whatever image I might now have before me *cannot* be the same as any that has preceded it. Now, the response to Bradley's objection we need not consider here. I would only point out that *if* Bradley is right, then for this reason alone associationism would fail. And it would fail because one of its central tenets is that what is revived in my mind through the relation of resemblance just *is* the image that was originally experienced.

Leaving this difficulty, let us consider the second (and more serious) technical complaint. Resemblance, we

---

[3]   I have considered these objections in Ferreira 1996b.

should recall, is an essential component within the theory of the association of ideas, since both the building-up of psychical habits and the revivification of ideas presuppose it. However, when we look closely at this mechanism we see that it cannot possibly do the work the theory requires of it. Simply put, the problem is that resemblance is a *two-term* relation. And in order that the mind apprehend this relation *both* terms must be before it at once. But, Bradley asked, if this is the case, how can the associationist possibly claim that it is through the relation of resemblance that a *present* impression or idea calls up an *absent* one from the psychical storehouse? Bradley's answer was that, if the ideas are truly *resembling* (in the only sense which the theory could tolerate) then both ideas must be simultaneously before the mind. However, if both are already present then clearly the one idea cannot be said to 'call up' or 'revive' the other. To do both of these things at once is impossible; and thus, Bradley claimed, the theory must be rejected as incoherent (Bradley, 1922, pp. 320–21).

I would mention, though, that while these 'technical' objections were seen by many as sufficient reason to reject associationism, they were not for Bradley the most troubling aspect of the theory. Far more problematic, he believed, was the fact that associationism ultimately placed the force of reason – not in the nature of *things* – but in the contingent *mental habits* of individual subjects. Having declared that the contents of our experience are discrete and disconnected, the associationist is, according to Bradley, in possession of no real criterion according to which one factual inference may be seen as more appropriate – more *rational* – than another. Given that the contents of sensuous experience are seen by this theory as wholly discrete and radically pluralistic, the theory can identify, Bradley claimed, no criterion of rational inference other than the previously established inferential patterns (mental habits) within the minds of individual subjects. In other words, the standard of rationality for me can only be what I have previously been conditioned to believe. And, while I might momentarily question whether or not my most recent inference is 'correct' (in the sense of being consistent with the complete set of mental habits that comprise my idea of an objective universe), I am in possession of no criterion of truth which is deeper than what my prior (and wholly contingent) experience has accumulated. But since such an internal standard of 'rationality' is determined according to arbitrarily established associative habits (that is, habits which reflect the idiosyncratic subjective conditions under which each of us lives), there can come to be as many 'rationalities' as there are diverse, idiosyncratic experiences of the universe.[4] Each is as valid as the next, and none can lay greater claim to truth than any other.

I would add here that the radical subjectivism entailed by this theory may not be overcome by claiming that reality somehow 'causes' (in the long run) a 'convergence' of associations within the minds of all subjects.

---

[4] It may at this point be objected that there is a criterion of rationality which is being ignored here. One might argue that it is always the collective experience that provides the standard according to which my individual associations can be measured, and that the *community* of language users ultimately provides a criterion of rationality to which the individual is always subject. However, this objection fails to realize that any persuasive force that the community might be able to exert upon me can only exist if I have been conditioned to believe that collective opinion is more reliable than my own. And this belief is still wholly contingent upon my individual (and idiosyncratic) mental habits.

To appeal to the idea of 'causality' (something which the theory claims we have no given impression of and which is the mere projection of our individual mental habits) as the means by which all subjects might ultimately arrive at the same empirical knowledge is, Bradley argued, inconsistent. It is inconsistent because to appeal to what has been acknowledged as an arbitrarily established (and ultimately unjustifiable) mental habit as that which overcomes arbitrariness is to view causality in two different and mutually exclusive ways.

We may conclude our brief consideration of empiricist associationism, then, by saying that through its reduction of much of the structure of the experienced world to a series of mental habits within the minds of individual subjects, it radically subjectivizes the sinews and joints which the real universe seems (pre-theoretically) to possess. And, according to Bradley, once the presupposed unity of experience has been exploded by philosophical theory there is no way to put it back together. It is at that point, he believed, theoretically impossible for us to determine any real correspondence between the structure of the universe and the subjective representations of that universe within our individual experience. And with this move the empiricist associationist has undermined the possibility of a meaningful criterion by which we might order our inferences as 'good' and 'bad', 'right' and 'wrong', or 'better' and 'worse'.

II

I would now like to consider the attack made by the English idealists on what were sometimes referred to as 'formalist' theories of inference. The problem we immediately encounter, though, is that the object of attack seems ill-defined. And I say this because the epistemological interpretations of the different species of formal logic have themselves been many and varied; there just does not seem to be a single line of thought such as we find in empiricist accounts of inference. Still, while the criticisms that were made in works like Bradley's *Principles of Logic* and Bosanquet's *Logic or the Morphology of Knowledge* were largely directed at the book tradition of syllogism, both writers seemed to think that their principal complaint also applied to the new formalism as advocated by Russell and Whitehead (Bosanquet, 1911, vol. 2, pp. 40 ff. Also Bosanquet, 1920, pp. 147–56, and Bradley, 1914, pp. 288–309). And in what follows we do find, I believe, an objection that applies to both older and newer doctrines.

Now formal logic, according to both Bradley and Bosanquet, appears to have as its first concern the identification of patterns of inference and logical equivalences by which we may test the *grammatical* consistency of any argument. And, so long as the formalist confines himself to this activity, he is engaged in an activity that is not objectionable. However, when the formalist attempts to transform his principles of grammatical consistency into a larger philosophical theory – a theory which purports to provide an accurate account of our pre-theoretical reason – intellectual confusion, they claimed, is sure to follow.[5] But, why

---

[5] We must remember that when the idealist writers spoke of 'formalist theories of inference' they meant something very different than we generally do today. The idea of a formal system as an 'uninterpreted' language consisting of a logical alphabet and set of transformation rules they would have found incoherent. For them all talk of 'formal' systems entails the *interpretation* of such systems (both intended and unintended), and thus a philosophical theory.

would an enormously heuristic device like formal logic be seen as so problematic when carried over to the theory of knowledge?

There appear to be two complaints here: the first (and most easily understood) objection is made against formalism's claim that there exists a finite number of valid patterns of inference. This doctrine is objected to because it seemed to the idealists that there were many intuitively valid inferences that we could point to which do not conform to one of these formal patterns; and to condemn such inferences as *wholly* invalid struck them as unjustified. According to the idealist authors, the inferential transition between judgements was brought about by relations of *content* (and not mere form); and thus there could be no exhaustive 'list' of valid patterns of inference (Bosanquet, 1911, vol. 2, pp. 201–202. Bradley, 1922, pp. 268–71). This objection seems fairly clear cut and the basis of the complaint is not difficult to follow. However, the second problem I notice seems more obscure. It appears that the idealists want to challenge any claim on the part of formal logic to have established the 'objectivity' of its inference forms. While it will take some time to explicate this charge, the idealist authors argue that the formalist conception of logical implication is one which (like associationism) diverts the course of reason from direction by the structure of things – by the given contents of our experienced world. And, thus, when formalism's confused conception of logical implication (and its all-or-nothing doctrine of validity) is allowed to influence the theory of knowledge, we are forced to understand our actual deductive inferences either as the unpacking of merely conventional meanings or vacuous tautologies.

But in order to understand these charges let us

immediately turn our attention to the question of formal implication and validity. Since it is a fundamental assumption of virtually every species of formalism that one proposition is 'implied by' others only if it may be validly deduced from them, it is crucial to understand both how the formalist understands validity and how his position differs from that of the idealist.

Now, that there is such a thing as 'logical validity' is, of course, agreed to by all. However, whereas Bradley and Bosanquet see this relation as something which derives from the *entire* structure of premises and conclusion (including what is not explicitly stated), formalism believes that there is a logical form – an empty container, if you will – that is fundamentally different from the contents which fill it up. This is not to say that this logical form may exist in isolation from all content. Few have been willing to go this far. However, it does mean – on virtually every interpretation – that form is one thing and content another, such that *whatever* content we put into the form, when the appropriate relation between premises and conclusion obtains, we have a valid inference. But what is the 'appropriate relation' that would bring about such validity? Again, there seems to be agreement between both sides that validity (and hence implication) is comprised of a 'truth preserving' relation between premises and conclusion. That is, an argument is valid if and only if the truth of its premises guarantees the truth of its conclusion.

There arises at this point, however, an enormous difference between the formalist and idealist conceptions of validity and implication.[6] Although idealism

---

[6] Bradley's discussion of 'validity' – while implicitly discussed throughout

agrees that when we intuit the relation of validity between premises and conclusion we are apprehending a fundamental structural relation between them that – given true premises – will not allow the conclusion to be false, it rejects formalism's claim that such a relation may hold between a set of premises and conclusion that contains a member which could not possibly be true. In short, while idealism wholly embraces the notion of logical validity, it rejects formalism's absolute differentiation between validity and soundness. But let us consider why this fundamental component within formalist accounts of inference is repudiated.

To begin, we should note that Bradley and Bosanquet see the formalist's rigid distinction between form and content as one that is not only metaphysically unjustified but utterly misleading when we try to apply it to actual inferences. They argue that, if it were the case that *any* content could be put into the shell of a valid argument form (let us say, a syllogism in Barbara), then there really does not exist any relation of implication between the *content* of the premises and the *content* of the conclusion. Or to put the matter somewhat differently, if form and content are *really* external to one another, then when we recognize that one proposition can be legitimately inferred from another (or others) what is being seen as following from or implied by the *form* of the premises is not the *content* of the conclusion, but only *its* form. In order that we recognize that both the form *and* content of the conclusion stand in the relation of validity to the premises we must be sure that the contents we put into

his *Principles* – is the explicit topic in the last two chapters (cf. Bradley, 1922, pp. 561–95; cf. also pp. 597–621, and pp. 695–8). Perhaps the most direct account by Bosanquet is to be found in Bosanquet, 1883; cf. pp. 69–73; also cf. Bosanquet, 1922, especially pp. 70–104.

the 'place holders' of a valid argument form may legitimately reside there. And *this, it was argued, is almost
always an open question*. Thus, it was claimed that, in
its zeal for certainty, formalism attempts to know *in
advance* of any thorough understanding of the
meanings of our propositions whether they actually can
stand in the relation of pure logical implication
(Bradley, 1922, pp. 521–34; also Bosanquet, 1920, pp.
162–5). However, according to the idealists, it is only
at the *end* of the road travelled by material knowledge
that the relations of implication between various judgements can be known. But let me illustrate these difficulties with some examples.

Let us consider the following syllogism: 'All hairy
bipeds are great philosophers'; 'Bonzo the chimpanzee
is a hairy biped'; 'Bonzo the chimpanzee is a great
philosopher'. Here we have a clearly valid but (equally
clearly) unsound argument. And the argument is valid,
we are told – not because it asserts either that the
premises or conclusion *are* true (or even that they ever
could be true) – it is valid only because it claims that *if*
the premises are true then the conclusion must be true
as well; or again, it is valid because it is 'truth
preserving'. But what do the idealists have to say about
such an interpretation?

The essence of their complaint seems to be this: while
it is true that validity is a relation of 'truth preservation', such an argument cannot be valid because there
are members of the set of propositions comprising the
argument that *cannot possibly be true* (at least in the
sense required). And what we, in fact, apprehend here
as constituting the relation of validity between premises
and conclusion is something very different from what
the 'substitution instance' suggests. It is claimed that

what we *really* apprehend in our intuitive grasp of the validity of this argument form is a structural interpenetration of contents taken from *other* judgements – judgements whose contents are now being suppressed and replaced by the contents of the present assertions (Bosanquet, 1883, pp. 70–73; and Joseph, 1916, pp. 331–3; also pp. 370–71). And further, we are told that it is only because of our own *incomplete knowledge* of the meaning of the contents of the propositions now before us that we could entertain for a moment the possibility that this could be a valid substitution instance for the form in which it is placed.

Now, let us follow out this point by considering some aspects of our knowledge of implication and validity. We must remember that in order to understand that an argument is valid we must be able to test it for validity. And according to the English idealists, to undertake this test (at least with any actual judgements we might make) we must be able to first think of a situation in which the premises are (or could be) true; and second we must carry through this experiment to see if there is anyway that the conclusion could – in light of the true premises – still be false. However, we are also told that certain premises cannot really take part in such a test; and this because, even when considered in a purely hypothetical fashion, there are some premises that cannot possibly be true. For example, if one of my premises is 'All hairy bipeds both are and are not great philosophers' I have before me a *contradiction*; and since a contradiction is necessarily false (and ultimately unthinkable) then I know that it cannot be truth preserving – it has no truth to preserve (Bradley, 1914, pp. 219–44; also Bosanquet, 1912, pp. 223–34; and Joseph, 1916, p. 13). Indeed, it was claimed, any premise that cannot be true has no capacity to imply anything.[7]   And further, it was argued, not only is the openly contradictory premise incapable of implicatory force, so too is the proposition that ascribes *contrary* predicates to a subject which is incapable of accepting them. But let me attempt to explain this point.

Even the most committed formalist recognizes that – if we are to interpret a formal language at all – we must, to some degree, be sensitive to the contents of our assertions.   And this because many contents present themselves – even on their minimal interpretation – as *logically exclusive predicates*. While it is clear that I may ascribe to the same subject (at the same time) properties like 'is old' and 'is happy', it is equally clear that this may not be done with properties such as 'is red all over at time T_1' and 'is blue all over at time T_1'. We could, of course, multiply examples here indefinitely. However, according to both Bradley and Bosanquet, the real difficulty that needs to be confronted is that we must be able to understand the degree to which contrariety (which on their view disrupts validity) may be present within any of our assertions.

The problem that is raised here is, I suggest, far more serious than it might appear at first glance. Although we might all agree that an assertion like 'An object is both red all over at time T_1 and blue all over at time T_1' contains logically exclusive terms (and is thus 'necessarily false') what about 'Canada is south of the United States' or 'A chimpanzee is a great philosopher'? Can we with any real confidence claim that there exists a 'possible world' – a world of 'thought' if not fact – in which these conditions may without contradiction or

---

[7]   Of course, one may certainly devise a formal *algorithm* in such a way that necessary falsehood does not preclude a narrowly conceived formal validity (cf. Langford and Lewis, 1959, pp. 235–62, and pp. 438–85).

contrariety stand alongside one another so as to be true of some state of affairs? I suspect that in the case of these last two propositions there are some who would answer 'Yes, so long as we know that there is no essential property of the grammatical subject that stands in the relation of contradiction or contrariety to an essential property of the grammatical predicate'. But, even if we are willing to accept as intelligible the metaphysics of essential and accidental properties, we are still faced with the problem of ascertaining what are and are not the essential properties of the various phenomena we apprehend in our assertions. And this, it was argued, is something that can only be progressively (and never perfectly) determined.

I would summarize the idealist criticism here as follows: It is impossible to know that an argument is perfectly valid based solely upon its form. We must also know that the contents we assert as standing in these (purportedly) pure formal relations can, in fact, legitimately do so. And, unless we are willing to embrace a thoroughgoing conventionalism about our thought and language (or *per impossibile* have surveyed every instance of the phenomena in question), the *full* meanings of our terms (and their ultimate logical status) must remain unknown. While we might at first believe that certain ideas can coexist within meaningful propositions, a deeper analysis of our meaning sometimes shows that this is not the case. That is, if we really think through the meanings of our terms we might find that we have on our hands predicates which – at some stage of development in our thought – openly repel one another and refuse to be combined in the manner which the argument form suggests. Thus, it was claimed, there is no possible way that a formal theory of impli cation can do what it claims. A knowledge of complete validity demands a thorough appropriation of meaning; however, meaning is something that is not created by us; it must be progressively *discovered* through the unfolding of experience. And short of a complete discovery of this intensional content, the perfectly valid inference must remain elusive.[8]

Now, there are a number of ways in which the formalist may defend his conception of validity and implication here. However, I shall mention but a few, and these only in outline.

The first way in which one may deflect the idealist attack here is just to embrace a thoroughgoing conventionalism; that is, one may claim that there are no 'deep' and 'hidden' meanings which we must discover in order to grasp the 'true' logical compatibility between predicates in any proposition. It might be claimed that we need only make ourselves aware of what we have collectively *agreed to* (something reflected in our ordinary linguistic practice) and the problem is solved. This is, of course, a very simple statement of what can be a rather complex position. However, to respond in this fashion is, I suggest, just to concede the point at issue. According to the English idealists, if it were true that we merely *create* (rather than discover) what it means for something to be a 'chimpanzee' or a 'philosopher' or 'Canada' then, the idea of an *objective* criterion of rationality to which we are all subject *is* blown to the winds, and we must be willing to live with all that such a view entails.

---

[8] For the idealists *all* terms have both intension and extension; there just are no 'purely referring terms'. I have discussed this point in Ferreira, 1996a; cf. also, Bosanquet, 1911, vol. 1, pp. 47–62; and Bradley, 1922, pp. 59–63, pp. 168–84; and pp. 642–6).

Another response that might be made is that which appeals to 'possible worlds parables'.[9] For example, it might be claimed that, even if idealism is right in its claim that necessarily false propositions can imply nothing, there is still a way by which we can test for validity without appeal to the contingent domain of meaning which we encounter in this the 'actual world'. It has been argued that we may know specific propositions to be valid substitution instances of an argument form if we can think of a 'possible world' in which these things – the contents as asserted by premises and conclusion – could be true. Now, there is one sense in which Bradley and Bosanquet completely agree with this statement; they too would claim that it is only through an act of thought that we can discover relations of implication and validity. However, I think that the contemporary understanding of what it means to 'think of a possible world' is quite different from what the idealists had in mind. And, while Bradley and Bosanquet never commented on the possible worlds idiom, their response (given what they *did* say about the relation between mental images and logical ideas) would be obvious.

What the advocate of 'possible world parables' most often means by 'think' here is really *imagine*. That is, he takes it as a test of logical possibility that we can mentally *picture* certain things as taking place. And, while it certainly is true that I can picture a chimpanzee writing a brilliant commentary on the *Critique of Pure Reason*, or imagine driving north through the snow-fields of Canada's Northwest Territories only to eventually come to the arid deserts of southern Arizona,

---

[9] For a discussion of this sort of validity testing see Bradley and Swartz, 1979, pp. 121–7.

to pictorially imagine something is not the same thing as to actually *think* it. And, according to the idealists, to make the activity of mental picturing the arbiter of logical truth is not only to confuse the psychical image with the logical idea, it is to cast doubt upon the existence of an objective criterion of rationality in a fashion which is, perhaps, even more extreme than that of the avowed conventionalist.

The last objection I would consider here is, perhaps, the one that would most commonly be made. Here we might imagine a defender of the formal validity–soundness distinction as saying something like the following:

All of this talk about the 'meanings' of our terms is nonsense. While these objections might apply to syllogistic logic, they don't touch us today because our logic is wholly *extensional*. We don't care about meanings (at least in your sense); we only care about the truth and falsity of our propositions; and we say this because *all* of the essential logical apparatus can be accounted for in this manner. And further, the only lesson that formal logic has for the theory of knowledge is this: if you *assume* the truth of certain things, then what you have assumed may be legitimately *restated* in certain other ways. The idealist 'logic' which you describe conflates induction and deduction and thus fails to grasp the very elementary point we are trying to make; and that is simply that, whatever is said in the conclusion of any valid argument has *already been said* in the premises. (And we can make any conclusion follow from our premises so long as we are willing to assume enough in them.) Our inferred conclusion is nothing more than a *tautological* restatement which is utterly nonproblematic so long as we do not violate the basic rules governing the transformation of one way of saying something into another. Hence, all of these 'objections' you raise are really much ado about nothing.

Now, there are various responses that can be made to this account of implication. However, given space limitations, I shall mention only two which, while not as fully articulated by Bradley and Bosanquet as by later writers, are present in their work nevertheless (Bosanquet, 1902, pp. 166 ff).

First, it might be said, that modern formalism's claim to have articulated a wholly 'extensional' logic by focusing only on truth and falsity is quite mistaken. Such a concentration does not avoid meaning or intension; it just focuses on one *aspect* of intension while avoiding the rest. And, while this manoeuvre may allow modern logic to evade some of the problems the idealists raised, its philosophical 'victory' here has been purchased only at the cost of trivializing its conception of logical implication. Through its almost complete suppression of intension it has destroyed the threads of *relevancy* between propositions such that it is forced to see as 'logically equivalent' expressions like 'If there is fire then there is heat' and 'If 2+2=5, then Eliot was a better poet than Joyce'.[10] In addition to this, its insistence on an absolute deductive–inductive distinction has made its logic inapplicable to the world of fact. As Mill pointed out, deductive inference on

---

[10] This criticism was explicitly and forcefully made by H. W. B. Joseph and Brand Blanshard (cf. for example, Blanshard, 1962, pp. 157–63. And Blanshard, 1939, vol. 2, pp. 374–87. Cf. also Joseph, 1916, pp. 96–7; Joseph, 1932, pp. 430 ff; Joseph, 1933, pp. 435 ff; Joseph, 1934, pp. 318 ff. For a somewhat different view see Harris, 1987, pp. 23–47).

such an interpretation becomes either the articulation of a *petitio principii* or a report on linguistic convention, with the *true* burden of human reason being thrown back onto induction. But recognizing that the theory of pure inductive inference was hardly in better shape, Bradley and Bosanquet were forced to ask 'Has the theory of knowledge been aided by such a logic?'

Certainly they did not think so (Bosanquet, 1920, pp. 31–69, especially pp. 45–50). Not only on this view are our deductive inferences reduced to mere restatements of what we (in some sense) already know, but our inductive inferences are (once more) reduced to the expression of subjective mental habits. What is really required, they claimed, is that we seriously reflect upon the conditions of intelligible discourse. And if we undertake this task we shall come to some very different conclusions about the possibility of perfect validity and pure a priori inference (Bosanquet, 1911, vol. 2, pp. 226–30).

III

While my purpose in this paper has only been to indicate the sense in which Bradley and Bosanquet saw the complete separation of inductive and deductive inference as leading to indefensible views in the theory of knowledge, something more, I think, must be said about their positive doctrine. And, while space limitations demand that I be brief, I think that the following comments might help to clarify some of the criticisms already considered.

If we are to understand the positive doctrine of inference that developed in the works of Bradley and Bosanquet we must always bear in mind that they rejected entirely the starting point of both empiricism and formalism. For both of these writers, experience began – not with the apprehension of a given manifold of diverse and disconnected sense particulars (or externally related objects) – but with a felt unity of experience. To be sure, this original unity contains sensuous differences. However, these differences are not (at least not at first) fully distinct and specific. Sensuous immediacy, on their view, does not provide us with the fully determined particular; rather, it presents contents which begin to show their particularity and individuality only as they are brought into fuller and more complete relations with one another. That is, only so far as I can take the experience that is before me at any one moment and see it within the context of my larger experience does the specificity that I assume characterizes that given moment actually become consciously grasped. We should therefore realize that, for the idealists, to consciously apprehend objects (at all) is to have judged. It is to have said (implicitly at least) 'Reality is such that...S is P'. Or put otherwise, to judge is to locate within the totality of experience the precise place held by the contents of my present awareness.

The key word here, though, is 'context'. According to the idealist doctrine of judgement and inference our assertions (which are usually far more complex than the superficial grammatical form shows) are capable of exhibiting to varying degrees their place within the system of experience. And this they do by progressively developing within themselves their systematic relations to other judgements (Bosanquet, 1920, pp. 4–20; and Bosanquet, 1911, vol. 2, pp. 185–207. Bradley, 1922, pp. 470–501, and pp. 597–601). Some judgements exhibit this systematicity only to a slight degree; others so deeply implicate themselves within our larger experience that we cannot consistently think them as false. And, for both Bradley and Bosanquet, the activity of inference (both deductive and inductive) was understood as just that transition within our experience by which a judgement, previously seen in (relative) isolation, becomes contextualized within this larger whole.

But let me provide a brief example by which these ideas might be made clearer. If while walking in the woods near my home I spot a tree which I recognize as *cornus florida,* the flowering dogwood, I might, indeed, judge 'This tree is a flowering dogwood'. It is important to notice, though, that when I so judge there are really two things before me. First, there is the explicit judgement (the proposition as asserted), and second there is the *context* out of which it is taken. In other words, in addition to what is being overtly asserted, there is always an assumed world from which my judgement, so to speak, 'hangs'. And in so hanging from my world the explicit assertion sets into motion reverberations along the lines of its content. For example, both 'this tree' and 'flowering dogwood' have within my experience a deeper meaning than I initially apprehend. And after making my original judgement these deeper aspects of meaning begin to come to light. For example, it could be that in allowing the deeper significance of my original terms to rise into my awareness, I encounter the following idea attaching itself to the larger meaning of 'flowering dogwood': 'The flowering dogwood is indigenous to the north-eastern US.' That is, through my desire to understand how my first judgement related to the real world which is its condition, I search my experience for the fuller meaning of my terms. And, in this case, I recall something I had learned years before.

Now, we may certainly treat this new proposition as a second 'premise' in a chain of argument; however, we should be aware that I am really only elaborating and expanding one of the ideas (flowering dogwood) that comprised my original judgement. I would also point out that, while there has already been a transition in knowledge which has set the stage for the fuller determination of my original assertion, any inference is still only implicit. And it is only with my next thought that I will have actually made the process explicit and thereby made the inferential transition complete. That is, through the apprehension of the expanded meaning of my original judgement (which we may understand as having taken the form of a second premise) I suddenly *see* something which – while there all along – I had not yet noticed. In now asserting 'This tree is indigenous to the northeast US' I have explicitly related my original assertion to the reality which conditions it and I have thus inferred. Or to restate this matter in much simpler terms, through allowing the implicit (and ultimately inexhaustible) meaning of the terms with which I began to come into my consciousness I have *contextualized* this judgement in a manner whereby I more fully and concretely apprehend the significance of the terms of my premises.[11] And while there are many fine points we

---

[11] It must be noted here that there is, according to the idealists, not only conceptual continuity in any actual inference, there is also genuine novelty. All of the terms as they were originally apprehended in my premises have been *altered* so as to exhibit relations that were not at all present (at least in the subject's understanding) before the inferential transition (eg., Bradley, 1922, pp. 434–7. Also, Bosanquet, 1920, pp. 24–30).

may add to the theory, this is really the crux of the doctrine.

The important point behind the theory of 'degrees of validity' and 'degrees of truth' seems, then, to be this: *So far as* I can ground any judgement within the structure of experience as a whole, I am in possession of a *valid* inference and a *true* judgement. And, while every inference is capable of a fuller grounding and deeper contextualization within the system of experience, we must recognize that not all judgements are equal. The least valuable inferences, (in the sense of being the least valid and least true), are those which – because of their relative isolation within the larger system – show themselves as easily falsified. Hence, what we ordinarily consider 'contingent assertions' are really, on this theory, judgements whose logical ground remains (relatively) external to the judgement itself. Given one set of conditions such a judgement is in harmony with the real; given a different set, its truth is blown to the winds (Bradley, 1893, pp. 320–24; also Bradley, 1922, pp. 555–7).

Our most valuable inferences, on the other hand, are those which, through exhibiting their place within the entire system of experience, have become 'stabilized' and hence are (relatively) immune from falsification. The more contextualized a judgement is the more we find that judgement 'locked-in' to the larger system (and progressively approaching 'timelessness' in its truth). Indeed, as we progress up the ladder of validity we see our assertions becoming so stable that (at the top anyway) they are understood as 'necessarily true'. But they are 'necessarily true' *not* because they are tauto-logical restatements of what our premises already explicitly contained (on the contrary); the highest of these judgements may be understood as 'necessarily true' because, in being so deeply implicated by the larger system of experience, any effort to deny them would simultaneously deny the very basis upon which the denial has been put forth – the system as a whole. And while there is always a degree to which our apprehension of the relation of such a judgement to the complete system may be deepened, such assertions are (when seen as so demanded by their conditions) as close to perfect validity (and absolute truth) as we can get.

We must bear in mind, though, that as finite beings our inferences always fall short of exhibiting their *complete* ground; thus there will always be a degree of *in*validity (and *un*truth) which infects them and from which they cannot escape. Since we can never know the *full* manner in which our terms relate (both to one another and the reality which conditions them), there is always the possibility that the larger reality within which they are made will betray them as incapable of maintaining themselves as they are presently understood (Bradley, 1914, pp. 256 ff).

I would conclude my brief discussion of the positive vision of inference that was developed by Bradley and Bosanquet, then, by emphasizing the following points: to infer was for these writers just to take a judgement and exhibit its ground; that is, we infer when we take the contents of any assertion and make them less abstract through a process of progressive contextualization which is both deductive and inductive, analytic and synthetic at once. Our inferences are analytic (and deductive) in the sense that they are engaged in the perpetual 'unpacking' of the meanings of the experienced contents of our world. And these same inferences are synthetic (and inductive) in that they bring to

the light of conscious awareness the bonds of identity –
the organizational principles – which hold together the
differences which our analyses have made apparent
(Bradley, 1922, pp. 471–86. Bosanquet, 1911, vol. 2,
pp. 91–6). And while one aspect or the other may be
dominant in any assertion, both are present in all our
inferences.

These are, of course, difficult and controversial ideas
that require a much fuller explication than I can provide
in such a limited space. However, I hope that it is clear
from this discussion that the idealist doctrine of
inference at least *purports* to have found a middle
ground between the extremes which contemporary
philosophy persistently places before us. For example,
while idealism agrees with the anti-foundationalist
when he repudiates the idea of privileged viewpoints
from which a completed knowledge may be had, and
while this same idealism applauds the rejection of
theory-neutral 'givens' that can (so the foundationalist
claims) provide us with indubitable knowledge, it is the
lesson of the idealist doctrine of inference that there *is*
yet such a thing as higher and lower and better or worse
when it comes to our knowledge of both fact and value.
(And here the idealist sides with the foundationalist.) It
was the continual claim of both Bradley and Bosanquet
that, just because all knowledge is less than perfectly
true does not mean that it contains no truth at all. And
just because all knowledge is condemned to perpetual
revision and reformulation does not mean that some
formulations are not better – are not more *objective* –
than others. And if there is only one lesson that we
might learn from an extended encounter with the
English idealists and their doctrine of inference it is that
there are, indeed, many more theoretical choices open

to us than the recent debate would suggest.

REFERENCES

Brand Blanshard, *The Nature of Thought*, 2 vols (London: Macmillan, 1939).

————, *Reason and Analysis* (LaSalle: Open Court, 1962).

Bernard Bosanquet, 'Logic as the Science of Knowledge', in Haldane and Seth (eds.), *Essays in Philosophical Criticism* (London: Longman and Green, 1883).

————, *Logic or the Morphology of Knowledge*, 2nd edn, 2 vols (Oxford: Clarendon Press, 1911).

————, *The Principle of Individuality and Value* (London: Macmillan, 1912).

————, *Implication and Linear Inference* (London: Macmillan, 1920).

F. H. Bradley, *Appearance and Reality*, 2nd edn (Oxford: Clarendon Press, 1897).

————, *Essays on Truth and Reality* (Oxford: Clarendon Press, 1914).

—————— , *The Principles of Logic*, 2nd edn, 2 vols (Oxford: Oxford University Press, 1922).

—————— , *Collected Essays* (Oxford: Oxford University Press, 1935).

Raymond Bradley and Norman Swartz, *Possible Worlds* (Indianapolis: Hackett, 1979).

Phillip Ferreira, 'Bradley on the Intension and the Extension of Terms', in W. J. Mander (ed.), *Perspectives on the Logic and Metaphysics of F. H. Bradley* (Bristol: Thoemmes Press, 1996a).

—————— , 'Bradley's Attack on Associationism', in James Bradley (ed.), *Philosophy After F. H. Bradley* (forthcoming Bristol: Thoemmes Press, 1996b).

H. W. B. Joseph, *An Introduction to Logic*, 2nd edn (Oxford: Clarendon Press, 1916).

—————— , 'A Defence of Free Thinking in Logistics', *Mind*, vol. 41 (1932), pp. 424–40.
—————— , 'A Defence of Free Thinking in Logistics Resumed', *Mind*, vol. 42 (1933), pp. 417–43.
—————— , 'A Last Plea for Free Thinking in Logistics', *Mind*, vol. 43 (1934), pp. 315–20.

C. H. Langford and C. I. Lewis, *Symbolic Logic*, 2nd edn (New York: Dover, 1959).

John Stuart Mill, *Collected Works*, vol. 9 (Toronto: University of Toronto Press, 1979).

IDEALISM, HUMANISM AND THE ENVIRONMENT

T. L. S. Sprigge

I

Ethical Humanism
The word 'humanism' has had several different meanings in its day. At present it tends to refer to a commitment to an ethic and philosophy of life based on considerations of human welfare rather than religion. However, for present purposes I wish to use it in a somewhat different sense. In fact, I shall distinguish two main types of humanism, ethical humanism and metaphysical humanism, and consider how they are related to each other and each to idealism.

By 'ethical humanism' I shall refer in the first place to the view that the sole thing which really matters in the world, so far at least as anything we can affect goes, is the quality of human life. Such humanism may be classically utilitarian and hold that the one thing which counts in favour of an action or practice is that it favours human happiness and the one thing which counts against an action is that it has adverse effects on human happiness.[1] However, 'ethical humanism'

---

[1] 'Happiness' and 'unhappiness' being somehow defined in terms of pleasure and pain. Difficulties in finding the best formulation of this hedonistic utilitarian point of view need not concern us; we all know the general type of view I have in mind.

covers all other types of ethic and general outlooks on life for which all that ultimately matters is the character of human life. Thus an ethic for which the one thing which really matters positively is the promotion of human self-realization or excellence, however these are understood, is, in my sense, a form of ethical humanism as also doubtless are various forms of what have been called virtue ethics. The one thing which makes an outlook a form of ethical humanism is that nothing really matters for it except the type of life enjoyed, or activities engaged in, by human beings.

However, I want the term to cover rather more than this. First, I would call 'ethically humanist' a view which thinks that there is nothing that matters nearly so much as features of human life, so that other things only have a quite minimal importance compared with it. Thus I should count as a form of ethical humanism any view which allows that, other things being pretty well equal, so far as effects on humans go, we should favour practices which don't cause animal pain, but which insists that, in real conflicts between animal and human welfare, human interests, except perhaps of the most negligible kind, should always outweigh the animal ones, and that, with this slight qualification regarding animals, effects on human welfare are the only determinants of right and wrong.

A more important addition to the extension of the term 'ethical humanism', as I shall use it, will allow it to apply to certain forms of theism. According to what I shall call theistic ethical humanism God has made the world entirely or almost entirely as a scene in which the human drama may unfold itself; consequently our duties are solely to other human beings, to ourselves, and to God Himself. As to the last it may impose duties towards God, such as that of appropriately worshipping him and loving Him, but for my purposes we will still be in the realm of ethical humanism if our duties towards God do not imply any duties towards the non-human creation, except as means to the realization of the right kind of human value.

Clearly such theistic ethical humanism can and does take various alternative forms. But they are united by the fact that what makes an action wrong is *either* its adverse effects on oneself as a moral being *or* the lack of appropriate concern it shows for other humans *or* that it offends God, which, for the most part, will be because of its failure to respect one's own intrinsic worth as a human being or that of other human beings. In short, theistic ethical humanism, unlike secular ethical humanism, doesn't limit what matters to facts about human beings, for God is what matters supremely, but since God's purposes, so far as we need to know them, concern what happens in human life, (including perhaps appropriate worship of Himself), the position may be described as a form of ethical humanism. Here again, we may extend our concept somewhat by allowing as a form of qualified theistic ethical humanism a view which regards our divinely ordained duty as enormously much more dictated by the requirement of proper respect for the intrinsic value of human beings, and perhaps especially ourselves as human beings, than of concern for the value of anything else, except God Himself.

For the sake of completeness I should perhaps add that, for my present purposes, an outlook will be one of ethical humanism if to God are added other super-natural beings, as for example, the Virgin Mary, conceived as still now existing, to whom we have duties apart from those to human beings, towards ourselves, or to God as such. Likewise polytheistic religions will be teaching a humanistic ethic, if they require either *no* or *minimal* concern with what happens in the non-human natural world, except insofar as it affects human interests, including therein their right relations to the gods.

II

Nonhumanism:
(A) Animal Rights; (B) Deep Environmental Ethics
There are two main points of view which challenge ethical humanism understood in the very broad sense I have attempted to explain. First, there is the philosophy of animal rights, or other outlooks which, without talking about animal rights, or perhaps rights at all, seek to give animals a much higher moral status than does any form of ethical humanism. For convenience, I shall call all such positions 'philosophies of animal rights', even though some main proponents of the type of position to which I am referring, for example Peter Singer, avoid the term 'rights'.[2]

The second point of view which challenges ethical humanism is what I shall call 'deep environmentalism'. This expression was first introduced into philosophy by Arne Naess together with the contrary expression 'shallow environmentalism' (Naess, 1973, pp. 95–100). To be more accurate, Naess worded the contrast as

---

[2] It is a more suitable expression than 'animal liberation' because that is a demand for change in the status quo, and therefore an outlook which would cease if its ideal were achieved, whereas a belief in animal rights, like a belief in human rights, will still have point, however successfully the required reforms are reached, as labelling one of the ideals on which society will then be successfully based.

between 'the deep long-range ecology movement' and 'the shallow ecological movement', but 'deep ecology' has acquired a more limited meaning than suits my purposes.)[3] Both ethical positions were concerned with conservation and preservation of much of wild and semi-wild nature, and with the prevention of various types of pollution. But the shallow environmentalist is concerned with these matters solely because he sees dangers to human welfare in the extinction of too many species, in the lack of recreational space, the exhaustion of the resources needed for modern civilization, and in the threat to the natural infra-structure of healthy human life. In contrast, the deep environmentalist is concerned, not only with such matters, but also with the threat to aspects of Nature which matter in themselves, not only for humans. This will doubtless include the concerns with animal welfare promoted by the philosophy of animal rights. But it also concerns itself with the conservation of areas and aspects of wild and semi-wild nature, (because wild humanly untamed nature is the home of intrinsic values which do not consist in their use, even their recreational use, or their imaginative or aesthetic appeal, to human beings) and to the preservation of species, animal or plant (both because each species has its own particular kind of intrinsic value, and because it makes its own contribution to the total eco-system of life on earth, which has a value quite independently of the needs of individual humans or animals).

---

[3] Apparently in current environmental ethics circles, 'deep ecology' now tends to refer to that form of deep environmentalism for which the proper attitude to nature only arises when we think of the natural environment on which we depend as a continuation of our own bodies, so that in a rather mystical way we come to regard the whole of Nature as our own body.

There are various forms of deep environmentalism, some more individualist, some more collectivist or holistic, some associated with one meta-ethic, some with another, but I do not have space, nor is it necessary here, to distinguish the different types. Holmes Rolston III provides a main statement of the type of ethics I have in mind (Rolston, 1988: see also Appendix B).[4]

What all deep environmentalists, as I understand the term, have in common is that they hold that there are intrinsic values in Nature, which we have a moral obligation to take into account, quite apart from, or rather in addition to, and as sometimes qualifying, the interests of individual humans or individual animals or any one species, such as our own. There is, doubtless, some impressionistic vagueness as to the precise sense and reference of the word 'Nature' here, but we may take it roughly as referring to the non-human physical world in those parts and aspects of it least, or not at all, interfered with by man, the object of moral concern being in particular those parts and features of the earth which are least humanized, and at most risk of being so.

I shall use the term 'nonhumanism' for the inclusive disjunction of animal rights philosophy and deep environmentalism. That is, the nonhumanist rejects the claim that all that really matters, or matters to more than a very negligible extent, is human welfare or excellence, or some other value realized only in human life, either because he thinks that what happens to sentient animals matters a great deal or because he thinks that what happens in nature, quite apart from the quality of the lives of humans and animals, matters a great deal, or because he holds both. It would be a bad mistake, of

---

[4] For a somewhat different form of deep environmentalism see Taylor, 1986.

course, to suppose that nonhumanism discounts the claims of human welfare or excellence; it only objects to an excessive prioritizing of these. What nonhumanism is against is not human beings but ethical humanism as I have described it. Nonhumanism based on animal rights claims is fairly different from nonhumanism based on deep environmentalism, and the claims of the two can enter into prima facie conflict, but a synthesis of them is surely possible, and in fact those sympathetic to the one do tend to be sympathetic to the other.

Now the point of all this laborious talk about ethical humanism and nonhumanism in a paper on idealism is that there is a strong inclination to suppose that philosophical idealism implies a solely humanistic ethics and that this, which I shall argue is mistaken, affects some people's attitudes to idealism. In particular those with any sympathy either with animal rights or deep environmentalism, especially the latter, are often inclined to see idealism as their humanistic enemy.

This may partly spring from knowledge of the actual ethical outlook of some idealists, but it probably springs more from what is assumed to be the only possible ethical position for an idealist. This is because idealism is likely to be associated with a form of humanism, distinct from ethical humanism, namely metaphysical humanism, and it is assumed, not unreasonably, that metaphysical humanism implies ethical humanism.

III

Metaphysical Humanism

Various kindred doctrines are meant to be covered by the expression 'metaphysical humanism'. Of these the simplest is the thesis that nothing actually exists except streams of human experience and that all factual truths either assert something about such actual streams or about what would occur in such a stream as a result of something else occurring in the same or another stream. However, I should also include under the heading of metaphysical humanism various views which supplement what may seem the rather meagre ontology of such a simple form of humanism by including one or more of the following: (1) human minds, regarded as something distinct from their experiences; (2) mental acts, regarded as something additional to mere experiences, and (3) the contents and internal objects of human experiences and mental acts as something distinct from the acts or experiences themselves. However, for simplicity I shall take these as all covered by such expressions as 'human experience' or 'human minds and their experiences'.

Metaphysical humanism is likely also to be enriched by including in the realm of factual truth not just categorical propositions about the existence and character of such mental things but also various hypothetical or subjunctive conditional propositions whose antecedents and consequents would concern nothing else. Even so, there will be no actuality except human experience.

There are some further ways in which I shall enlarge the extension of the term 'metaphysical humanism'.

(i) I shall classify as a qualified metaphysical humanist a philosopher who holds that, although there may be, perhaps must be, things-in-themselves other than human minds and their experiences, nothing is knowable about them except that they are the otherwise unknowable determinants of these.

(ii) Likewise I shall regard a philosopher as a qualified

metaphysical humanist if he thinks that all factual truth concerns minds and their experiences and suggests that if there are any other minds, truths about them are of negligible importance, not just ethically, but for the internal purposes of human knowledge.

(iii) I shall regard a philosopher as an implicit metaphysical humanist if, in his account of factual truth, he seems virtually to forget about the possible existence of anything other than human minds and their experiences, if, for example, he reduces everything to minds and their experiences and implicitly always seems to assume that all minds are human.

(iv) Finally, I shall call a philosopher a metaphysical humanist if he believes that nothing exists except human minds and their experiences, except a cosmic ego whose life is lived through human minds (possibly experiencing them in a unity denied to each human mind taken separately). I may anticipate my discussion of how idealism of various types stands to humanism by the suggestion in advance that Fichte and Croce, and some would say Hegel, approximated to metaphysical humanism of what we might call this absolute type.

Objections to metaphysical humanism may be of two types.

First, there are those who object to it on the basis of what they regard as the common sense belief that there are many things beside minds and their experiences, in particular the physical world and all that it contains, which are neither minds nor their experiences, nor their merely internal objects.

But there is a second group who may go along with the idealist claim that nothing exists but minds and their experiences, but who believe it a mistake to suppose or imply that all minds are human. Such other minds might be supernatural minds, but the minds most relevant to the concerns of this talk are animal minds.

Now we need some term for a philosophy which would replace human by 'animal-or-human' wherever metaphysical humanism says 'human'. It is difficult to find a suitable term for this, because to speak of such systems as metaphysically 'animalist' makes them sound much more heartily physical in their ontology than they are. Expressions which suggest themselves are 'persons', 'selves' and 'subjects' but each of these has inconveniences which I shall not tire the reader with listing. I shall therefore give a radical switch to the normal meaning of the word 'vitalism' and call such theories metaphysically vitalist since they hold that nothing exists except the minds of living creatures and their experiences.[5] For my purposes it does not matter whether or not some plants are allowed to have experiences by such a theorist; the claim is not that everything in the phenomenal world commonly regarded as living has experiences which go to fill up reality as it truly is, only that reality has no ingredients which are not of this type. Thus a panpsychist, for whom reality is made up, not just of the experiences of individuals commonly recognized as living, but also of experiences pertaining to individuals commonly regarded by Western twentieth-century man as inanimate, is not a metaphysical vitalist in my sense.

[5] If a faint association with Bergson is suggested by the use of this word, that is not altogether inappropriate, since Bergson, while having an essentially experientalist orientation, certainly did not have a humanistic one. Thus he explicitly complained that too many philosophical systems 'appear as though existing in a world where "neither plants nor animals have existence, only men"' (Mullarkey, 1993). See Bergson, 1959, p. 1253, also p. 1292 and p. 1425. However Bergson's position is close to panpsychism and therefore not a form of vitalism as I am understanding it.

But what of supernatural beings, such as angels and devils? Can these be among the living beings whose experiences make up reality for the vitalist? It will be convenient to bring them in under this umbrella because the minds of such creatures are conceived of as pretty similar to those of humans or animals. But what of God? I shall regard Him also as living in a relevant sense if, and only if, He is conceived of as an individual with His own stream of consciousness.

Before going any further I should just like to mention a more exotic ground on which each of metaphysical humanism and vitalism might be challenged, namely on the ground that existence of a kind pertains to various so-called abstract objects, or also or instead cultural objects such as those Karl Popper ascribed to a third world, which can exist, whether they are experienced or not. However, if these are the only things a philosopher allows to exist besides the experiences of living beings I shall count him or her as a metaphysical humanist too. For I am concerned mainly with theories as to what exists concretely, in a way in which such objects are not supposed to do even by their proponents. However, we shall see shortly that forms of humanism and vitalism which allow for such non-concrete objects do have some extra resources for countering certain ethically motivated objections to them.

Returning to my main line of thought I now point out that of our two types of nonhumanist the concerns of the animal rightist are not threatened by an idealism which is vitalist rather than humanist, while the concerns of the deep environmentalist are not assuaged by the counting in of animal along with human experience. It is very likely that most animal rightists are not vitalists, but since metaphysical vitalism takes animal minds and their joys and sufferings as on an ontological par with human minds and their joys and sufferings, metaphysical vitalism can live very happily with it. On the other hand, vitalism does prima facie seem to sort ill with deep environmental ethics because so much of what the latter regards as intrinsically valuable in nature is apparently denied even any genuine reality, let alone value, by vitalism.

Having now, I hope, sufficiently clarified what I mean by metaphysical humanism, and metaphysical vitalism, and acknowledged that the first threatens ethical nonhumanism in both its aspects and the second in one of its aspects, let us now see how far various forms of idealism are really equivalent to some form of metaphysical humanism or vitalism, and where so, whether the *prima facie* opposition they pose to nonhumanism is a real opposition.

IV

Metaphysical Idealism, Humanism, and Vitalism
The relations between idealism and animal rightism is a much easier subject than the relation between idealism and deep environmentalism. So I shall start by considering only the first.

All that I need say on the logic of the matter is this: there is no reason whatever for the animal rightist to think that metaphysical vitalism stands in any kind of opposition to his moral position. The vitalist may concede that the minds of animals are as like or as unlike human minds as the animal rightist would like to suppose, and therefore in principle he can say that the welfare of animals matters in the same way as does the welfare of humans, to whatever extent the animal rightist may claim. Now it seems that the *most familiar* (please note the emphasis) forms of idealism are all in effect, if not in so many words, either metaphysically humanist or vitalist. So the question how metaphysical idealism stands to animal rightism is really the question how far such standard types of idealism takes a humanist and how far a vitalist turn.

If we stand apart from history and ask how far idealism should lean more towards humanism or more towards vitalism, we must say that it depends on what the grounds of idealism are. But before doing this, it is worthy of remark that the one school of philosophy which chose for itself the label of humanism in anything like a relevant way was pragmatism, as developed by certain thinkers. The philosopher who most gloried in it was F. C. S. Schiller, the one British pragmatist, likewise (so far as I know) the one British philosopher who regarded himself as a follower of William James. However, James himself did at times adopt the term 'humanism' as an expression for his own pragmatism-cum-radical empiricism. Both these pragmatists could, in fact, be called idealists; however, my concern in this paper is more with those philosophers one most immediately thinks of as covered by this term.

Although not the only form of idealism, the most common form of idealism claims that the physical world exists only as an object for minds. Now it appears to me that there are two main types of ground on which such an idealism is argued for, though most historical idealists probably make some use of each type of argument.

The first type of argument claims that we cannot conceive of a physical world without sensible qualities such as can only exist as contents of consciousness or objects of some mind's experience. I shall call idealisms in which this type of argument is most prominent sensory idealism. Sensory idealism is usually associated with the general claim that there is something self-evidently self-defeating in the attempt to form the conception of an unperceived physical object. The second type of argument for idealism claims that we cannot conceive of a physical, or perhaps of any, world which is not structured by categories which exhibit it to the reflective intellect as its own handiwork. I shall call this rational idealism.

The two great founding fathers of idealism are Berkeley and Kant. And by and large Berkeley's idealism is of the sensory type, and Kant's of the rational type (see Appendix A). Thus for Berkeley our intellect plays no more part in determining the character of the physical world than it does for the most straightforward realism. His idealism is simply the discovery, through close attention to its character, of what it really is, a system of ideas, which, since they are not produced by us, must be produced in us telepathically by God. For Kant, in contrast, the fact that the physical world only exists for us is evidenced by the way in which it answers to principles which only an intellect could impress on it, our own intellect for Kant, the intellect of a universal self for later German idealists.

Now since animals are commonly thought of (perhaps questionably) as having a rich sensory experience, but poor intellects, it seems clear that for sensory idealism they, qua minds, can be taken as just as real as ourselves, for the sensory is for it the most basic feature of mind and the physical world can be present to them largely as it is to us. Rational idealism, on the other hand, dwells so exclusively on intellectual category-using forms of mind that it can hardly bring itself to take non-rational minds seriously at all and certainly will not allow that they are among the minds for whom the physical world exists. Thus for the sensory idealist we are sharers to some great extent of a common world with the animals, while for the rational idealist non-rational minds are an ontological embarrassment and certainly not sharers of a common world with us.

Does it follow from this that a sensory idealist will be a metaphysical vitalist and the rational idealist a metaphysical humanist? Well, I think it follows, at least, that there will be a strong well-grounded tendency for each to move in this direction.

Berkeley would seem to be a theistic vitalist. (Thus he refers quite often to presumed animal experience to make his points.) It is not so clear that Kant is a metaphysical humanist, for I do not find his views about animal experience too clear, but he is certainly close to being a metaphysical humanist of what I called a qualified kind, qualified, that is, by the postulation of things in themselves, and the dim vistas beyond humanism which these open up. And some of his followers moved in the direction of an unqualified metaphysical humanism. The clearest example is Fichte.[6] For Fichte there is no realm of things in themselves to put a qualifier on either humanism or vitalism, and upon the whole it seems clear that for him the universal Ego lives out its life solely in the struggles of human beings in a physical world, which is

---

[6] The most accessible account Fichte gives of his philosophy is in the First and Second Introductions to his *Wissenschaftslehre*. The English reader may find these in Fichte, 1982.

simply their own posit and has no existence except for them.

Thus the logic of the various positions, as I have charted them, seems to correspond fairly closely with the historical facts about idealist philosophers. The nearer they are to Berkeley and sensory idealism, the more ready they are to give animal minds a serious place in their ontology, while the nearer they are to Kant the less ready they are so to do.

Let me illustrate this point further by considering a few particular examples. Schopenhauer regarded himself as the true heir to Kant, and there is some justice in this claim. But there is also something much more Berkeleyan in his thought than one will find in Kant. For Schopenhauer the physical world is presented to us pictorially by our understanding, and then as a separate stage we apply concepts to it by reason. We have understanding in common with the animals though reasoning is exclusive to ourselves. This shared understanding with the animals makes Schopenhauer take the reality of animal experience very seriously, and an object of serious moral concern. Here is quite a striking contrast with Fichte.

Let us compare in the same way two later British idealists, T. H. Green and F. H. Bradley. Green is certainly much closer to Kant than is Bradley and the case for idealism on his part is entirely a matter of showing how the natural world is the construction of rational relational thinking. Animals are hardly granted anything worth calling an experience at all, because they have no intellect which can connect one experience and its contents with another, and, for Green, experiences unrelated by a synthesizing mind are scarcely conceivable.

Bradley on the other hand has far more use for arguments of a Berkeleyan and sensory kind than Green, and has a good deal to say about animal experience and thinking. Although Bradley is hardly an animal rightist, indeed he is not much of a human rightist either, it is clear that he thought animals proper objects of moral concern.

> It is monstrous to say that for us man has no more right than lower animals or inanimate nature. It is also monstrous to say that these have no right as against him. The covering of a hideous world with the greatest possible number of inferior beings so long as they are human is not the end – even for us. (Bradley, 1983)

As for Hegel, I shall avoid chancing my arm by ascribing any view to him in this connection, though I may have something to say later as to how Hegelianism stands to deep environmentalism.

My general conclusion is that idealism of the more sensory and Berkeleyan type tends to be a form of metaphysical vitalism, while idealism of the more rationalist and Kantian, and ultimately Fichtean type, tends to be a form of metaphysical humanism. Therefore the animal rightist has some cause to be hostile to the more rational type of idealism, and no cause at all to worry about the more sensory Berkeleyan type of idealism.

V

Idealism & Deep Environmentalism: Opening Remarks
Things are different, and much more difficult, when we move to the relation between idealism and deep environmentalism. Certainly deep environmentalism

has some ground for suspicion of both humanism and vitalism. The deep environmentalist is concerned to extend moral status beyond humans and animals to other parts and aspects of nature and to demand respect for them. Doubtless from the deep environmental point of view metaphysical vitalism is better than metaphysical humanism, but he or she may still think that it hardly does justice to the wonderfulness of nature, since it seems to make of nature a mere spectacle in animal or human minds.

The metaphysical vitalist might try to meet these objections by introducing denizens of something like Popper's third world, a resource I have allowed him parenthetically above. He may suggest that it is a simplification to say, eg., that a great work of art only exists, and can only have value, as the content of individual human minds. It is, indeed, somehow a creation of human minds but has a reality which outstrips their contents and a human mind may be judged for its ability to appreciate it rather than the art object judged by the actual experiences in which it is registered. And such a metaphysical vitalist may say that the great works of nature, which we have been cultivated to appreciate, may exist and be valuable in the same way, and thus have an existence and value which goes beyond what humans, and still more what animals, may register.

Doubtless this can bring the metaphysical vitalist-or-humanist rather nearer to positions espoused by deep environmentalists. All the same, I doubt if it will really satisfy him, since part of the wonder of nature, or aspects of nature, for him is precisely that it or they are in no sense human creations.

We could sum up the deep environmental response to

idealism, as idealism is often conceived, as the charge (in the words of Santayana) that idealism exhibits 'cosmic impiety'. Whatever Kant may have said, the wonder of the starry heavens does seem to be belittled if it is reduced to a system of ideas in the minds of humans or animals, and the amazingness of the long course of the evolution of life on this earth seems to be trivialized if made into a story human minds tell themselves (for in this case animal minds hardly come into it) for the better prediction of their own experiences or as a not literally true background for thoughts about human progress.

To get something of the spirit of deep environmentalism consider the following passage from Holmes Rolston's *Environmental Ethics*. Having insisted on the value which has its home in many aspects of nonhuman life, both at the individual and at the collective level, Rolston goes on to extend the intrinsic values present in nature well beyond the bounds of life:

> Nonbiotic things have no information in them, no genome, much less sentience or experience. There are no cells, nor organs, no skin, no metabolisms. Impressed with the display of life and personality on Earth, we correctly attach most of our ethical concern to persons and to organisms; but we may incorrectly assume that [so-called] mere things are beyond appropriate and inappropriate consideration.
>
> A 'mere thing' can, however, be something to be respected, the project of projective nature. Crystals, volcanoes, geysers, headlands, rivers, springs, moons, cirques, paternoster lakes, buttes, mesas, canyons – these also are among the natural kinds. They do not have organic integrity or individuality; they are constantly being built, altered, their identity in flux.

But they are recognizably different from their backgrounds and surroundings. They may have striking particularity, symmetry, harmony, grace, story, spatiotemporal unity and continuity, even though they are also diffuse, partial, broken. They do not have wills or interests but rather headings, trajectories, traits, successions, beginnings, endings, cycles, which give them a tectonic integrity. They can be projects (products) of quality. The question now is not 'Can they suffer?' or 'is it alive?': but 'What deserves appreciation?'.

In nature there is a negentropic constructiveness in dialectic with an entropic teardown, a model of working for which we hardly yet have an adequate scientific, much less a valuational, theory. Yet this is nature's most striking feature, one that ultimately must be valued and of value. In one sense we say (with Hume) that nature is indifferent to planets, mountains, rivers and trilliums. But in a more profound sense nature has bent toward making and remaking these objects (=projects), and millions of other kinds, for several billion years. These performances are worth noticing – remarkable, memorable – and they are worth noticing not just because of their tendencies to produce something else, certainly not merely because of their tendency to produce this noticing in certain recent subjects, our human selves. They are loci of value so far as they are products of systemic nature in its formative processes. The opening movements of a symphony contribute to the power of the finale, but they are not merely of instrumental value; they are of value for what they are in themselves. The wonders of the heavens and the marvels of Earth do not lie simply in their roles as a fertilizer for life or a stimulator of experience. There is value wherever there is positive creativity.

In Mammoth Cave, in a section named Turner Avenue, there are rooms laden with gypsum crystals spun as fine threads, a rare formation known as 'angel hair'. So fragile are these needles that humans passing through and disturbing the air destroy the hair-thin filaments. This part of the cave is closed, never visited by tourists and only on exceptional occasions by mineralogists. A nonbiotic work of nature (a kind of dirt!) is here protected at the cost of depriving humans of access to it. This park policy is partly for humanistic reasons: to preserve angel hair for scientific research. But it also involves an appreciation of angel hair as a project of systemic nature. Angel hair counts morally in the sense that natural value here lays a claim on human behaviour.

It was once the practice in Yellowstone National Park to put soap into certain geysers (altering the surface tension of the water) in order to time the eruptions conveniently for tourists. For almost a century the Park Service at Yosemite built an enormous fire on the lip of Glacier Point at dusk. 'Indian Love Call' was played, and the fire pushed over the cliffs to the ahs! of spectators. But the spectacle has now been discontinued as inappropriate. (Rolston, 1988, pp. 198–9)

Holmes Rolston's concern is that we should be sure to leave a great deal of Nature to carry out its own operations without interference from humans. And this is not just because it is satisfying for perhaps obscure psychological reasons to know that there is much going on on earth (or for that matter elsewhere in the cosmos as man extends his dominion) but because these

processes really have an intrinsic value of their own
which we can spoil. (I must say parenthetically that
deep environmentalism owes us an account of disvalues
in nature as well as positive values, for to hold that the
value in nature is always positive seems to rob the
conception of value of much point. And if some aspects
of nature have a negative value may there not after all
be something to be said for a good deal of human
activity in improving nature in a Capability Brown
manner? However, I cannot in this talk enter deeply
into just how deep environmentalism ought to be
developed, and must restrict myself to the question
whether it has good reason for being hostile to idealism
as committed to a humanist, or at least a vitalist,
metaphysics.)

In this connection it must be said that, however much
idealist metaphysics of certain sorts may encourage the
kind of ethical humanism, or even vitalism, which
Rolston is challenging, much popular and philosophical
opinion, of a quite non-idealist kind, also finds the
ethics of deep environmentalism absurd. For many
non-idealists about fact are in effect idealists and
humanists, or at most vitalists, about value. They find
it absurd, without quite being able to explain why, to
suppose that anything apparently non-sentient can be
beautiful or wonderful in any sense which is not a
matter of the feelings it produces in humans or kindred
observers – for example, a magnificent mountain range.

Deep environmentalists challenge this account in
various ways. Suppose someone says that some area of
unspoilt country only has value for one who enjoys
visiting it or at least thinking of it. But, says the deep
environmentalist, seriously to value something is to
think that it is valuable in itself. It is rather human taste

which is to be evaluated according to its ability to respond to values in such things than human taste which gives things value.

However that may be, the deep environmentalist is likely to be profoundly suspicious of vitalism and humanism as trying to make something which they think has independent value into a mere content of the mental state of a human, or possibly an animal.

Now leaving aside various problems about deep environmentalism which may arise with whatever metaphysics it associates itself, how far is idealism of itself inimical to it?

A likely suggestion is this: insofar as idealism takes a humanist or vitalist form it is inimical to deep environmentalism. And certainly this tends to leave it with little respect for nature as having any value in itself. Thus Fichte depicts humankind as continuing to carry out its one grand plan 'until all matter bears its stamp...' and human spiritual unity is attained.[7]

If, however, it takes a more 'objective' form for which the mind-relatedness of nature consists in the fact, not that it only exists for a human or animal mind, but rather that it is itself mind-impregnated, then it may seem that we have a metaphysics actually favourable, perhaps even unconsciously believed in, by most deep environmentalists. For, after all, the view that nature and the bodies of all sorts which it includes are pervasively mind-impregnated sounds like just that kind of pantheism towards which the quasi-mystical feelings many people feel in certain solitary places of great beauty or grandeur seem to point.

---

[7] Quoted in White, 1993, p. 22.

VI

Deep Environmentalism, Berkeley and Phenomenalism
However, before we move on to reflections on how a
non-humanist and non-vitalist objective idealism stands
to deep environmentalism, I should like to say a word
as to whether metaphysical humanism and vitalism are
really so hostile to deep environmentalism as they may
at first appear.

How, first, does Berkeleyism stand to deep environmentalism? Well, a main reflection lying behind
Berkeley's idealism is precisely the sense that Lockean
or Cartesian physical realism deprives nature of everything that is appealing about it.   Once we realize that
nature is not a remote cause of our ideas but is actually
composed of ideas such as ours, then everything which
constitutes beauty is a genuine part of it.   And, it would
be quite in the spirit of Berkeley to say that the beauty
of mountain scenery or of the sea striking against rocks
and filling and then emptying the pools there, is really
out there, along with the shapes, the colours, and the
spatial unities.   Ah, but the deep environmentalist might
say, all the same you are only seeing something (on
your theory), when you look at such a scene, which
vanishes when you or other observers are away.   To
this Berkeley, of course, has the ready reply that it will
remain there for God's 'vision'.[8]   Thus Berkeleyism

---

[8]   Admittedly, there is considerable difficulty in knowing quite how to
conceive God's vision (or rather multi-sensory awareness) on Berkeley's
account. It is proper enough, indeed, that God should never be reduced
to something easy of conception by us. Still, if God is to serve the present
role we do have to think of Him as sensorily experiencing things in a way
which is somewhat similar to ours. But is His vision of things a vision as
from no particular position in space and is that really conceivable, and, if
so, does it make God's vision of things a way in which things as they are
for us can exist without us? Or does He view everything on every scale
from every possible position? I will not pursue this further but it does raise
certain difficulties for Berkeleyism.

coheres in some respects very well with the requirements of deep environmentalism. The only trouble is that God's ideas must include visions of all that the deep environmentalist finds unsatisfactory too, such as fields dominated by monocultural agriculture. But perhaps that backs up the case for Berkeleyan deep environmentalism by motivating us to help keep the earth a good place for God to look at.

However, if God is dropped from Berkeleyism and is not replaced by any other kind of Absolute, leaving us with the phenomenalism of J. S. Mill, C. I. Lewis and A. J. Ayer, and even Edmund Husserl, then I think that we have a theory which is not only vastly implausible in itself but really is guilty of cosmic impiety, bringing the amazing immensities of nature down to our own level. I wonder how many readers will recognize the following quotation in this connection.

Where I seem to differ from some of my friends is in attaching little importance to physical size... I take no credit for weighing nearly seventeen stone.

My picture of the world is drawn in perspective, and not like a model to size. The foreground is occupied by human beings and the stars are all as small as threepenny bits. I don't really believe in astronomy, except as a complicated description of part of the course of human and possibly animal sensation.[9]

How does a Kantian position bear on all this? If we stick to the first critique, and rescind from the rather dubious room for religious faith made by the second critique, then I think perhaps the emotional response to

---

[9] From a talk given in 1925 by Frank Ramsey to a Cambridge discussion group (Ramsey, 1931, p. 291).

the immensities of the physical universe which becomes most appropriate, is that of Herbert Spencer, that is, a kind of vague obeisance to the unknowable (Spencer, 1862, pt. 1). Perhaps some qualifications of this can be drawn from the third Critique but I am afraid that, if so, I must let them pass.

VII

Absolute Idealism and Nature: The German Case
When idealism becomes absolute there seems no reason why it should privilege human and animal felt reality above all other apparent components of the universe. But the fact is that it has often tended to do so. Listen to Bradley on this matter, writing to William James about the latter's humanism.

> You must remember that I was brought up in that development of Kantianism which ended in Humanism or at least was said to end in it. That there was no reality beyond human experience and no possibility of copying or following anything from the outside was a sort of watchword even. 'No Transcendence' in short.
> For myself I have had in some respects to diverge from this "Humanism" as I received it...[10]

Fechner's arguments to my mind don't *prove* much more than does Shelley's Sensitive Plant and the visions of the later part of his Prometheus. But so far as I was concerned they helped to take me back to a wider form of pantheism. I don't see *any* connection

---

[10] Letter from F. H. Bradley to William James, 15 October 1904. It is quoted in Perry, 1935, vols. 1 and 2, pp. 488–99, and in Sprigge, 1993, p. 589. Bradley's letters to James are in the Houghton Library, Harvard.

in principle between Absolute Idealism and the giving of the highest place to human beings. That strikes me as a one-sidedness which came historically but is not logical at all.[11]

Even if the connection between absolute idealism and humanism is, indeed, historical rather than logical, it is still of some interest to look at some historical forms of absolute idealism and consider how far they have or have not been metaphysically humanist in character. (For the remainder of my discussion I shall drop reference to vitalism, as what will concern us mainly is the contrast between metaphysical humanism, with or without a tincture of vitalism, and positions which reject both.)

The most evidently humanist of the German absolute idealists was surely Fichte. Fichte thought that Kant's postulation of things in themselves, which act upon us in some unknown way to provide the matter for the world which our intellect constructs for itself according to its own structure, was quite unnecessary.[12] If the knowable physical world is something whose form we construct unconsciously why should not the matter likewise be something upon which we determine unconsciously too? Thereby we avoid the completely unnecessary hypothesis of things in themselves, and are left simply with our own indubitable existence and those hidden depths to it of which we are dimly conscious. Of course there is an external world or non-ego but this exists only as what the ego posits, and does so for reasons of which the general character can be

[11] Letter from F. H. Bradley to William James, 3 February 1909 (Perry, 1935, p. 638, and Sprigge, 1993, p. 592).

[12] Actually he insisted that Kant was wrongly construed as having ever thought this. See Fichte, 1982, pp. 58–60 (*Gesamtausgabe*, vol. 1, pp. 487–8).

deciphered. For the ego wants to live a life of moral worth and this it can only do if it has obstacles to overcome, and the external world it posits consists precisely in those obstacles whose overcoming is most morally valuable at its current stage of development. But how is it that each ego shares a non-ego, as seems evident, with other egos? Fichte has two related answers. One is that moral development is something which can only occur in a community, so that the different egos need to posit a shared non-ego giving them a common environment in which to work out their moral destiny. Secondly, Fichte became clearer, as his thought developed, that the ego which is working out its moral destiny in each of us is really a single ego living out a multiplicity of connected lives.[13]

Fichte's philosophy therewith constitutes the birth of absolute idealism. But though certainly absolute it is also sometimes quite reasonably called subjective idealism, since it conceives the natural world as only existing for the subjective experience of finite individuals, all somehow expressions of a single world self or universal Reason. Thus it is, as I said above, a form of humanism.

Absolute idealism took a less metaphysically humanist turn with Schelling, whose continually shifting forms of idealism tended to become more 'objective'; with the Absolute or God not simply dreaming the physical world as the scene of moral endeavour but rather expressing itself in a parallel dialectic both in mind's arising in nature and in nature's appearance to mind. Still, the ultimate point of it all seems to have been conceived as the Absolute's coming to consciousness of itself in the human mind, implicitly

[13] See Fichte, 1982, p. 75 (*Gesamtausgabe*, vol. 1, p. 505).

in art and explicitly in philosophy, so if not precisely metaphysically humanist, in our sense, it is certainly an anthropocentric view of the universe. Still Schelling's philosophy played its role in that mystical love of Nature which was a main feature of German and later British Romanticism.

What of Hegel? Just in what sense he was an idealist is controversial. Did he think that the nature which mediates between the dialectic of pure concepts and the dialectic of human history was only an object for a subject, more specifically the human subject in which the Absolute comes to self consciousness, *or* did he think it always there for an absolute subject transcending the human mind, *or* did he think of it in much more realist terms as existing objectively as that from which mind (in particular, the human mind) emerges dialectically? In short, was his position as much sheerly humanist as Fichte's?

Whatever the answer to this question, a matter on which it might be thought something of a disgrace that a major philosopher should leave experts on him so unclear, he was certainly a metaphysical humanist in a somewhat broader sense. For it seems evident that the whole point of the dialectical process from pure Being to Spirit was that the Absolute should come to self-consciousness in the human mind, in particular (it would seem) in the mind of Hegel. I must admit to joining Santayana in finding this a somewhat paltry conception of the ultimate point of the world. But, however that may be, it is decidedly humanist in the sense in which deep environmentalists are so concerned to reject. And certainly some philosophers in the Hegelian tradition have been metaphysical humanists in the same sense as was Fichte. This seems undoubtedly true, for example, of Benedetto Croce.

Before moving to consider some Anglo-American idealists from this point of view I should mention in passing that the social holist aspect of Hegelianism is often unconsciously echoed in the work of rather less than completely deep environmental ethicists.[14] Such environmentalists present it as their central claim that the identity of human beings, individually and as a race, is, in large part, a matter of their place in the larger bio-system, and that, therefore, the human good is not separable from the good of that system. This is evidently rather akin to the social holism often associated with absolute idealism, extended beyond the human community to the larger biotic community. However, it does not directly bear on the main issue of my present concern which is how far idealism can recognize values in nature, whether more individualist or more holistic, which only involve humans as their potential destroyers or preservers.

VIII

Absolute Idealism and Nature: The British Case
For a major absolute idealist who (as we saw from the letters to James from which I quoted above) felt uneasy with a human-centred view of the universe, then (the strange figure of Gustav Fechner, 1801–87, apart), one must turn to Britain, in fact to Bradley, noting along the way that T. H. Green and Bosanquet would seem pretty humanist in the vague broad sense to which I have been moving.

---

[14] This is really a summary of the ecological humanism advocated by Andrew Brennan (Brennan, 1988). See Sprigge, 1991 for a discussion of his views.

For Bradley the most likely view of the world was that it consisted of finite centres of experience united in one absolute experience together with whatever was posited in such centres. However, he thought it just possible that there was a certain amount of experience in the Absolute which was not focused into finite centres of experience, and which might be what appears to us as Nature. He also seems to have been willing to countenance the view, somewhat akin to Leibniz's and anticipating Whitehead, that the reality behind the physical world in general consists of innumerable finite centres additional to those which constitute the consciousness of humans and animals.[15]

In certain respects this type of absolute idealism becomes very like the vision of the universe of the process philosophers, Whitehead, Hartshorne, and their followers.[16] This being so, it is worthy of note that a number of philosophers have developed a version of what is effectively a form of deep environmentalism based on their process philosophy.

But there is something somewhat unsatisfactory about this from the point of view of the deep environmentalist. The way in which this is so has been well described by Clare Palmer in a thesis on the subject of which I had the good fortune to be an examiner.

For the process philosopher what the physical world really consists of is innumerable flows of feeling or

---

[15] I cannot develop any further account of Bradley on nature here, but as someone who is to quite an extent a Bradleyan I will say on my own behalf that a Bradleyan type of absolute idealism seems to call for a panpsychist approach to nature. (Actually in A. E. Taylor's Bradleyan phase this was the view he took.) To a great extent the kind of panpsychist absolute idealism which appeals to me, as likely to be the truest, is developed by Josiah Royce, but here again I must simply record the fact.

[16] The main differences are over the nature of time and the precise sense in which everything is unified in God or the Absolute.

experience. The stream of our own consciousness is just one of these. It must not be thought, however, that for this sort of panpsychism the inner reality of the history of every physical object is an individual stream of experience; this is certainly not supposed true of most macroscopic objects. The result is that the real articulation of the physical world is (supposedly) into units which feel their own existence is on what, from a physical point of view, is an extremely small scale. Rocks, ecosystems, mountain ranges and even trees have no inner consciousness of their own. For the most part it is only submicroscopic particles which do so. As for human and animal consciousness this is something for Whitehead which 'wanders around the interstices of the brain' occupying only a minute part of it at any one moment.

The result is that hardly any of the units which seem valuable to the deep environmentalist have any inner experience of their own being. This, it seems, limits the support such panpsychism can offer a deep environmental position.

This can only be done if we return to Fechner and hold that much larger units of physical nature have an inner spiritual existence of their own. However, there is no space to develop this point further here.

Perhaps after all the absolute idealist should take a rather different tack. He should say, perhaps, that in some way or other the inner being of the physical world at large is certainly psychical, but that we can hardly claim that what we experience in the world as most valuable is what is most independently valuable in itself. On the other hand, in finding beautiful and appealing what we do, we are not relating to mere nothingness as we effectively are for phenomenalism. Moreover, the feeling of unity with the cosmos which sometimes come to us from aspects of nature is a cognitively correct awareness, for as parts of nature we really are parts of a unitary spiritual whole. In some sense we are experiencing what Spinoza described (in an early work) as the 'knowledge of the union that the mind has with the whole of Nature'.[17] It may be doubted whether the inner life of the constituents of majestic snow-clad mountains feel better to themselves than do the consituents of a rubbish dump, but the feeling of unity with the cosmos especially prompted by the contemplation of the one may be calculated to inspire a deeper and more valid sense of how we stand towards the cosmos.

I have dwelt, probably to the reader's advantage, so much on the views of others that I have only been able to hint here at my own. My main conclusion is that absolute idealism, conceived as the view that Reality is 'a single Experience, superior to relations and containing in the fullest sense everything which is' (Bradley, 1968, p. 246), need not be, and should not be, in any way metaphysically humanist or vitalist, and that there is no reason therefore for those, like the deep environmentalists who are repelled by ethical humanism or even vitalism, and by metaphysical humanism or vitalism as implying it, to regard absolute idealism in general with suspicion; indeed they should recognize it rather as their best metaphysical friend, since it gives grounds for recognizing as cognitively valid the pantheistic feelings towards nature which often inspire them. But as to precisely how these positions (absolute idealism and something approximating to deep environmentalism) may be unified, and

[17] Spinoza 1985, p. 11 (*Tractatus de Intellectus Emendatione*, §140).

what is the justification of each taken both separately and in tandem with the other, I have only been able to provide some hints of a position which, up to a point, I have developed elsewhere. I end simply with the reminder that deep environmentalism, and such pantheistic absolute idealism as may be associated with it, owe us some reflections on the topic of disvalue as well as positive value in nature. An idealism like Fichte's might have certain advantages here in taking the traditional view that nature is something to be used and overcome rather than preserved as such. Still, my own sympathies lie more with those who emphasize the majesty of non-human nature as a feature of the Absolute.

Appendix A

There is another distinction between idealisms which tends to go together with the one outlined in Section 4. The first has a fairly naive one-level view of truth of what can, roughly speaking, be called a correspondence type. The second tends to identify truth, so far at least as it is something ever knowable, with what can be validated by the use of certain criteria; thus it is never a simple report on how things are independently of our thought. 'The fundamental proposition for such idealism' in its strongest form, (I quote from an old book) 'is that nothing can exist for intelligence which is not its own product' (Watson, 1882, p. 154).

Thus Berkeley's view of truth is basically a common sense correspondence or what one might call an absolute one. It is true that Berkeley offers no particular theory of truth, but he is certainly not out to challenge a common sense correspondence one. His claim is not that our concept of truth needs revision, but simply that the truth about the world is in some respects different from what we are unreflectively inclined to think.

Kant, on the other hand, presents an idealism which is mainly of the rational type, for it is mainly as the work of our intellect that the natural world reveals itself as phenomenal. And in effect he has a two-level view of truth. So far as truth of the first common-or-garden types goes, judgements possess it, not because they correspond with how things are independently of our thought, but because in them intelligence has unconsciously constituted something out of unknowable raw unconscious data which satisfies its own internal requirements. Kant does, however, in effect hold that there is a second type of largely unknowable truth, of a more absolute kind, which would concern these raw unconscious data and their source. More radical followers of Kant tend only to allow for truth of the first kind.

Appendix B
Tom Regan lays down as a condition which must be met by a properly environmental ethic (in effect, by what I call 'deep environmentalism') that it ascribes moral standing to some non-human beings, and that among these some must be non-conscious (Regan, 1982, p. 187). He sums up the tenets of deep environmentalism (calling it 'deep environmentalism') further thus:

Central Belief: Nature, including its varied and complex ecological systems, has value in its own right, apart from human interests.
Norm Regarding Permissible Action: We are not to treat nature as though it had value only as a means to human ends, but are always to treat it in ways that

display recognition of, and respect for, its inherent value.

Appropriate Motives and Attitudes: We are to interact with nature in a spirit of reverence and love, regarding the natural order with that respect appropriate to its independent value (Regan, 1982, p. 212).

REFERENCES

Henri Bergson, *Oeuvres* (Paris: Presses Universitaires de France, 1959).

F. H. Bradley, *Essays in Truth and Reality* (Oxford: Clarendon Press, 1968).

————— , 'A Note on Christian Morality', ed. Gordon Kendal, *Religious Studies*, vol. 19 (1983), pp. 175–83.

Andrew Brennan, *Thinking about Nature* (London, New York: Routledge, 1988).

J. G. Fichte, *The Science of Knowledge*, translated Peter Heath and John Lachs (Cambridge: Cambridge University Press, 1982).

John Mullarkey, *Bergson and Perspectivism*, Ph.D dissertation (University of Warwick, 1993).

Arne Naess, 'The Shallow and the Deep, Long-Range Ecology Movement. A Summary', *Inquiry*, vol. 16, no. 1 (1973), pp. 95–100.

Ralph B. Perry, *The Thought and Character of William James: As revealed in unpublished correspondence and notes, together with his published writings*, vol. 2 (Boston: Little Brown and Company, 1935).

Frank P. Ramsey, *The Foundations of Mathematics*, ed. R. B. Braithwaite (London: Routledge and Kegan Paul, 1931).

Tom Regan, *All That Dwell Therein* (Berkeley: University of California Press, 1982).

Holmes Rolston, *Environmental Ethics* (Philadelphia: Temple University Press, 1988).

Herbert Spencer, *First Principles* (1862; London: Watts and Co., 1937).

Baruch Spinoza (trans. E. Curley), *The Collected Works of Spinoza*, vol. 1 (Princeton: Princeton University Press, 1985).

Timothy L. S. Sprigge, *James and Bradley: American Truth and British Reality* (Chicago: Open Court, 1993).

————— , 'Some Recent Positions in Environmental Philosophy Examined', *Inquiry*, vol. 34, no. 1 (1991) p. 110.

Paul Taylor, *A Theory of Environmental Ethics* (Princeton: Princeton University Press, 1986).

John Watson, *Schelling's Transcendental Idealism: A Critical Exposition* (Chicago: S. C. Griggs and Company, 1882).

Alan White, *Schelling: An Introduction to the System of Freedom* (Cambridge, Mass: Yale University Press, 1993).

NOTES ON THE CONTRIBUTORS

Leslie Armour is a graduate of the University of London. He now lives in Canada and is Professor of Philosophy at the University of Ottawa. He has taught at various universities in California, Ohio, and Ontario. His books include *The Rational and The Real*, *Logic and Reality*, *The Faces of Reason* (with Elizabeth Trott), *The Conceptualization of the Inner Life* (with E. T. Bartlett III), *The Concept of Truth*, *Being and Idea*, and *Infini-Rien: Pascal's Wager and the Human Paradox*.

Paul Coates is Head of Philosophy at the University of Hertfordshire. He has published articles on thought and conciousness and on Kripke's sceptical paradox. He is currently working on issues concerned with the philosophy of mind and perception.

Donald Davidson is Professor of Philosophy at the University of California in Berkeley. He is author of *Essays on Actions and Events* and *Inquires into Truth and Interpretation* and other books and articles.

Daniel D. Hutto is Senior Lecturer in Philosophy and Cognitive Science at the University of Hertfordshire. He has published many articles in the areas of philosophy of psychology and epistemology.

Phillip Ferreira is Associate Professor of Philosophy at Kutztown University of Pennsylvania. He has published numerous articles on F. H. Bradley and British Idealism.

Michele Marsonet is Associate Professor of Logic and Philosophy at the University of Genoa, Italy. His books include *Science, Reality and Language*, and *The Primacy of Practical Reason*.

Tom Sorell is Professor in Philosophy at the University of Essex. He is the author of *Scientism: Philosophy and the Infatuation with Science* and is editor of *The Rise of Modern Philosophy*.

Timothy L. S. Sprigge was Professor of Logic and Metaphysics at the Univeristy of Edinburgh from 1979 to 1989. He now teaches there part-time as an Endowment Fellow and is Professor Emeritus. His books include *Facts, Words and Beliefs, Santayana: An Examination of his Philosophy, The Vindication of Absolute Idealism, Theories of Existence, The Rational Foundations of Ethics*, and *Bradley and James: American Truth and British Reality*.

Guy Stock is Honorary Lecturer and Tutor in the University of Dundee and Honorary Senior Lecturer in the Universities of Aberdeen and St. Andrews. He has edited (with Anthony Manser) *The Philosophy of F. H. Bradley* and (with James Allard) *F. H. Bradley: Writings on Logic and Metaphysics*.

Fred Wilson is Professor of Philosophy at the University of Toronto. He is the author of *Psychological*

Analysis and the Philosophy of John Stuart Mill, and *Empiricism and Darwin's Science*.